THE NEW RULES OF
CORPORATE CONDUCT

THE NEW RULES OF CORPORATE CONDUCT

Rewriting the Social Charter

Ian Wilson

Q

QUORUM BOOKS
Westport, Connecticut • London

Library of Congress Cataloging-in-Publication Data

Wilson, Ian, 1925–
    The new rules of corporate conduct : rewriting the social
charter / Ian Wilson.
        p.   cm.
    Includes bibliographical references and index.
    ISBN 1–56720–249–7 (alk. paper)
    1. Social responsibility of business.   2. Industries—Social
aspects.   I. Title.
    HD60.W55   2000
    658.4'08—dc21   99–33204

British Library Cataloguing in Publication Data is available.

Library of Congress Catalog Card Number: 99–33204
ISBN: 1–56720–249–7

First published in 2000

Quorum Books, 88 Post Road West, Westport, CT 06881
An imprint of Greenwood Publishing Group, Inc.
www.quorumbooks.com

Printed in the United States of America

The paper used in this book complies with the
Permanent Paper Standard issued by the National
Information Standards Organization (Z39.48–1984).

10 9 8 7 6 5 4 3 2 1

For Adrianne, my wife,
whose writing challenged me,
whose caring sustained me,
whose love inspired me.

Contents

Illustrations

Preface

There is a tide in the affairs of men,
Which, taken at the flood, leads on to fortune;
Omitted, all the voyage of their life
Is bound in shallows and in miseries.
                    William Shakespeare, *Julius Caesar*, IV, iii

The world is passing through the most sweeping political and economic restructuring of the post–World War II era. This condition is pervasive, tumultuous, and continuous. Country after country, and institution after institution, is being swept into the vortex of these changes. The old boundaries—between industry and industry, economy and economy, corporations and governments— are shifting and becoming more permeable. Information technology is transcending our previous limitations of time and space. As a result, everywhere we are confronted with the prospect of a prolonged period of social, political, and economic adaptation to new roles, new responsibilities, new relationships.

Much has been made of the social and political implications of these changes. With the collapse and fragmentation of the Soviet Union, the whole focus and rhetoric of political analysis and debate has changed. Francis Fujiyama interpreted the event as "the end of history." And Samuel Harrington suggests that future clashes will center more on cultural than on national or ideological divisions. With the rising economic power of Japan, China and the "Asian tigers," we are told by some that the third millennium ushers in a "Pacific century," as the center of economic and political gravity shifts from Europe and North America to the Far East.

It is, however, the implications of these changes for the corporation— particularly the large, private, multinational corporation—that I want to address in this book. As the primary form of economic organization in most countries, the corporation stands to be deeply affected by this transformation of its landscape.

It has much to gain and much to lose in the foreseeable future, for it stands at the intersection of two of the major thrusts of the current restructuring.

On the one hand, the current *economic* restructuring—the reshaping of the global economic landscape—has been triggered in large part by the production, marketing, and investment strategies of multinational corporations and the new global flows of trade, capital, and technology. Patterns of national comparative advantage and economic development have undergone radical shifts. Growth prospects (or the perception of them) have changed. Global competition, in new and old industries alike, has intensified.

At the same time, a *political* restructuring has been gathering momentum, redrawing the boundary between the public and private sector as nations struggle to define the most appropriate roles for government and business in this new world. Privatization, deregulation, and a shift toward more market-oriented systems have been hallmarks of the past decade. In the process, there has been a subtle but marked shift of responsibilities and public expectations toward the private sector. Despite widespread skepticism about the responsiveness and social performance of private corporations in the past, they have been given the benefit of even greater doubts about the effectiveness of state-owned corporations. The net result of recent power shifts has thus been to open up new opportunities and give greater latitude for private decision making.

The new challenge for the corporation therefore is to respond successfully and simultaneously to these two thrusts. It must both maintain (if not gain) position in an increasingly competitive world and respond to the new societal expectations of its responsibilities. Balancing the corporate effort to manage these often conflicting demands will call for executive leadership and vision of the highest order. Viewed in this light, *the next decade will be a critical testing time for democracy, market systems, and (by extension) the private corporation.*

The challenge is not, of course, entirely new. The social and economic setting for the corporation has always been in a state of flux; and the corporation is always changing, adapting to new conditions, and new demands. The process of corporate renewal and reformation—that is, literally a *re*-formation—should be a constant condition. So we should not talk of this challenge as if it were a crisis, although there will always be critical moments. Crisis implies the prospect of a definitive resolution: Either the fever breaks, and health is restored, or there is a decline, a worsening of the sickness, and eventual death. Rather, the pattern here is one of challenge and response—thesis, antithesis, synthesis—evolution rather than revolution—with the changes being, for the most part, slower and more subtle than we might sometimes hope for or than our rhetoric might imply.

Nevertheless, I believe that it is no exaggeration to suggest that the next ten years will be a defining—or, more exactly, a redefining—stage in this evolutionary process. The bar of societal expectations of corporate performance is being raised; the challenge has become global; and the stakes are high. It is no longer just a matter of the standing and reputation of individual corporations. At issue is the stability and success of the corporate form of organization as a whole in this latest round of experiments in democratic market systems.

The linkages among corporate performance, economic progress, and political stability are tight and compelling. Take two examples from vastly different contexts. In Russia, we can clearly see how dependent the future of democratic institutions in that country is and will be on the social responsiveness of the new economic order in which private enterprise is being accorded (albeit slowly) a growing role. Profiteering or a failure to supply the promised consumer goods would likely be primary causes of social unrest and consequently of the withering away of the experiment in Western-style capitalism. In the United States, further movement toward deregulation and privatization is most surely contingent on the scope and sincerity of corporate efforts to meet new societal demands and on the success of the private sector's self-policing of its own ethical behavior. For instance, the Clinton administration's proposed "hands-off" policy on the future course of electronic commerce would no doubt quickly be reversed if the consuming public were to encounter a persistent pattern of false claims, "ripoffs," and invasions of privacy.

Of course, other factors outside the control of corporations will influence the outcome. Ethnic conflicts and a resurgent nationalism might lead to counterrevolution in Russia. Social divisions or international crises might cause the United States to swing back toward a more activist role for government. Nevertheless, my conviction remains that corporations themselves must play the critical role in determining these outcomes. To paraphrase the younger William Pitt, "Corporations can save themselves by their efforts, and democracy by their example."

For much of the 1990s, the tide has been running in favor of corporations. However, trend is not destiny. The question remains: Will they take this tide of new expectations "at the flood" and ride it to fortune? Or will they miss their timing, or misjudge the social mood, and then be caught in the backwash of public disenchantment and a drastic reversal of public fortune?

This book is dedicated to an examination of these assertions and a search for answers to these questions. In structure, the book is built around three key components: the changing societal context of the corporation; the nature of the new rules of corporate conduct that are emerging from these changes; and the outlines of a corporate agenda that these new rules appear to suggest.

In the first section, we look both backward and forward at the societal context for the corporation, because it is this context, with its ever-changing values and expectations, that determines the rules under which corporations must operate, for corporations are social, as well as economic, institutions. They operate under the terms of two charters: the formal written charter that establishes the corporation as a legal entity and determines its responsibilities to its shareowners; and the unwritten charter of societal expectations which determines the terms under which the public and a variety of stakeholder groups grant legitimacy to the corporation.

Starting in the mid-1960s, a convergence of forces—demographics, afflu-ence, education, and technology—created a tectonic shift in social values, the rise of a variety of "movements" (e.g., minorities, youth, women, the environment), and what I have termed the "shaking of the seven pillars of business." It was during this period that the "corporate social-responsibility movement" started to develop, molded by a mix of new regulations, interest groups' pressure, and corporate initiatives.

Now a new set of forces is coming into play. For the next ten years at least, four formative forces are most likely to shape social values and public expec-tations of corporate performance worldwide:

- The "power shift" in public–private sector relationships—the converging forces of democratization, market systems, deregulation, and privatization.
- Globalization of trade, production, and technology—and ideas, culture, and expectations.
- Economic restructuring—at the global, national, industry, and corporate levels.
- The transforming forces of information technology.

In looking to the future, we are inevitably confronted with major uncer-tainties that make forecasting a risky and sometimes unproductive exercise. We are better served by contemplating a range of alternative scenarios, which effectively cover the envelope of uncertainty. With this in mind, this section closes with the depiction of four possible futures that might arise out of these uncertainties, each with a different paradigm of the corporation:

- *Transformation*, in which the corporation emerges as an agent of social change.
- *Reregulation*, in which the corporation becomes a regulated utility.
- *Neomercantilism*, in which the corporation is viewed as a national competitive weapon.
- *Turbulence*, in which the corporation becomes a populist target.

These, then, are four possible contexts in which the "new rules" might develop.

The second section of the book examines the nature of these new rules in the context of seven aspects of corporate performance: legitimacy, gover-nance, equity, environment, employment, public–private sector relationships, and ethics.

Legitimacy requires a rethinking of the purpose of the corporation and the role of profit in its operations and decision making. Profit is a means, a motive, and a measure; but it is not the purpose of the corporation. Social legitimacy—the corporate equivalent of consent of the governed—will be fully earned only when the corporation views itself as an institution that has both a social purpose ("to provide needed goods and services") and an economic driver ("to the profit of society and itself").

Governance entails a broad review of the whole system of corporate accountability, constituency rights (and responsibilities), and checks and balances. The guiding principle of the future is that the corporation must be thought of, managed, and governed more as a community of stakeholders, and less as the property of investors. In both corporate and political systems, there will be a strong drive toward broader diffusion of power, clarifying and increasing lines of accountability, and placing greater emphasis on due process.

Equity (or rather, the perception of equity) will be, as the past decade has shown, a hot issue in times of great change that create the potential for both great gain and great pain for individuals and institutions alike. In the recent past, there have been great and growing disparities in the distribution of both gains (e.g., compensation increases) and pains (e.g., layoffs, employment insecurity). Thus the pressure on corporations to achieve greater equity in sharing both the gain and the pain—and in the treatment of stakeholder interests—will almost inevitably grow.

Protection of the environment enters a new phase with the emergence of environmental issues on the global scene and with the growing recognition that business is the only mechanism powerful enough to produce the changes necessary to reverse environmental and social degradation. Corporations, too, are recognizing that an underlying logic links the environment, resource productivity, innovation, and competitiveness. As a result, environmental action by corporations is moving from a reactive to a proactive stage: It is becoming a central, rather than a peripheral, part of their operations, as more and more corporations adopt strategies rooted in ecological principles.

Employment—job creation and employment security—will be a critical issue for most nations as they face both economic restructuring and a global labor surplus. As a primary creator of jobs, the corporation will be judged by its performance in dealing with both the quantitative (the number of jobs created) and qualitative issues (e.g., quality of working life) covered by the new rules. Meeting these requirements while satisfying consumer expectations for price stability and improved standards of living will be one of the major challenges facing corporate management.

Public–private sector relationships are at the heart of the "power shift" currently underway around the globe. If corporations are to ride the crest of this wave, they must be prepared to contribute, by policies and actions, to the redefinition of appropriate roles for government and business in this new society. In particular, they must provide answers to such questions as, How far should privatization be pushed? What role should regulation play? How will or should "capitalism" change?

Ethical behavior has always been an integral part of society's expectations of corporate performance—but one where perhaps the greatest amount of public cynicism has existed. There is little doubt that ethics will play an increasingly important role in the new rules, if for no other reason than that this cynicism must be reversed if the power shift is to play out successfully. Trust is also crucial to establishing sound relationships with all stakeholder groups; and trust can only be built on a strong ethical foundation.

The final section of the book lays out the beginning of an agenda of changes that corporations might adopt in response to these new rules. This agenda calls for a substantial transformation in the character, policies, and social roles of the corporation—a transformation as great as that which already differentiates the corporation of today from that of the 1950s. It is an agenda that demands much of corporate leadership. But it is an agenda that must be acted upon, for at issue is the stability and success of the latest round of experiments in democratic free-market systems.

In content, the book is partly descriptive, partly prescriptive, but mainly exploratory. It is clearly descriptive in its attempts to recreate the history of the past twenty-five years in its analysis of the forces for change and in its discussion of corporate actions already taken. It tends to be prescriptive, both in establishing a conceptual foundation for the corporation's social purpose and legitimacy, and in its suggestions for the unfinished agenda for corporate change. But the book should be seen as predominantly exploratory, as befits any work that emphasizes the future rather than the past. It invites the reader to join in a voyage of exploration into future possibilities.

In focus, there may be a bias toward emphasizing the United States experience, although I believe that the trends are increasingly global. The bias, if there is one, arises from my forty years of business experience in that country. But it is a bias I have tried to correct, to reflect the fact that globalization—of economic activity, of political experience, of information, even of societal expectations—is a predominant force of our times. It would be disappointing to me, and misleading in fact, if this analysis were construed too narrowly with regard to its geographic relevance.

Acknowledgments

This book is the product of more than forty years of experience in the corporate world, within the United States and elsewhere around the globe. The ideas expressed in it owe much, therefore, to what I have learned from those with whom I have worked along the way.

At General Electric, in the course of a twenty-five-year career there, my ideas about the place of the corporation in society were shaped and tested by the many exchanges I had with Virgil Day, Dick Anton, Don Watson, and many others. In particular, I owe a great deal to Reginald ("Reg") Jones, who was GE's CEO from 1971 to 1981 and showed all of us how a corporation should behave in the political arena.

My consulting work at SRI International brought me in contact with many lively and diverse intellects—among them, Pat Henry, Art Chait, Eilif Trondsen, Gene Thiers, and Peter Davis—and provided me with the opportunity of greatly expanding the range of my experience. In my thirteen years with SRI, I was privileged to work with management teams in many of the world's leading corporations, not only in North America, but also in Australia, Norway, Finland, Argentina, Venezuela, Japan, Singapore, Indonesia, and the United Kingdom. To all of them I owe a debt of gratitude for the ideas, different perspectives, and the encouragement they gave me.

As an avowed "futurist," I have also benefited greatly from the lessons I have learned from some of the pioneers in this field, including Ed Cornish, founder and president of the World Future Society; the late Bertrand de Jouvenel and Willis Harman; and Arnold Brown, Bill Halal, and Graham Molitor.

My thanks go to the Virginia Center for the Creative Arts. On two occasions, the center provided me with the time, space, and stimulation to initiate and persevere with this book—once when the original outline was developed, and then again toward the end of the journey when I most needed an impetus for the final thrust.

Finally, I owe more than I can adequately express to my wife, Adrianne, to whom this book is dedicated. Her writing ability and loving presence constantly both challenged and sustained me throughout the long gestation period for this work.

Part I

THE CHANGING BUSINESS ENVIRONMENT

— 1 —

Retrospect: The Birth of the "Corporate Social Responsibility Movement"

> If we would know where we are going, we should first consider where we are, and how we got there.
>
> Anon.

Corporations operate under the terms of two charters: a formal, written, legal charter; and an unwritten, but critically important, social charter. The written charter establishes the corporation as a legal entity and determines its responsibilities to its shareowners. But it is the unwritten charter of societal expectations that determines the values to which the corporation must adhere and sets the terms under which the public grants legitimacy to the corporation.

A good starting point for our exploration of the changing corporate social charter is a brief retrospect at the past thirty years, a period of continuous and sometimes tumultuous change which radically reshaped the societal context—and the rules governing corporate conduct—for the corporation.

It is a critical but often overlooked point that the corporation is a social, not merely an economic, institution. It has a social purpose, not in the sense of being a social-welfare organization, but of serving society's economic needs. It supplies the goods and services that society requires; it provides employment for the labor force; and—at its best—it raises the standard of living of consumers and provides the resources that we can apply to the creation of a more civilized and dynamic society.

So the societal context is important, indeed critical, to the corporation. Through the values that its people hold and the expectations that they have, society exerts a powerful force in determining the policies, the strategies, and the organizational culture that corporations adopt.

THE EXPANDING ARENA
OF SOCIETAL EXPECTATIONS

Over time, people's expectations of corporate behavior have expanded and grown vastly more complex and demanding (see Figure 1.1). Start with the simplest precorporate transaction between individual buyer and seller—say, the purchase of a pan by a housewife from an itinerant tinker. Here, it is safe to say, only two parties were involved; information was equally shared; and the dominant considerations were, indeed, economic—quality, price, and value—with an ethical assumption that there was no cheating involved in the transaction. Over time, however, as first the small enterprise and then the large company became the principal form of economic organization, the number of interested parties multiplied, the relationships became more complex, and the interests of more and more constituencies were involved.

As a result, the societal expectations of what is considered "acceptable" corporate performance have expanded progressively along four axes. The simple buyer–supplier relationship has increased in complexity on both the supply and demand sides. In place of the individual maker–seller, there are now diverse groups of employees, managers, and shareowners; chains of suppliers, dealers, and distributors serving the corporation; and, more recently, alliances with strategic partners, some of whom might even be competitors. On the demand side, in addition to the individual consumer, now more sophisticated and demanding, buyers can also include public entities, other corporations and cooperatives. New constituencies—governments at all levels, interest groups, communities, even the public at large—also now hold a stake in the well-being and social performance of the corporation.

Compared with the relatively slow evolution of these changes (spanning the past two centuries of the industrial age), movement along the other two axes has been more recent and more rapid. Starting early in this century and accelerating in the past twenty-five years, legal, political, moral, and social values have created the standards by which corporate performance is now judged. Even more recently, a transnational dimension has been added to an already complex picture, as the globalization of economic activity has led corporations to expand beyond the national boundaries of their home country. As a result, the typical corporation now finds itself challenged to meet multiple, sometimes conflicting, standards and expectations of diverse societies.

This expansion of constituencies and interests has progressively enlarged the social role and importance of the corporation, broadened its responsibilities, and underscored the fact that it must reflect the society's shared values—social, moral, political, and legal, as well as economic. Building the corporation on a foundation of economic values alone has never been a satisfying solution, either for its members or for society. Now it is not even a viable option.

With the expansion of constituencies has come the need to reflect *their* expectations and values in corporate performance. As societal values have

Figure 1.1
The Axes of Expanding Societal Expectations

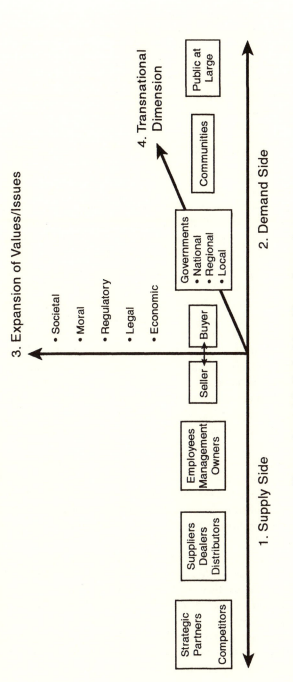

changed, they have become embodied in legislative and regulatory requirements on the one hand, and in a growing network of special interest groups on the other. In the process the distinction between economic and social considerations has become blurred. For example, the economic issue of resource conservation is variously defined also as a political–regulatory issue, a social issue (in terms of consumer behavior), an environmental issue, and even a moral issue of preserving resources for future generations.

THE SIXTIES AS A TURNING POINT

However, while this expansion of societal expectations and corporate responsibilities has developed gradually over time, there have been periods in which there have been noticeable spurts in activity. The trust-busting activities of Senator Sherman and President Theodore Roosevelt around the turn of the century was clearly one such period. Another was the Depression and the resulting New Deal legislation of Franklin Roosevelt in the 1930s. A more recent defining period occurred thirty years ago, in the late 1960s and early 1970s, when we saw the emergence of the movements of those times—minority rights, women's rights, consumerism, environmentalism, anti(Vietnam) war—whose agendas formed the basis for yet another movement: the corporate social-responsibility movement.

As we look back on the post–World War II era, we can see that the 1960s were clearly a turning point in social history. If ever there was such a thing as a cultural revolution, this was it. This was one of the most turbulent periods in American history; the earlier consensus appeared to have broken down completely; and, as writer John Cogley put it, "forces new to American life were unleashed, terrifying to the old, unsettling for those who thought they had achieved stability, and bruising for the young."

The period of 1965 to 1970 was in some important respects a watershed period. Since then, the streams of our social thinking have jumped their old courses and started to flow in different directions. I refer to our thinking about such key relationships as those between man and woman, the individual and institutions, the majority and minorities, business and society, and the economy and ecology.

When we seek the causes of this turning point, we must look beyond the explanation that was often so glibly offered at the time—that this was the product of an acute form of "generation gap" or more specifically, "a few radical kids on campus." No doubt, "the kids" of the baby-boom generation reflected the changes in their most extreme form; their sheer numbers made their ideas felt on campus and beyond; and they *were* the cutting edge of the future. To that extent, demographics were a factor. But the youth of that time did not set the changes in motion.

The real causes of these changes were many, but they start with the fact that society was in the midst of a major historical transition. This transition was of a magnitude that has been equaled perhaps only two or three times in previous history: once, when man the hunter and herder became man the settled farmer; again, when urban living (civilization in its literal sense) made its appearance; and more recently, when agricultural society was transformed into industrial society. The latest transition took us from an industrial to what we then called a "postindustrial society," using the term coined by Daniel Bell. For the United States in particular, a country whose economic strength had been built on manufacturing, the change to an economy built primarily on services (communications, transportation, utilities, banking, education, and wholesale and retail trade) was suspect and threatening, as if this was not a legitimate foundation for a world-class economy. We had difficulty in believing that, using only one-third (at that time) of our labor force, we could produce all the material goods our society needed—all the food, fibers, and ores; all the buildings; all the machines, consumer goods, and other products.

This changing *character* of work—from being essentially "things oriented" to "services oriented"—accounted to a large extent for some of the changing *attitudes* toward work. For one thing, particularly in the growing managerial and professional segments, people came to want to be regarded not as "hands" (an industrial term) but as "brains" (a postindustrial term).

A further characteristic of this new society—one that bore directly on the changing value systems of the time—was the interaction among high and increasing levels of affluence, education, and technology. These three forces were not, of course, new to society, but they seemed, like a nuclear reactor, to reach a critical point where a new chain reaction of values, attitudes, and behavior started.

In the decade of the sixties alone, affluence (measured by incomes over $15,000 in then constant dollars) doubled. This change in income levels set in motion major changes in patterns of consumer spending and saving. It also led to changes in ways of thinking about one's self and one's world. We saw this most noticeably perhaps in the increasing emphasis that was being placed on quality rather than mere quantity—the switch from "more" to "better." It is also possible to trace some of the changing views of work and leisure back to this root, for in an affluent society there was no longer quite the same grinding necessity to strive for survival and security as there had been during the Depression. We seemed to be raising our sights to a higher level where we could begin to choose among types of work (selecting those that seem most personally rewarding) and to consider leisure as a valid activity in its own right. Finally, it was this sense of affluence and choice that contributed in part to a growing sense of impatience with the progress (or lack of it) we had made in resolving our social problems—a "lower frustration tolerance," as I termed it at the time, with all forms of economic hardships, social injustice, and inequity.

As with affluence, so with education. The significance of this force lay only partly in the physical manifestations of more schools, higher expenditures, and changing curricula and methodology. Of at least equal importance were the attitudinal changes triggered by the fact that more students were completing high school and attending college. The better-educated person tended for instance to have more self-respect; wanted to be treated more as an individual; was far less tolerant of authoritarianism and organizational restraints; and had different and higher expectations of what our social institutions could and should do.

Finally, there was technology. Probably nothing has been more characteristic of advanced economies than the application of technology to industrial systems. The popular belief was that it would continue to be a distinguishing characteristic of the postindustrial society—but that it would be technology with a difference. One might say that the high-water mark of the "old" technology occurred in 1969, with the landing on the moon while millions around the world watched. That event convinced us that, given the will and the money, nothing was now *technically* impossible.

Yet, starting at almost precisely the same time as this celebration of a supreme technical triumph, there was as never before a widespread questioning of the value, the pace, and the extent of technological progress. At one level we developed a heightened awareness of the negative environmental and societal consequences of some technical developments and started to insist that, in this field too, "better" should replace "more" as our motto. At another level there was the beginning of a movement that asked the question, "Do we *have* to do it simply because we *can* do it? Does 'can' imply 'ought'?" This in effect substituted a moral for a technological imperative. Certainly this questioning attitude has profoundly affected our approach to nuclear power, supersonic transports, and more recently genetic engineering.

Together, these forces combined to shape what I called a "New Reformation"— a reformation or reordering of our public and private value systems. This paradigm shift could be summed up as a major shift in emphasis

- From considerations of quantity ("more") to considerations of quality ("better").
- From the concept of independence, toward the concept of interdependence (of nations, institutions, individuals, and all natural species).
- From mastery over nature toward living in harmony with it.
- From competition toward cooperation.
- From the primacy of technical efficiency toward considerations of social justice and equity.
- From the dictates of organizational convenience toward the aspirations of self-development in an organization's members.
- From authoritarianism toward participative management.
- From uniformity and centralization toward diversity, decentralization, and pluralism.

Looking back on this period with the benefit of hindsight, it is all too easy to dismiss some of the values and beliefs of the time as naive and mistaken.

Certainly, the changing economic and political environment of the next thirty years has done much to blur the clarity and sharpness of these value statements and to change national and personal priorities. But the fact remains that this era did give rise to a whole set of new movements, and these movements in turn began a rewriting of the corporate social charter. From that beginning there was no turning back. As the title of one of Thomas Wolfe's books reminds us, "You can't go home again." In this sense, the watershed analogy holds good. For all the twists and turns that the flow has taken and despite new channels that have opened up, the streams of our social thinking have continued to flow in a different direction and expectations of corporate performance have changed.

THE ASSAULT ON BUSINESS VALUES

The corporation as the prototypical institution of the industrial society was quick to feel the impacts of these changes. However inclined businessmen may have been to relegate "changing values" to academia and the campus, the subject matter could not be confined within these boundaries. Take for example one phrase among many that summed up the spirit of those times: quality of life. First used by President Lyndon Johnson at a University of Michigan commencement, it was initially dismissed by many as a "nice abstraction" or a "popular political slogan." But it quickly took on connotations, the significance of which corporations could not ignore—quality of products, quality of working life, and quality of the environment.

In the product arena, this quality evoked new expectations of styling, new concerns for safety, and new questioning about the social acceptability of products—nuclear power, supersonic planes, or tobacco. In short, it became the rallying cry of the whole consumerism movement.

In the work arena, many of the younger, better-educated employees, particularly those moving into managerial and professional ranks, were looking for a new depth of challenge and meaning in their work. They wanted to have more responsibility and say in what they did and how they did it. Believing that education is a career-long activity, they wanted their work experience to include opportunities for further education and self-development. Being more conscious of their individualism, they were more insistent on individualized treatment in their daily work experience and in the choice of salary and benefit programs available to them.

In the environmental arena, the concept of quality started with a basic concern over pollution and its control. But it rapidly developed into a broader concern over the preservation of ecological balance—a recognition of the need for a systems approach in defining the relationships between nature and human activity. From this emphasis on environmental quality also sprang the questioning of technological progress mentioned earlier and the search for a definition of "balanced growth" in both economic and population terms.

I commented at the time that "we are witnessing a shaking of the 'seven pillars of business,' those basic values we have, up till now, considered to be the eternal verities undergirding our business system—growth; technology; profit; managerial authority; technical efficiency; 'hard work'; and company loyalty."[1] It was not my contention, then or now, that there was likely to be a wholesale rejection of these values; only that each of these supposedly immutable qualities was being redefined and rebalanced with a set of countervailing values. For instance

- The concept of economic growth as an unqualified good was being seriously modified, both in our private thinking and in public-policy decisions, by considerations of quality and "balance." Significantly, it was under the Republican administration of President Nixon that the White House's National Goals Research Staff issued a report entitled "Toward Balanced Growth: Quantity with Quality."
- Even technology, the major dynamic of our growth, was subject to challenge on the grounds of our need to improve our control over safety, environmental degradation, and social stability. Again, it was no mere coincidence that during this period Congress established its own Office of Technology Assessment.
- Profit had always been a popular target of populist attacks. What was new in this period was the increasing power of public-interest groups on the lookout for corporate excesses and the growing popularity of the notion of corporate social responsibility—as well as competition—to act as a check on corporate power.
- The legitimacy of managerial authority was being called into question by employees—and other corporate constituencies—demanding greater participation in the decision-making process.
- Technical efficiency—in job structure, production methods, and the operation of products and systems—was no longer considered to be an unqualified good, an end in itself. It needed to be balanced, so the reasoning went, with considerations of the human factor, human scale, organizational culture, and stability.
- The concept of work, in the sense of work done "in the sweat of thy face" (or, some would add, "the numbness of thy mind"!), started to be redefined and replaced by the notion that the character of work was itself changing, demanding more of the minds rather than the physical strength of employees.
- And finally the concept of company loyalty was weakened, both by the realities of career mobility and by the "whistle-blowing" belief that the public interest must be paramount, overriding corporate considerations.

Many corporate executives of that time would have been inclined to dismiss such a discussion of values as being more appropriate to the classroom than the boardroom. If so, events quickly disabused them of such a notion as these changing values made their impact felt both on the corporate image and on the bottom line.

In retrospect, we can see that, starting in the mid-1960s, there was a rapid decline in the public standing of the corporation. Harris Polls of the time reveal an escalating distrust of corporate leadership based on the perception that these leaders had too much power and were too self-interested. To be sure, the private corporation was not alone in this loss of public confidence. If misery loves company, corporate executives could take comfort in the fact that this erosion of confidence extended to virtually all large institutions, and certainly included government, unions, and the military.

That, however, was not the end of the story. These changing values did not remain just a sociological phenomenon but became a political force that spawned a new surge of legislative and regulatory activity, the likes of which had not been seen since the 1930s. A raft of new agencies sprang up (e.g., the Consumer Product Safety Commission, Environmental Protection Agency, Occupational Safety and Health Administration, Office of Technology Assessment), new regulations were promulgated, and the bottom-line impact of all this activity soon became apparent. A study by the Center for the Study of American Business, for example, estimated the cost of federal regulatory activity in 1976 at $65.5 billion, made up of $3.2 billion in administrative costs and $62.3 billion in compliance costs.[2] Regardless of the merits or otherwise of this spate of regulations, their impact on the corporate bottom line succeeded in getting the attention of executives and directors.

THE CORPORATE RESPONSE:
FROM REACTION TO PROACTION

Initially, the corporate reaction to these perturbations in its business environment was one of disbelief and almost of outrage. We must remember that the period that proceeded the 1960s was one of post–World War II prosperity, the political tranquility of the Eisenhower years and the "silent generation," and the social conformity of "the man in the gray flannel suit." In that environment the corporation had been regarded as a powerful mechanism for raising the standard of living, and a corporate career as the best way to realize the American dream. Surely, there had been criticisms of "big business" from the likes of Senator Estes Kefauver and, later, Ralph Nader. But these were generally aberrations from the opinion of the general public and easily (or so it was thought) rebutted.[3] Now something new and unsettling was spreading in the land: Urban riots and campus protests were in the headlines daily. As the unrest spread and affected mainstream society, it became less easy to dismiss it as the product of "a few radicals" on campuses or in the cities.

Disbelief soon gave way to a siege mentality, for indeed many corporations were in a state of siege in those years. Consumer boycotts proliferated, even on an international scale, as Nestlé found, with the global reaction against its marketing of milk formulas to babies in developing countries. Corporate recruiters found themselves heckled and barred from campuses. Politicians picked up on the legislative implications of the new social movements, and executives found themselves defending the status quo in congressional hearings designed to lay the foundation for a new round of legislation to enforce corporate social responsibility. Even annual meetings, which had hitherto been tranquil events, became epicenters of protest as consumer advocates, spokespeople for shareowner rights, and even church groups took more activist postures on issues as diverse as nuclear power, arms sales, South Africa, and environmental protection. Confronted with such an onslaught, a few companies, more prescient than others, started to experiment with responses to the new demands. But most tried to hunker down in the hope that the storm would pass.

But the storm did not pass. The need for response became overwhelming, and gradually the siege mentality gave way to experimentation and improvisation in corporate efforts to blunt the force of these attacks. First, and most obviously, there was no escaping the task of compliance with the new regulations. So companies established new components, promulgated new policies, expanded internal training and communications programs to promote compliance, and started, tentatively, to speak out in an effort to influence public opinion and government policy.

Individually and collectively, large corporations started to build their positions and go public on these new issues. For instance, The Business Roundtable, comprising the chief executive officers of more than one hundred major corporations, published a statement on corporate responsibility that showed both how far business had come from its earlier position and the gap that still existed between its current stance and the full expression of the new societal expectations.[4] On the one hand, it quoted with approval the opinion of Reginald Jones, the former chairman and CEO of General Electric, that "public policy and social issues are no longer adjuncts to business planning and management. They are in the mainstream of it. The concern must be pervasive in companies today, from boardroom to factory floor."[5] On the other hand, it made very clear the corporate adherence to the primacy of profit and its relationship with shareholders: "As providers of risk capital, shareholders make the corporation possible. . . . Any approach to corporate responsibility must begin with the practical recognition that the corporation must be profitable enough to provide shareholders a return that will encourage continuation of investment." Nevertheless the debate had been started, and positions were changing—on both sides.

A few pioneers, like Clark Abt, the head of Abt Associates, even experimented with various forms of social audit, or social accounting, in an attempt to put dollar figures on the social benefits and corporate costs of businesses' activities dealing with the new social concerns. The early efforts in this field were, of necessity, simplistic and somewhat naive—and satisfied neither side. Opponents, the traditionalists, attacked it as a deviation from the economic underpinnings of the corporation. Advocates viewed the efforts as a public relations gimmick, and were resentful of attempts to quantify the results of social programs in the very dollar terms they were attacking. Not surprising, these early efforts have gone nowhere as yet.

Far more successful and widespread were attempts to amplify the traditional annual report with straightforward descriptions of a company's efforts to deal with social issues. One of the earliest and most successful efforts was that of General Motors who in 1971 held a conference for a group of prominent educators and representatives of foundations and investment institutions "to explain the progress General Motors has made in a number of areas of public concern, and to obtain the participants' thoughts as to the Corporation's activities and goals in these areas." A record of the presentations and discussion at this conference were published, and GM has continued to issue an environmental, health and safety report to the present day.[6]

However, most corporate responses in the early 1970s were still largely reactive, playing "catch-up" in a game whose rules were being set by the corporate critics. It was only toward the end of that decade that some of the leaders in this field had moved toward a more proactive, rational, and institutionalized approach. The Business Roundtable statement mentioned earlier documented some of the details of this new organizational approach to the problem (see Box 1.1). But the two key elements that gave the approach its proactive character were first an expansion and an increased sensitivity of the planning framework; and second the adoption of a systems approach to business–society issues.

Let me illustrate with examples drawn from my experience at General Electric. In 1967 the company established a Business Environment Studies component to track these new and unsettling developments and to provide a more complete framework for the company's strategic planning, adding social and political dimensions to the more traditional economic and technological forecasting. As we analyzed the course of events in that tumultuous decade, we encapsulated one key finding in a simple, straightforward phrase: "Without a proper business response, the *societal expectations* of today become the *political issues* of tomorrow, the legislated *requirements* of the next day, and the *litigated penalties* of the day following" (emphasis added).

The lessons we hoped would be learned from this finding were twofold. First, there was an obvious and dramatic narrowing of the options open to a company as this sequence progressed. The earlier a company moved, the more maneuvering room it had. Nowhere was this progression more obvious, or more unfortunate for business, than in the development of the civil-rights campaign from the late 1950s through 1973 (see Table 1.1). Similar examples could be cited for product quality, occupational safety, land-use planning, and pollution control.

BOX 1.1

Elements of the Corporate Response to Societal Demands

Many companies now include the whole spectrum of corporate social objectives in strategic planning. This requires planners to consider not only

Table 1.1
The Evolutionary Sequence of Societal Expectations of Business Performance

Without a proper business response,	Business options	The example of civil rights
Societal expectations of today become	Semiautonomous	Sit-ins of the late 1950s
Political issues of tomorrow,	Defensive	1960 platforms of both parties
Legislated requirements of the next day,	Compliance	1964 Civil Rights Act
And *litigated penalties* the day following.	Pay penalties (ordered or negotiated)	1973 EEOC backlog of 60,000 cases

economic and technological trends and events but also social and political; to study not only the expectations of shareholders, employees, customers, and suppliers, but also those of the community and the public. . . .

Some companies have established committees of the board of directors to deal with corporate responsibility issues. Such committees provide guidance to management in defining the company's role, assessing the effectiveness of performance, and recommending changes. . . .

In companies which have developed a structured approach to matters of responsibility, staff groups (often including an officer of the company) examine and raise questions related to these issues. They seek to encourage employees in all sections of the business to recognize public policy as part of their regular work and call on them for analysis of the particular issues in their area. . . .

Companies have also found it useful to have such policy instruments as

- a written code of conduct
- a written policy on disclosure
- well-defined corporate policies with regard to such matters as executive compensation, fair pay, equal employment opportunity, personal privacy, freedom of expression
- a continuing focus on corporate impact on the environment, health and safety in the workplace, and the impact of plant openings and closings on communities and employees
- continuing concern about product quality, acceptable pricing policies, and ethics in advertising

- a high priority for high level attention to the size and direction of corporate philanthropy
- a program designed to inform, sensitize, and train present and future management to deal with public policy and corporate responsibility issues.

Source: The Business Roundtable, "Statement on Corporate Responsibility" (Washington, D.C.: The Business Roundtable, October 1981).

The second lesson was that simply identifying the early warning signs of a new social demand did not necessarily dictate the launching of a new corporate response—a preemptive strike, as it were. Not every new demand became politicized. So careful tracking of developments was necessary. However, it remained true that early warning did present a company with options—to act (and, if so, how and when) or not to act—and with the advantage that, even if legislation and regulation did follow, a decision to move proactively—to put in place voluntarily what might later be compulsory—would stand the company in good stead, from both a practical and a public-relations point of view.

This last point is borne out by experience. In the late sixties, General Electric was clearly playing "catch-up" on equal employment opportunity for minorities. However, in 1970 it was quick to pick up—and act on—the signals of a developing women's rights movement. In fact, it had issued its own affirmative-action guidelines in this area *before* the Equal Employment Opportunity Commission had developed its own. And even though the commission later filed suit against the company based on the results of history, not on the adequacy of the new company policy, both sides agreed that the company's early action had done much to ameliorate the situation. From the company's point of view, it made negotiations on the suit and compliance with the resulting order that much easier. And the fact that operating managers were now essentially conforming, not to new regulations, but to new company policy, made the transition to the new rules smoother and less stressful.

The other element that was starting to make corporate responses more proactive was the adoption of a systems approach to these new issues. Professor Raymond Mack of Northwestern University once advised Illinois Bell to deal with equal employment opportunity as it would a rate case. In GE, we took a similar tack: We adopted a systems approach to business–society issues. By this we meant that the company's response should

- Take a multifunctional, interdisciplinary analysis of the problem, its impacts, and its solutions.
- Examine both the internal and the external environments of the company in an effort to relate the subsystem (the company) to the larger system (society) of which it is a part.
- Identify the opportunities as well as the threats inherent in the developing situation.

• Use the basic management principles of goal setting, accountability, and (most important) measurement of performance in meeting the new rules.

Talking management's language in this way made sense. It became easier to integrate the new performance standards into the normal running of the business. And even the most reluctant managers were apt to change their behavior when they knew that their performance in these areas was now to be measured and reflected in the reward system.

SPRINGBOARD TO THE FUTURE

One product of the tumultuous period of 1965 to 1980 was the emergence of what some have called the "corporate social responsibility movement." The progress that we made then—and we *did* make progress—toward creating a more perfect alignment between corporate behavior and changing societal values was initiated by the activists of those days, codified in new laws and regulations, and finally shaped by the actions of the more progressive companies.

But the scene is ever in motion. There is no point of stability and equilibrium. Where we are now is not a settled end point but a springboard to the future.

NOTES

1. Ian Wilson, "Toward a New American Paradigm: Its Significance for Business," speech to the American Marketing Association's 2d annual Social Indicators conference, Washington, D.C., February 23, 1973.

2. Robert DeFina, *Public Policy Expenditures for Federal Regulation of Business* (St. Louis, Mo.: Center for the Study of American Business, Washington University, 1977).

3. See Appendix A, "The Debate on Bigness."

4. The Business Roundtable, "Statement on Corporate Responsibility" (Washington, D.C.: The Business Roundtable, October 1981).

5. *Business and Society: Strategies for the 1980s* (Washington, D.C.: U.S. Department of Commerce, 1989).

6. *Progress in Areas of Public Concern* (Detroit: General Motors Corporation, February 1971).

— 2 —

Prospect: Formative Forces and Alternative Futures

The new rules of engagement—the rewritten terms of the social charter—will build upon the past we have examined but will be shaped by the forces of the future that have still not yet fully developed.

A new set of forces is now coming into play. For the next ten or more years, the four key formative forces that are most likely, on a global basis, to be shaping public expectations of corporate performance are (see Figure 2.1)

- The "power shift" in political (and geopolitical) relationships.
- Globalization.
- Economic restructuring.
- The transforming technologies of the Information Age.

Of course, many other factors—including demographics (the size of cohorts, age–sex mix), economics (jobs and income), and specific events such as political changes, natural or manmade disasters, and technology breakthroughs—will play a part in this process. But these four represent the main lines of force along which the issues in the revised corporate social charter will most probably be arrayed.

In the following pages we take a brief look at each of these four key formative forces, not so much to define what they are (for they are already widely recognized), but rather to highlight the social issues and questions they are likely to raise for the private corporation.

POWER SHIFT

I use the term "power shift" to cover a cluster of disparate yet related trends that are redrawing the political and geopolitical maps of countries and the world. In this cluster I would include

Figure 2.1
Formative Forces of the Future

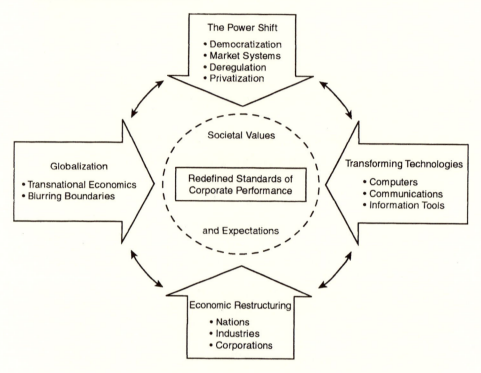

- The restructuring of geopolitical relationships that has followed the collapse of communism, the disintegration of the Soviet Union, and the burgeoning of power and influence in Japan and a unifying Europe.
- A movement toward democratization of political systems and greater reliance on multiparty systems and popular elections.
- A growing preference for market systems rather than government planning and control as the driver and guide of economic activity.
- A corresponding movement toward deregulation, predominantly in economic areas such as financial services, airlines, communications, and energy (more so than in social areas such as health care and welfare).
- The movement toward the privatization of previously public institutions and services, from garbage collection to education to the postal service.

The combined effect of these trends is to shift the balance of power between nations and between institutions in our societies.

These trends are global, though not universal, in reach. But their pace, scope, and even definition vary from country to country. Deregulation of financial services has proceeded further and faster in the United Kingdom than in Japan. The targets of privatization are different in France, Mexico and New Zealand. Poland and the Czech Republic have made more progress toward institutionalizing a market economy within their borders than have countries in the former Soviet Union. And certainly democracy means different things to different nations. For instance, as *The Economist* once noted, the meaning and implied policy priorities differ in North America and Western Europe from those in Singapore and Japan: "This is the crux of the disagreement between the Asian authoritarians and Western democrats. The Asians think that the economy comes first: a government's first duty is to keep the country competitive; democracy and all the rest should be thought of in terms of how well they serve economic development."[1]

But, however defined, democracy is on a global growth curve. The human-rights advocacy organization, Freedom House, noted as far back as 1992 that democracies had become an absolute majority of the 171 nations that it monitors.

Looking at these trends from the corporate point of view, one might conclude that they are promising and entirely favorable. And indeed the long-term effects of declining superpower confrontation and an end to the arms race should encourage the opening of new markets and a shift in national spending priorities toward social services and economic and infrastructure development. Privatization should provide new business opportunities. Deregulation should relax the strictures of government controls. And the underlying force of the move toward democratic and market systems has been people's interpretation of the history of the post–World War II period and their conclusion that democratic capitalism *works*. In particular, the economic successes, first of the United States and West Germany, then of Japan, more recently of Singapore and the United Kingdom, have provided successive waves of evidence of the competitive and social advantages of market-based capitalism and of its engine, the private corporation.

There are, however, two caveats that must be entered in this picture. First, trend is not destiny: There is no inevitability—indeed there is considerable uncertainty—that these trends will continue on course. And second, with these new opportunities and greater freedom for the corporation, there come greater responsibility and more demanding expectations. In fact, the two provisos are interlinked: continuity of these favorable trends is, to a large extent, dependent on companies discharging these new responsibilities, exercising greater self-restraint in the pursuit of profit, and meeting the new expectations in a socially acceptable manner.

There is an inherent fragility and instability in the transition to new democratic and market systems, as events in Algeria, Venezuela, and Russia have demonstrated. Democracy does not automatically produce stability or prosperity, nor does economic growth automatically give rise to open political systems. The transition is often brutal, and the new institutional infrastructure takes time to develop. What role, if any, can corporations play in easing this difficult transition?

Despite widespread disenchantment with governments' ability to manage change, people have not given up entirely on the public sector, and their desire for regulatory protection remains high in many areas. Financial collapses such as the savings-and-loan crisis in the United States, Western Europe's struggle with high levels of unemployment, or new concerns about workplace safety or toxic pollution can quickly modify, or even reverse, the thrust toward deregulation. How far can corporate initiatives and self-regulation go toward meeting these public concerns?

In many countries there is an underlying tension between public cynicism regarding corporate performance and the expectation of major benefits from shifting responsibilities from the public to the private sector. Indeed, the argument can be made that public expectations of corporations are actually *declining*, not expanding. Lapses in corporate performance seem to be greeted with an equal mixture of outrage and resignation ("What can you expect of profit-hungry companies?"). This is an explosive mixture of sentiments. What can corporations do to defuse this tension?

In some cases the public may have unrealistically high expectations for corporations to achieve quick results from economic reform, deregulation, or privatization moves. But, as we have seen in country after country, economic success may not quickly follow political reform. Can corporations hope to inject realism into these expectations without being accused of self-interest and a *lack* of responsibility?

There are obvious questions and legitimate public debate as to the adequacy of "pure" private-sector solutions to many of today's problems (e.g., trade, national competitiveness, education and health care). It is clearly superficial to insist that "the market" can be the total solution. But what should be the corporate view of the right role for government in such areas? And how should these views be made public?

In the face of such challenging questions, there is an overwhelming need to work toward a clearer definition and understanding—on the part of the public, corporations, and governments—of just what are the appropriate roles and responsibilities of the public and private sectors in this new economic and political order. Without such a public agreement, societal expectations of what corporations can and cannot reasonably be expected to achieve will prove to be unrealistic and are almost certainly doomed to result in frustration and reaction.

GLOBALIZATION

We are virtually at the point of living, if not in a global society, at least in a global economy. Global flows of trade, production, finance, and technology are rapidly breaking down the national boundaries of our existing economies. International competition among countries is driving governments toward a convergence of legal systems, accounting procedures, taxation, and regulation. In the process, something close to a global business monoculture is emerging. And the private corporation, quick to seize the opportunities presented by these trends, has now become, de facto if not de jure, a global institution.

At the same time, with even greater and more direct impact on societal expectations, new technologies and increased travel are driving the "globalization of information"—a worldwide flow of facts, ideas, fashions, experiences, values, and expectations. We may not yet have attained the cultural commonality of Marshall McLuhan's "global village," but we are rapidly approaching, on a global basis, the speed of communications attainable in such a local community.

In the 1950s Adlai Stevenson spoke of the "revolution of rising expectations" in the developing countries of the world. Forty years later, in all too many cases, those expectations remain frustrated and unfulfilled. Now, this global flow of information is combining with the power shift and the increasing international reach of corporations to give new impetus to a revolution of globalized expectations. Just as corporations search out and seek to adopt the best competitive practices of other companies, so people in more countries are able to identify the "best societal practices" of corporations around the world and to shape their own expectations of what should be achieved in their own countries accordingly. More people in more places want world-class goods and services. But they also want world-class working conditions and social services. There is an increasing tendency for Japanese workers to expect a reduction in working hours, as is the case in Germany and the United States; for women in the European Community to move for the adoption of American-style antidiscrimination practices; and for Malaysian and Venezuelan refineries to be prodded to adopt the environmental protection standards of industrialized nations. In these and other ways, globalization should in the long run raise both expectations and living standards.

There is however a shadowed side to these developments. In the short run at least, the globalization of trade and production can lead to the restructuring of industries and economies. Restructurings lead to the disruption of established patterns of employment and community development. And these disruptions lead to social unrest and political backlash. We have seen this pattern repeated in country after country, even in the United States, as in the heated debate over the North American Free Trade Agreement (NAFTA). In a thoughtful treatise on this subject, Harvard University economist Dani Rodrik argues that we should not trivialize the costs of trade to domestic social peace. Comparing social outlays and economic openness in different nations in the postwar era, he calculated that government expenditures increase almost precisely in proportion to the risk posed by trade to a particular economy. Countries with small economies and large dependence on trade, like Sweden, Belgium, and Austria, developed extensive welfare programs to cushion trade's domestic impacts. Those with large economies and less dependence on imports, such as the United States and Japan, had smaller social cushions. Rodrik concludes that "the social welfare state is the flip side of the open economy." Now, with corporations free to move to countries with lower costs of labor and lower taxes, the burden of these transitions is increasingly being borne by workers. Protectionism is not the answer, but "neither should we treat trade liberalization as an end in itself, without regard to how it affects broadly shared values at home."[2]

Even greater volatility and upheaval flow from the free movement of capital throughout the world. Interest rates, exchange rates, and stock prices in various countries are intimately interrelated, and global financial markets exert tremendous influence on economic conditions. The global flow of capital is vital to economic development, but financial markets are inherently unstable. With some hyperbole perhaps, even so respected a financier as George Soros was moved to say, in the wake of the 1998 Asian currency "meltdowns," "The global capitalist system is coming apart at the seams." The choice before us, Soros asserted, was between regulating global financial markets internationally and leaving it to each individual state to protect its own interests as best it can.[3]

Clearly, it is mainly in the political arena that the issues Rodrik and Soros raise will be debated and resolved. But corporations will be called upon to take a stand in these debates and will influence the outcome by the policies they adopt to deal with the problem within their own walls. What position should they take on repairing the social cushions that might protect both employees and communities against the sharpest effects of trade-driven restructuring? To what extent should corporations weigh social costs in their global strategy decisions, and what responsibility should they assume for meeting some portion of these costs?

Levels of pay and working conditions still vary considerably from country to country, and these variations play a considerable role in influencing corporate decisions about the location of plants and other facilities around the globe. The realities of the local labor market work to perpetuate these differences. But economic progress and international comparisons will over time work to moderate them. How should corporations meet both competitive needs and rising societal expectations with some level of integrity and consistency in their compensation systems on a global basis?

Similar differences in product and environmental standards pose nagging questions for corporate decision makers. For example, should products that are banned for health, safety, or environmental reasons in one country be exported to other countries where no such bans exist?

Ethical behavior is absolutely central to any judgment of corporate character; and here one might think there is little room for deviation or disagreement as to what is right. In large areas of conduct, this is true. Yet, at significant points, what is acceptable in one country turns out to be frowned upon in another. A classic example is the difficulty that U.S. corporations have had in balancing compliance with U.S. legislation banning bribes to foreign-government officials with the practical need, in many countries, to "grease the way" in order to get even the most routine official act performed. By whose standards should corporate codes of conduct be judged?

This brings up the larger question of how to resolve the sometimes conflicting claims of the various national interests with which the global corporation must now deal. Specifically, in any conflict between the interests and policies of the "home" country and those of a "host" country, how should the corporation act? To whom is the corporation responsible, and for what? And, on a related matter, should the corporation ensure that there is representation of offshore interests in its decision making, through the international make-up of its senior management and board of directors?

ECONOMIC RESTRUCTURING

Economic restructuring has become a cascading and perturbing force, destabilizing old institutions and threatening old habits, values, and expectations. Driven largely by the other three forces (deregulation–privatization, globalization, and technology), restructuring has hit successively at the national, industry, and corporate level:

- There has been a massive shift in the distribution of global economic activity as nations have moved up the curve of economic development, with the industrial countries moving into information-related services and the less-developed countries taking on more of the world's mining and manufacturing activities.
- Industry after industry has been radically restructured as the "rules of the game" (and the game itself) have been changed by the entry of new competitors, the increase in product substitution, changes in consumer values, and the blurring of boundaries between industries.
- The physical and, even more, the cultural outlines of corporate organization and performance have changed under the combined impact of mergers, joint ventures, leveraged buyouts, alliances, new strategies, and the drastic slimming ("downsizing" or, euphemistically, "rightsizing") of organizations.

The shock that these changes have given to established expectations of corporate performance would be hard to exaggerate. Every stakeholder group has had to revise the calculus by which it reckons its particular segment of the social charter—diminishing expectations in one area, raising them in another, but changing them almost universally.

No group has had to adjust its expectations more than employees. And for most the net adjustment has been downward. In many countries, the expectation of secure employment has been rudely shattered. In the United States, for instance, in the ten years between 1982 and 1992, the Fortune 500 companies shed 3.7 million jobs, almost one out of every four. And the restructuring and downsizing still go on, even in a period of economic growth, as announcements in the business press report almost daily. Similar shakeouts have already occurred or are in store for the future in state-owned corporations in Latin America and the former Communist bloc and in the European Community, as companies prepare for the unification and deregulation of markets and the full impact of the introduction of a common currency, the euro, and (still in the future) in the currently job-rich services sectors.

Consumers have been perhaps the greatest beneficiaries of this competitive restructuring, as might be expected from a trend whose basic thrust is to increase competition and market orientation. However, while restructuring has the long-term effect of increasing consumer choice and curbing price inflation, it also produces short-term macroeconomic disruption in growth patterns, thereby slowing the rise in consumer incomes. Also, since most consumer income is job dependent, consumers are hit by the same employment cutbacks and insecurity as employees.

Shareowners too have benefited for the most part from booming stock markets during the 1980s and 1990s. But for many it has been a wild ride filled with uncertainties; and there were casualties, particularly in real estate and financial services, as restructuring-induced competition pricked the balloon of unrealistic expectations, Significantly too shareownership is undergoing its own form of restructuring as institutional investors, with different needs and expectations from those of the individual investor, continue to gain market dominance and start to wield their power in dealings with corporate management.

Restructuring has had the effect of binding suppliers more closely to their corporate customers as competition demanded improvements in the efficiency of the *total* production system, including the logistics of materials and parts (e.g., "just-in-time" delivery). There have been obvious costs as well as benefits in this increasing interdependence, and suppliers' expectations reflect this change—for example, through their demands for greater trust, openness, and sharing of information in joint decision making involved in the design, manufacturing, and delivery of component parts.

With this economic restructuring therefore has come a realignment of relations between the corporation and its stakeholders and a series of challenges to corporate performance, including

- Balancing demands for job creation, job security, and improved working conditions against the need to meet increasingly fierce competition.
- Defining the form and limits of shared decision making with various stakeholder groups, in the face of demands for a greater say in the shaping of change.
- Providing expanded education–training programs to assist employees, managers, suppliers, and customers in adapting to new products–services, technologies, organizational structures, and strategies.
- Dealing with public policy proposals for a formal, written social charter (as in the European Community), spelling out the rights of stakeholders.

TRANSFORMING TECHNOLOGIES OF
THE INFORMATION AGE

The transforming technology of our age is that cluster of computer, communications, and related technologies that we refer to collectively and loosely as "information technology." It is the driving force that is transforming the industrial, mass-production economy into an information-rich, value-added economy. Paul Hawken reminds us in his prescient book, *The Next Economy*, that more is involved here than the rise of the semiconductor, fiber optics, modular telephone, "smart cards," and the like.[4] The ratio between "mass" and "information" is changing in *all* forms of economic activity, in *all* products and systems. Information is fast becoming the strategic resource. Information is power—economically, socially, and politically.

These technologies are truly transforming. They transform our economy and our society quite as radically as did the Industrial Revolution more than a century ago. A succinct and graphic summary of this transformation forms the introduction to an "Encyclopedia of the New Economy" in *Wired* magazine:

When we talk about the new economy, we're talking about a world in which people work with their brains instead of their hands. A world in which communications technology creates global competition—not just for running shoes and laptop computers, but also for bank loans and other services that can't be packed into a crate and shipped. A world in which innovation is more important than mass production. A world in which investment buys new concepts or the means to create them, rather than new machines. A world in which rapid change is a constant. A world at least as different from what came before it as industrial age was from its agricultural predecessor. A world so different its emergence can only be described as a revolution.[5]

These technologies also transform societal values and expectations, both directly and through their impact on the other driving forces. Information technology facilitates and expedites the process of globalization by speeding the flow of ideas and information across national boundaries. It is one of the most powerful drivers of economic restructuring through its redesign of business processes and the linkages it provides between functions, businesses, and institutions. And it helps shape the course of the power shift by leveraging the power of improved information flows, for instance, to improve the working of the marketplace and to strengthen the checks and balances of informed citizens in an effort to minimize (if not reverse) the growth of centralized government regulation.

More directly, these technologies change societal values and expectations through their impact on the diffusion of information, the nature of work, the structure of organizations, and the extent of relationships. Fundamentally, information technology changes our ability to know and to assess actions and events—increasingly on a global basis. Television brought the Vietnam War into the American living room; CNN made us real-time witnesses, and judges, of the Gulf War. There is now the very real prospect of "instant replay" of corporate events: Bill Gates's defense of his company, Microsoft, against antitrust charges; Mark Andreessen's launching of the Web revolution with Netscape; Steve Jobs's showmanship in his return to Apple Computer; and George Fisher's efforts to restructure Kodak. Interestingly, one important effect—particularly in the high-tech sectors of the economy—is to personalize actions to a key executive rather than depersonalize them as corporate events.

As the nature of work (the typical job) changes, so do workers' skills, needs, and expectations. Peter Drucker has noted that the information worker is a different type of employee from the manual worker and so must be managed differently. As we embrace the logic of the technology, we find we are breaking down the walls between functions and businesses. As one example, John F. Welch Jr., the CEO of General Electric, is striving to make GE the prototype of the "boundaryless company" in which the old bureaucratic and hierarchical divisions give way to more open systems and the freer flow of useful knowledge. As knowledge and information become more widely available (for example, through the diffusion of expert systems), the power of the ultimate user increases and intervening agents become "disintermediated." Thus, at one level, Welch's moves toward "boundarylessness" have helped to disintermediate whole levels of middle management; at another level, the increased availability of financial and travel information has disintermediated many brokers and travel agents as individual consumers complete transactions on their own.

The implications of these technologies for corporate market and competitive strategies are little short of shattering. The tectonic plates underlying many corporate strategies have shifted, and the old assumptions are no longer valid. However, our concern here is with the new corporate social strategies that will be needed to align organizations with the values, expectations, and behavior of these new societies.

We must first recognize that, with a societal transition as radical as this, the passage cannot be smooth and trouble free. Though the ultimate benefits are generally expected to be substantial and widespread, the individual, organizational, and societal adjustments to this transition that are required in the meantime will in the short run necessarily be disruptive, and the benefits will not automatically be evenly distributed. If we do not learn from the social mistakes in the transition in the nineteenth century from an agricultural to an industrial economy, we shall be condemned to repeat them.

As the primary driver of this technological revolution, the private corporation bears a heavy responsibility and demanding expectations for its role in easing this transition and helping preserve social cohesion and tranquility. One of the greatest threats to this cohesion is the possibility of a new and growing source of class division. In the past we referred to it as a division between the "haves" and the "have-nots"; in the future it might more appropriately be called a split between the "knows" and the "know-nots," between those who have, and those who do not have, the computer literacy, the flexibility, and learning capacity to survive in this new economy. What role can and should the corporation play in promoting improved and continuous education and training, both for its own employees and in the larger community of which it is a part?

Another effect of these technologies and the organizational restructuring that they set in motion has been to multiply and tighten the linkages between the corporation and its stakeholders. Networks of communications with customers, suppliers, distributors, and dealers are now routinely used to shorten product-development cycles, speed deliveries, reduce inventories, and in general increase efficiency. What impact do these closer ties have on the corporate governance and decision-making systems? How should one manage such a network of relationships to ensure a balancing of various constituency interests?

On a more personal level, individuals are increasingly aware of the build-up of vast dossiers of information about their purchases, lifestyles, education, family relationships, and credit and medical histories. While this information can be used to personalize product design, marketing, and service to the individual consumer, there is a growing sense that George Orwell's Big Brother has already intruded too far into our personal lives. What safeguards should corporations build into their information systems to ensure the privacy, security, and legitimate usage of personal information?

PARADIGMS OF THE FUTURE CORPORATION: ALTERNATIVE SCENARIOS

We can summarize the principal thrust of these four forces in shaping societal expectations of corporate performance as follows:

- The *power shift* has the effect of transferring responsibilities from the public to the private sector and of heightening demands for a broader power sharing in the decision-making processes of all institutions, including corporations.
- *Globalization* is raising the level of commonality in expectations between one country and the next as the "best societal practices" of corporations become globally known and establish a de facto global standard. It also increases awareness of global problems, most notably those related to population, the environment, and the division of economic resources.
- As one result of *economic restructuring,* there is a widespread yearning shared by most stakeholder groups for greater stability in relationships and for a more equitable sharing of both the gain and the pain caused by this restructuring.
- *Transforming technologies* heighten the value and expectation of access to information; radically change relationships within and between organizations; and reinforce the power of the other three formative forces.

However, there is nothing immutable and much that is uncertain about the trends in these formative forces. If we are to get a realistic perspective on the future challenge to corporations, we would do well to consider some alternate courses that these trends might take.

What are the critical uncertainties about the future course of these forces? This is not the place for a detailed analysis, but a quick examination would suggest the assessment in Table 2.1.

A useful set of scenarios can thus be structured around alternate outcomes for the two forces that would seem to exhibit the greatest uncertainty—the power shift and economic restructuring:

- Will the *power-shift* transition (to more democratic and market-oriented systems, privatization, and deregulation) continue and take firm root? Or will it succumb to countervailing forces, fail, and even be reversed?
- Will the multiple-level *economic restructuring* proceed successfully and relatively smoothly? Or will it result in considerable volatility and only partial (at best) success?

It can be argued that there is yet another critical axis of uncertainty: the nature of the corporate response to the challenge. Clearly the outcome will differ depending on whether corporate actions are seen as "responsive" or "reactive." However, in the proposed scenario structure, corporate respon-

Table 2.1
Uncertainty Assessment of Key Formative Forces, 1998–2010

Key Forces	Assessment	Rationale
Power shift	Most uncertain	The inherent uncertainty of any sociopolitical transition is magnified by the extent of the structural problems to be dealt with and the potential strength of backlash forces.
Globalization	Mixed	While ties of economic interdependence are virtually certain to increase, there is less predictability about the global financial system and international political relationships.
Economic restructuring	Uncertain	The magnitude of simultaneous restructurings (global, national, industrial, and corporate) raises major questions as to the timing, nature, and smoothness of outcomes.
Transforming technologies	Relatively predictable	The continued diffusion of information-based technologies and their impact on organizational and individual behavior is relatively predictable over this time frame.

siveness is associated with and contributes to the smooth evolution of the power shift, while reaction contributes to its failure.

The different outcomes for these two axes of uncertainty provide the underlying driving forces for four scenarios, called simply (see Figure 2.2):

- Transformation
- Neomercantilism
- Reregulation
- Turbulence

In the *Transformation* scenario, the world experiences over the next fifteen to twenty years a systemic transformation of the post–World War II political and economic environment, marked by the substitution of triad (United States–Japan–Europe) rivalry for superpower confrontation, sustained movement toward market systems and privatization, and improved international coordination on economic, trade, and environmental policies.

Trade- and technology-driven growth is sufficiently robust to provide the breathing space and resources needed for experiments in deregulation and

Figure 2.2
A Perspective on Alternative Futures

Power Shift

		Accomplished	Failed
Economic Restructuring	**Success**	***Transformation*** (Corporation as agent of social change)	***Reregulation*** (Corporation as regulated utility)
	Volatility	***Neomercantilism*** (Corporation as national competitive weapon)	***Turbulence*** (Corporation as populist target)

privatization (in Latin America, ASEAN, and former COMECON countries, for example) to develop and take root. In the advanced economies, this growth, coupled with accelerated reduction in defense spending, permits both a reallocation of resources to social and infrastructure projects and a pullback from the protectionist attitudes that had threatened to interrupt the progress toward increasing economic interdependence.

With these developments, societal concerns start to shift away from their obsession with job creation and income security to focus more on health and environmental issues, on measures to correct some of the excesses and imbalances of the economic boom of the 1980s and 1990s, and on government and business ethics. In the developed countries in particular, there is a growing sense of social healing, which leads to diminishing social tensions and increasing cooperation between business and the public sector.

Corporations continue to grapple with the problems of adjustment to the changing requirements of global economic integration and restructuring. But, with some easing of these pressures, and increasingly under the leadership of CEOs from the baby-boom generation, they become more responsive to societal concerns and expectations and thereby regain a measure of credibility and legitimacy to the point where they become recognized as primary agents of social change. Over time, progress toward new societal goals comes more from corporate initiatives than from government programs.

In the *Neomercantilism* scenario, the problems associated with global economic restructuring prove to be as persistent and difficult to resolve as many had feared.[6] Sluggish economic and employment growth in many countries gives new impetus to protectionist sentiment, a weakening of trade agreements, and the emergence of managed regional-trade blocs. Interregional trade conflicts are destabilizing, and the resultant instabilities are made even more volatile by competitive currency devaluations and deregulation of financial services institutions.

The political shift to democratic and market systems is thus more hesitant than in the *Transformation* scenario and is marked by some failed experiments and backtracking toward, for example, reregulation of financial services. However, most transitions stay the course, as people come together to find ways of "sharing the pain" through a difficult economic period (although monetary constraints necessarily circumscribe the expansion of social-welfare programs).

A new spirit of corporate openness—in both internal and external relations—leads to greater public recognition of the reality of their restructuring problems and to public-policy initiatives aimed at enhancing their global competitiveness. This neomercantilist policy avoids the dangers of overt government controls and industrial policy and views corporations as national competitive weapons to be honed and deployed in the global (and regional) economic struggle.

The *Reregulation* scenario is characterized by relative economic success and sociopolitical failure, though the pattern and balance between the two varies greatly from region to region. The global economy goes through a long and painful period of restructuring and adjustment, establishing new trading patterns in the process. It does, however, avoid falling into another world-wide recession and manages to sustain persistent, though regionally differentiated, levels of moderate growth.

This economic success comes however at the expense of the power shift. For one thing, the complexities of maintaining international financial equilibrium turn out to require a larger role for government management than market enthusiasts had suggested and worked for. For another, many of the national experiments in democracy are reversed under pressure from a public angry and frustrated over the persistence of economic pain (e.g., unemployment, declining incomes) and the absence of any apparent gain. For many, the choice once again appears to be democracy or economic success. Privatization becomes a less viable political option; and reregulation replaces deregulation as the new wave of political activism.

This reversal of the political tide is accelerated by corporate misreading of the implications of the power shift. Faced with increasing competition, and constrained by weak and cyclical profitability, corporations focus mainly on traditional economic issues, largely neglecting newer social claims and expectations. More and more, these expectations are translated into legislated requirements; and, in the process, large corporations in particular—which are perceived as rich but unresponsive—take on the characteristics of regulated utilities.

The *Turbulence* scenario is, as its name suggests, the most unsettling and challenging environment for both corporations and governments. The cumulative problems of simultaneous economic and political restructurings reach critical proportions, and the resulting tensions produce shock waves that shatter domestic tranquility and international cooperation.

Neither established nor new governments seem capable of handling the economic problems brought on by excessive public and private debt, trade imbalances, and declining defense expenditures. With growth weakening or declining, unemployment rising, and inflation an ever-present threat, the political reaction turns to policies of economic nationalism and populism.

The first victims are those experiments in privatization and deregulation that had seemed to many to offer the greatest hope for a new economic order, in developed and developing countries alike. Despite the prevailing lack of confidence in governments' economic-management capabilities, public distrust of corporations is even greater. The feeling prevails that moves toward more market-oriented systems have exacerbated the underlying problems and that the only viable choice is to return to the old course of managed trade, selective controls and regulations, and increased social-welfare programs.

Corporations become a primary target of populist sentiment and policy. Driven by competitive necessity, corporate restructuring efforts—with their inevitable fallout of workforce reductions—are bitterly resented as an affront to social equity and evidence of executive callousness. This bitterness finds legislative expression in measures to restructure corporate governance (e.g., board composition, employee rights), curb executive compensation, and increase employment security and benefits. Social responsibility thus becomes an imposed, rather than a voluntary, condition of corporate performance.

The purpose of these sketches of the future is not to paint detailed pictures, but rather to underscore the extent of the uncertainties that these formative forces entail and the differences they may create. There is a current popular misperception of historical inevitability about, for instance, the future of globalization and the surge to democracy—a belief that the end is foreshadowed and predestined in the beginning. No doubt, a historic break with the past *has* occurred; but, that does not guarantee a sure link with the future. Indeed, the very magnitude of the changes creates a turbulence whose outcome cannot be foreseen with any degree of accuracy. For executives to imagine that now the tide is running in their favor and that all they need to do is ride the wave of the future is dangerously to underestimate the challenge that confronts them and their companies.

NOTES

1. "Singapore: Competitive Order," *The Economist*, February 15, 1992, pp. 36–37.

2. Dani Rodrik, *Has Globalization Gone Too Far?* (Washington, D.C.: Institute for International Economics, 1997).

3. George Soros, *The Crisis of Global Capitalism* (Reading, Mass.: Public Affairs, a member of the Perseus Books Group, 1998).

4. Paul Hawken, *The Next Economy* (New York: Holt, Rinehart and Winston, 1983).

5. John Browning and Spencer Reiss, "Encyclopedia of the New Economy," in *Wired*, March 1998, p. 105.

6. "Mercantilism: The doctrine or policy that the economic interests of the nation as a whole are more important than those of individuals or parts of the nation, that a balance of exports over imports, with a consequent accumulation of bullion, is desirable, and that industry, agriculture, and commerce should be directed toward this objective" (from *Webster's New Twentieth Century Dictionary*, 2d edition).

Part II

THE NEW RULES OF
CORPORATE CONDUCT

What I refer to as the corporate social charter is, as the preceding chapters should make clear, an evolving phenomenon. It reflects the changing conditions of society and the economy and the changing values of consumers and the public. It is partly written in the form of legislation, regulations, and policy declarations.[1] But it is the (as yet) unwritten portion—the portion that reflects deep-seated but still not fully formed desires and expectations—that corporations would do well to monitor and respond to, if they aim to enhance their legitimacy and avoid the constraints of further regulation.

The "new rules" are not the whole of the social charter. They say nothing about (though they build upon) the vast array of expectations that have already found their way into legislation. Antitrust compliance, product safety, environmental protection, union rights, wage and benefits protection, occupational health, and all the other mandated requirements of corporate performance are taken as givens. What this section of the book focuses on are the seven issues—legitimacy, governance, equity, environment, employment, public–private sector relationships, and ethics—that now seem most likely to represent the next phase in the continuing rewriting of the corporate social charter.

I have chosen to frame each of these new rules as a simple declarative sentence. This may give the impression of greater certainty about future developments than I intend; but it has the great merit of focusing the discussion on specific proposals and actions that might be taken. And, indeed, we are not without guidance in these areas. Leading corporations are already beginning to respond to these new requirements and provide us with the outlines of a corporate agenda for the future. We can see that no one corporation has all the answers. But collectively these examples suggest the outlines of a private corporation as different in tone and practice from today's model as today's is from the model of the 1960s.

Looking back over the questions and issues likely to be raised by the four formative forces, we can begin to see the outlines of a revised social charter—the new rules that will govern corporate policies and strategies. To simplify and focus our discussion, we can codify these new rules under seven headings:

- *Legitimacy*: To earn and retain social legitimacy, the corporation must define its basic mission in terms of the social purpose it is designed to serve rather than as the maximization of profit.
- *Governance*: The corporation must be thought of, managed, and governed more as a community of stakeholders, and less as the property of investors.
- *Equity*: The corporation must strive to achieve greater perceived fairness in the distribution of economic wealth and in its treatment of all stakeholder interests.
- *Environment*: The corporation must integrate the practices of restorative economics and sustainable development into the mainstream of its business strategy.
- *Employment*: The corporation must rewrite the social contract of work to reflect the values of the new workforce and increase both the effectiveness and loyalty of employees and the corporation.
- *Public–Private Sector Relationships*: To ensure the success of the power shift, corporations must work closely with governments to achieve a viable and publicly accepted redefinition of the roles and responsibilities of the public and private sectors.
- *Ethics*: The corporation must elevate and monitor the level of ethical performance in all its operations in order to build the trust that is the foundation of sound relationships with all stakeholder groups.

NOTE

1. See, for instance, the European Social Charter in Appendix B. While this document is a statement of policy aims and principles, not mandatory requirements, the rights that it asserts for workers and citizens are presumed to be self-evident and accepted by all members of the European Community. It is also worth noting that the great majority of its 31 articles cover working conditions and thus directly affect corporate performance and policy.

— 3 —

Legitimacy:
Restating Corporate Purpose

New rule: To earn and retain social legitimacy, the corporation must define its basic mission in terms of the social purpose it is designed to serve rather than as the maximization of profit.

THE NEED FOR RETHINKING

Ask anyone what the purpose of medicine is, and you will be told, "To heal the injured and cure the sick," or "to ward off or ease the pain of physical suffering," or (in the modern idiom) "maintain health and 'wellness.'" Ask about the purpose of education, and the answers are, "Enculture the young," "train the workforce," "increase and transmit knowledge," and "promote self-development and lifelong learning." Ask anyone—consumer or educator, entrepreneur or corporate executive, economist or politician—what the purpose of business is, and, like as not, you get the monosyllabic response: "Profit"— sometimes elaborated as to "maximize profitability," or (again, in the modern idiom) "create shareowner value." I have a clear recollection of one corporate vice chairman who, when asked what the mission of his company (one of the Fortune 500) was, replied without hesitation, "To grow earnings per share 15 percent a year!" To the average corporate executive, such a response would appear both reasonable and obvious and any deflection from it would be treated as if the floodgates of socialism were being opened.

The contrast between these responses is startling and dismaying. If business can come up with no better definition of its social purpose than profit, it is little wonder that it is the object of so much public suspicion and skepticism at best and antipathy and outright hatred at worst. Corporations in particular have always been weak in what Kenneth Boulding termed "the affective domain." "No one," he once observed, "is likely to love either General Electric or the Federal Reserve!" However, I would argue that the business response is not merely unsatisfying: it is, quite simply, wrong. It does not, to my mind, reflect the facts of today's business environment.

However, it is necessity, not sentimentality, that calls for a more acceptable and accurate statement of purpose. The primacy, indeed the exclusiveness, that current statements give to profitability as the purpose of the corporation—embraced by advocates and condemned by critics—leaves little or no room for any policy or any action other than those which contribute directly and substantially to that purpose. The need for such a rethinking grows with every passing year, in part because the statement is out of touch with current reality, in part because it will be even more socially unacceptable in the future.

This rethinking is needed for both external and internal reasons. Externally, the broader corporate role that the power shift makes possible calls for a more elevated, more encompassing statement of purpose than this. Certainly, if the power shift is to succeed, as it does in the *Transformation* and *Neomercantilism* scenarios, corporations must stake out and articulate a new and stronger claim for their social legitimacy. Failure to do so, as in the *Reregulation* and *Turbulence* scenarios, will surely lead to the imposition by political fiat of new requirements and restrictions.

But there is an internal need too. Most corporations have become depersonalized to the point where energy levels are low, cynicism is high, and work fails to fulfill or excite. Managers and employees alike, particularly those in the ranks of what Peter Drucker calls the "knowledge workers" (who will soon form the majority of the labor force in many advanced economies) look for a purpose beyond making money for shareowners—a sense of mission that is more personally satisfying and organizationally effective.

It may seem surprising to start the list of new rules with one that has the appearance of being abstract and philosophical. But rethinking and restating the purpose of the corporation is neither an idle exercise in semantic quibbling nor a public-relations gambit. It matters, and it matters profoundly, not just in clarifying debate, but more important in determining action. It establishes values and priorities, influences strategy and action, and infuses the whole culture of an organization with a sense of passion and purpose. Depending on our definition, both societal expectations and corporate behavior will vary dramatically. Colin Marshall, when he was deputy chairman and chief executive of British Airways, made the point well when he said, "A corporate mission is much more than good intentions and fine ideas. It represents the framework for the entire business, the values which drive the company and the belief that the company has in itself and what it can achieve."

We need to consider the significance of this new rule at two levels: the overall purpose of the private corporation in modern society; and the specific purpose or mission of a particular company. Both are important. If we can, as a society, agree on the general statement, we can change both the climate of public opinion and the basic premise of corporate behavior. If individual corporations can define for themselves mission statements that are in tune with this basic premise, they will gain in both social legitimacy and organizational effectiveness.

RESTATING THE PURPOSE OF THE CORPORATION

Any restatement of the purpose of the corporation must start with recognizing the fact that it is a social institution, not simply and purely an economic organization. Certainly, its function is economic, but its purpose is social: It exists, like any institution, at the discretion of society to serve society's needs. On its ability to serve those needs depends its continuing claim to legitimacy.

Building upon that premise, I developed a statement thirty years ago while I was still at General Electric that seemed to me to encapsulate the true purpose of the corporation. Though much has changed in the meantime, this statement has stood the test of time, because it deals with some unchanging fundamentals. It comes in two parts, with the first part stating simply

The corporation is a creation of society whose purpose is the production of needed goods and services, to the profit of society and itself.

The second, perhaps more controversial, part of the statement continues:

As an institution of society, a corporation must reflect that society's shared values—social, moral, political and legal, as well as economic. It must change as society changes. However, as a dynamic institution, it can also seek to influence the ultimate form and expression of those changes.

Each element of that definition is needed and important, if the whole is to be an accurate reflection of reality.

The corporation *is* a social institution—a creation of society, not in the sense of being a social-welfare entity, but of serving society's needs. It is created by a charter that can be revoked either literally by legal action or figuratively by the action of the marketplace. Its principal activity lies in satisfying the *economic* needs of society through the production and distribution of goods and services in all their diversity—coal and chemicals, clothing and cars, transportation and entertainment, health care and software. And these goods and services must be *needed*. If they do not meet some individual or communal need, they will not be purchased, and the would-be supplier will have failed to justify its existence. Finally, if this cycle of events is completed successfully—and success is after all the aim—*both* the corporation *and* society must profit. This mutuality of interests is important and inescapable. If society benefits, but the business does not make money, then the corporation will go out of business—in the short run. Or, if society sees no benefit to itself from a corporation's activities, then in the long run (and the long run is what the corporation plans for) the business will not be profitable.

I have chosen to keep this basic statement terse and, some might say, mundane. This is intentional, for I did not want the statement to take on the trappings of idealistic rhetoric. I felt it better to keep it simple and within the bounds of recognizable reality. Within the phrase, "to the profit of society" lie many of the elements of social welfare that the idealist would wish for: a higher material standard of living; greater discretionary income; a better educated and healthier population; a stronger and more competitive economy; greater freedom of choice; and, yes, even a cleaner and more vital environment. These, I believe, are the stars to which corporations should hitch their wagons. They are realistic, achievable, and worthy—certainly more elevating than higher dividends for shareowners.

Arie de Geus, the former Royal Dutch/Shell planner, in his book *The Living Company* distinguishes between "economic companies," which are run as profit machines, and "living companies," which strive to perpetuate themselves by learning and adapting to the changing requirements of their environments more quickly than do economic companies. He cites a Royal Dutch/Shell study which showed that the average lifespan of a multinational corporation is now only forty to fifty years, much shorter than most of us would have guessed. One-third of the 1970 Fortune 500 companies had by 1993 either disappeared, been acquired, merged, or broken up. The study also found that the ability to return investment to shareholders seemed to have nothing to do with longevity: Profits were not a predictor or determinant of corporate health, but a symptom of it. De Geus concludes that "companies die because their managers focus on the economic activity of producing goods and services, and they forget that their organizations' true nature is that of a community of humans."[1]

Agreeing on a new definition of corporate purpose such as the one I propose is only a first step toward complying with the new rules. It is important, for it provides us with a statement of social purpose for the corporation more in line with that of other social institutions. And it implies a set of values that go far beyond the profit motive. But, for the new rule to have practical effect, corporations will have to move beyond these generic principles to develop their own statement of mission and purpose that captures the realities, values, and aims of their particular situation.

I have written elsewhere of "the power of strategic vision."[2] I defined "vision" as "a coherent and powerful statement of what the business can and should be [ten] years hence" (the time horizon varies, of course, with the nature of the business). Vision in this sense is anything but vague and impractical. It is the capstone of planning. It sets a direction and a destination. It is a force for focusing a company and motivating action throughout the organization. It is a tool that has been used with great effectiveness by leaders as diverse as Percy Barnevik of ABB Asea, Sam Walton of Wal-Mart, Akio Morito of Sony, Roy Vagelos of Merck, and Jan Carlzon of Scandinavian Airlines. Perhaps the best recent example of the power of vision in restructuring and reorienting a company has been the sustained use that Jack Welch has made of it throughout his tenure as CEO of General Electric (see Box 3.1). No executive has driven harder and more successfully toward the goal of increasing shareowner value. But none has recognized more clearly or communicated more effectively the need for a broader vision, a set of values, and a view of future possibilities that can inspire and motivate every member of the organization.

One of the first steps toward developing such a vision must be achieving agreement on the basic mission or purpose of the company. This is a statement that seeks to answer such basic questions as "Why are we here? What economic needs do we seek to satisfy? What is the basis for our claim to social legitimacy? What values do we espouse?" And here we have a great deal of evidence showing that leading corporations in the triad—United States, Europe, and Japan—have developed statements of purpose that convey a sense of mission beyond profitability. Consider the following examples.

British Airways (BA) aims "to be the best and most successful airline in the world," earning good profits in whatever it does by "putting people first." There is a sound commercial reason for this, but BA also advances the moral rationale that all of us, customers and employees alike, are people, and life would be better for all of us if we took a little more care of one another.

Johnson & Johnson, the world's largest health-care company, sets out its responsibilities to its various stakeholders in a document called "the credo," giving precedence to "the doctors, nurses and patients, to mothers and all others who use our products and services." Last in the list come stockholders and profit with the belief that if the company puts profits behind service profits will come.

J. Sainsbury plc, the U.K. supermarket chain, and ICL, the U.K. computer firm, both have mission statements based on the concept of service. Sainsbury's primary objective is "to discharge the responsibility as leaders in our trade by acting with complete integrity, by carrying our work to the highest standards, and by contributing to the public good and to the quality of life in the community." ICL's basic mission is "to succeed in the international market place by applying information technology to provide high-value customer solutions for improved operational and management effectiveness." And, in support of this mission, the company makes seven commitments: to change, to customers, to excellence, to teamwork, to achievement, to people development, and to creating a productivity showcase.

Borg-Warner Corporation, the U.S. diversified manufacturing and services company, and Matsushita Corporation, the Japanese producer of electrical products, both have statements of mission and purpose that accord with the values that the new rule embraces. Borg-Warner's 1982 statement began with

BOX 3.1

Welch's Vision for General Electric

From the day in 1981 that Dr. John F. Welch, Jr. ("Jack" to peers, employees, and the public) took over as chief executive officer of General Electric, he has articulated strongly, clearly, and constantly a vision for the company that stressed two central elements: a restructured portfolio, and a revitalized culture. The two elements are interlinked, and he has consistently implemented them in tandem, although for the first six or seven years, portfolio restructuring was his first priority.

His vision of a restructured portfolio embraces a basic concept and a central image. The basic concept is that GE will be only in those businesses in which it is (or can be) number one or number two (or, in the service businesses, has a substantial position) in the global market. Such a positioning, he argues, is needed not merely because of its greater profit potential, but because it is the only one that matches and challenges GE's resources and history and is a "stretch" goal that evokes the imagination, passion, and commitment of managers and employees alike.

The central image is a simple and memorable one of three interlocking circles: one represents the GE core or "heritage" businesses (for instance, lighting, major appliances, and turbines); another, high-technology products, such as medical systems, aircraft engines, plastics; and the third, high-growth services such as financial and information services and the National Broadcasting Company. The three circles are interlinked, with the core businesses requiring advanced process technology and strong service offerings, high technology needing a link to services, and services relying on the latest technologies to be competitive.

But it is the other element—the revitalization of corporate culture—that has evoked the most interest outside the company and posed the greatest challenge to Welch and the company. (He anticipated this challenge in a 1984 letter to me, in which he wrote that "from my experience, changing strategy and improving vision are a lot easier than moving culture.") Welch's vision of a revitalized culture focuses on achieving excellence and entrepreneurship, leanness and agility, and a "boundaryless" company— one which transcends petty functional boundaries. It envisages paring away bureaucracy, moving faster, and demanding (and making possible) the very best from everyone. The aim, as Welch is fond of saying, is to combine "the sensitivity, the leanness, the simplicity, and the agility of a small company, with the strength, resources, and reach of a big company."

the assertion that "any business is a member of a social system, entitled to the rights and bound by the responsibilities of that membership. Its freedom to pursue economic goals is constrained by law and channeled by the forces of a free market." However, it noted that "these demands are minimal, requiring only that a business provide goods and services, compete fairly, and cause no obvious harm." The company went on to assert that those requirements are "not enough for Borg-Warner. We do so convinced that by making a larger contribution to the society that sustains us, we best assure not only its future vitality but our own."

The Matsushita statement derives from the writings of the firm's founder, Konosuke Matsushita, who set the lofty goal of serving "the foundation of happiness through making man's life affluent with inexpensive and inexhaustible supply of necessities." "Profit," he asserted, "comes in compensation for contribution to society. Profit is a yardstick with which to measure the degree of social contribution made by an enterprise. Thus profit is a result rather than a goal."

Or take the example of British Petroleum Company (BP), now BP Amoco. Sir John Browne, the chief executive, has a clear philosophy and strategy that defines a role for BP Amoco that goes far beyond the production of oil and gas products. Browne believes that, for BP Amoco to thrive, the communities in which it does business must also thrive. To make that happen, Browne has insisted that the economic and social health of the villages, towns, and cities in which the company does business be a matter of central concern to the company's board of directors. He has also made social investment for the long term an important variable in compensating managers and employees.

What to do and how to do it is left to local BP Amoco business units. But regular reviews of their activities are held by regional executives: goals are set, and performance is measured against them. As a result, the company's community investments are diverse and extensive. They range from providing computer technology to control flooding in Vietnam, to replanting a forest in Turkey, to providing refrigerators in Zambia to help doctors store antimalarial vaccines. "These efforts," says Browne, "have nothing to do with charity, and everything to do with our long-term self-interest. I see no trade-off between the short term and the long term. . . . Our shareholders want performance today, and tomorrow, and the day after."

THE ROLE OF PROFIT

Despite these examples, there are at least three central issues raised by my phrasing of corporate purpose. First, if profit is not the purpose of the corporation, what then is its role? Second, should shareowner interests override those of other constituencies? And finally, which societal values should be reflected in corporate performance, and how?

There is probably no aspect of corporate behavior that can raise greater emotional response than the idea of "profit." It is at the heart of many attacks on the large corporation; and it is the most cherished concept of those who cast themselves in the role of defenders of the corporate faith. It is also an issue on which I find myself in frequent disagreement with both sides.

It is scarcely surprising that, when profit is positioned as the one true purpose of business, the conflict with social responsibility is most extreme. Businessmen (the male term is intentional here) and business apologists such as Milton Friedman and Theodore Levitt have been unequivocal in their argument that "the business of business is making money, not sweet music." "Business," Levitt once wrote, "will have a much better chance of surviving if there is no nonsense about its goals—that is, if long-run profit maximization is the one dominant objective in practice as well as theory."

But is this really the true purpose of business? A counterview comes from Andrew Campbell, director of the Ashridge Strategic Management Centre in the United Kingdom, when he states, "Business is not about squeezing the last drop out of suppliers and charging as high as possible a price to customers. This is the trader's mentality. This is short termism. This is not what business is about."[3]

A profit-maximizing company may also provide good employment opportunities for its employees, deliver good value to its customers, and expand business opportunities for its network of suppliers and distributors. But it will do these things (if we are to take this theory at face value), not because they are good things in themselves, but because they will lead to higher profits.

Now, while it may appear that the two theories are starting to converge, and that there is little practical difference between them, a chasm still remains. As John Kay, director of Oxford University's School of Management Studies, noted, "The shareholder value approach is fundamentally instrumental: meeting customer needs is a means not an end. . . . We do not need to have read Kant's moral philosophy to appreciate the difference between the person who proffers his friendship because he likes you, and the person who proffers it because he hopes to sell you double glazing."[4] The difference in thinking about means and ends will permeate the whole culture and actions of a corporation. At every level of the organization, in the mind and actions of every employee, there is either a clear-cut focus on a single, dominant financial goal or a broader recognition of the multiplicity of ends and constituencies that must be served.

In defining my own position, let me start by stating unequivocally that the private corporation must be in some sense and to some degree a profit-making organization: Without profit, its existence will be brief and troubled. But this does not require that profit should be its purpose—its reason for existence. It has a vital role as means, as motivator, and as measure, and this role is sufficient to demonstrate its importance in the business equation.

Profit provides the means—the resources for investment in research, new product development, plant expansion, and improved equipment. It is not the marginal or profitless corporation that creates new jobs, cleans up its environmental act, supports education and community activities, or does any other of the socially desirable things that people expect from business—because it can't afford to. Earning a profit and being socially responsible are not incompatible; they can be—indeed, *must* be—bound together.

Profit is a key motivator, for the corporation and the entrepreneur alike, to seek out new ventures. It is one of the incentives (not by any means the only one) that spur the application of intellectual creativity to the practical needs and problems of society.

And, finally, profit is a measure of the corporation's success or failure in performing its social role of meeting economic needs. In meeting these needs, it is essential that business earn a profit. More accurately, it is essential that the corporation feels it *can* earn a profit; the actual realization is the reward of the successful business only.

Profit is not even the only motivator of executive performance. Take just one example of executive decision making. In deciding to make contributions to education—a practice once assailed by shareowner suits, but now approved by the courts—corporations are motivated only marginally by profit. I recognize the argument can be made that such contributions help to ensure the stability and progress of institutions of higher education, and that this in turn will raise the education level of society and improve the caliber of the labor force on which these corporations will draw, thus enhancing their manpower and so their long-term profitability. But the chain of cause and effect between the actual contribution and the eventual, prospective profit improvement is so long and involved that it seems perverse to deny the existence of other motivating factors in order to maintain the exclusive purity of profit as the assumed sole motivator. Other examples abound. Providing day care, supporting community programs, developing employee education and training courses, establishing ombudsmen—in these and other cases, is it reasonable to explain corporate decisions solely on the basis of their drive for profits? Even if such actions are discounted as empty public-relations gestures designed to deflect public criticism, the door to a broader range of corporate motivators has been opened. And how are we to explain the fact that companies such as Ecover (the small Belgian manufacturer of cleaning materials) and The Body Shop (the U.K. beauty products retailer) have based their whole business strategies on an ecological foundation? That, most surely, was not the only route to profits; something else—some other values—were at work.

Nor is profit the *only* measure that corporations employ to gauge and report their success. Look at almost any annual report, and you will see that claims of sales growth, technological leadership, customer satisfaction, and employee development are also used as measures of performance.

Even with these limitations, the role of profit in the corporate equation is critical, though not the be-all and end-all. My argument is both with corporate spokesmen who would make profit the sole purpose of their enterprises and with corporate critics who see no redeeming social value in profit. We have to put profit in its correct perspective if we are to engage in any rational discussion of "corporate social responsibility"—past, present, or future. Agreeing with my definition of corporate purpose and my perspective on the role of profit does not eliminate debate over the social role of the corporation, but it does help to channel debate into more productive discussion of substantive issues if we can start from a shared philosophical and conceptual foundation.

SHAREOWNERS OR STAKEHOLDERS?

Turning now to the second question—should shareowner interests override those of other constituencies?—the first point to stress is that a company is a community of interests, and it cannot prosper unless it looks after the interests of *all* the members of that community. Shareowners are one—but only one—constituency. Other members of the corporate community include employees, customers, suppliers, dealers and distributors, and (increasingly these days) partners in strategic alliances—as well as the communities in which that company does business. *All* of these groups have a stake in the well-being of the company: *all* contribute to that well-being. This evident fact accounts for the growing popularity of the term "the stakeholding corporation."

This is not a new idea. As long ago as the 1950s Lemuel Boulware, who was at that time vice president of employee and community relations at General Electric, hammered away at the notion that management had to operate the business "in the balanced best interests of all contributor–claimants." Although his terminology was labored and inelegant, his aim was on target. And although he used the argument mainly to drum up community and labor support for his strong (some said "union-busting") union-relations policy, he did not hesitate to bring his message inside the corporation, reminding managers of the multiplicity of interests they are required to balance and protect. More recently, we have seen the growing popularity of the "balanced scorecard" as a strategic management tool for assessing and managing the whole range of stakeholder relationships, using a variety of both qualitative and quantitative measurements.

It is in many ways perverse to suggest that shareowner interests should take priority over all others, for this seems to fly in the face of this obvious multiplicity of corporate interests. The most compelling argument for this position is that shareowners are literally the owners of the business, and are free to do with it as they wish (within the limits of the law). At one time that was literally and persuasively true. Now, however, the force of this argument is considerably blunted by the fact that these "owners," both individual and institutional, are more aptly termed "investors"—people who consider themselves completely free to move their capital wherever it will earn the greatest return, and who, by no stretch of the imagination, feel involved in any sense of ownership. Further, as John Kay has pointed out, "If the business consisted purely of its physical assets, then I would find [this argument] fairly persuasive, but I don't think that is true. A company is its history, its structure of relationships, its reputation . . . and to say that shareholders own these things is kind of bizarre. They don't and couldn't."[5]

There is a distinction between creating social wealth and creating shareowner value—certainly in the short term. In simple terms, creating wealth involves producing more than you consume, adding value at every stage in the production and delivery system; it is socially beneficial, potentially benefiting all the stakeholders. Creating shareowner value, however, is targeted at maximizing benefits for only one constituency, although other stakeholders may enjoy some "spillover" benefits. In other words, the relationship between the two terms is not reciprocal: Creating social wealth necessarily entails benefits for shareowners, but creating shareowner value does not necessarily or equally benefit society and the other corporate constituencies.

In all these arguments, there seems to be an underlying bias toward the evident simplicity of "maximizing" as contrasted with the more complex task of "balancing." Economists for the most part tend to adhere to the theory that every business and every consumer acts to maximize something. But even a casual observation of our own everyday behavior reveals that we seldom act to maximize any one particular thing. More frequently, we seek to balance different and conflicting objectives and concerns. The same is true of corporations. True, balancing interests is often a difficult and sometimes frustrating task and not one that we can easily describe or explain. But it is one that we encounter daily, as parents, as citizens, and as employees, when we have to make judgments about competing claims on our time, our interests, or our money.

THE CORPORATION AND SOCIAL VALUES

Turn now to the third question: Which societal values should be reflected in corporate performance, and how? If the corporation is a social rather than a purely economic institution, it stands to reason that the way it operates should express not just economic values such as efficiency, productivity, economic value, and improved standards of material living, but a broader range of economic values that reflect the ethos of the times.

With the power shift from the public to the private sector has come a growing need for corporations to reflect qualities that we have up to now thought of as purely political values, with little relevance and appropriateness to the economic sector. In the future testing of democracy and the private corporation, governments will have to become more economically oriented, and corporations will take on more political connotations. As the prototypical economic expression of democratic systems, corporations will need to become more "democratized." Indeed, it is the very hope and expectation of greater democracy in *all* our institutions that is one of the major driving forces of social change in our age.

I realize that a word of caution and explanation is immediately called for here. I write of the "democratization" of the corporation in quotation marks, for I do not envisage that it will be transformed into a fully democratic institution in the political sense. The direct election of managers by employees, for instance, is not likely to come about in the foreseeable future. And yet I want the term to be taken seriously, for I believe that there will be growing social pressure on the corporation to give more explicit expression to traditional democratic values in its organization, policies, and culture.

What sort of values do I have in mind? Some are freedom, the dignity of the individual, equality, pluralism, justice and the rule of law, and the "consent of the governed." These are admittedly particularly Western democratic values and are far from being accepted or realized even politically in many areas of the world, such as countries as diverse as Russia, Singapore, China, and most of Africa. But the pattern is being set in what we now refer to as "the developed countries," and the globalization of ideas and information will tend to spread this pattern across diverse regions and cultures.

In the corporate context, the expression of these values will not exactly follow the political model; they will take on a form and a tone that fits the economic and organizational realities that govern corporate life. Thus, for instance, *freedom* can be thought of as one principle governing the employment relationship between an organization and its members. This relationship should be characterized by freedom of association and by expansion of the permissible arena for individual thought and action. As in the political arena, freedom is relative. Individual freedom of action is limited in the broader society by social and legal constraints and in the corporation by the requirements of business goals and organizational structure.

Clearly, the corporate limitations are more restrictive; yet even here the constraints are loosening. Certainly our social and economic system is built in part upon the idea of maximizing the degree of freedom in the association between employer and employee. At one end of the relationship, "slave labor" is assuredly proscribed, and we have laws in place to try to ensure that both parties are free to choose whether to enter into a contract of employment. At the other end—at the termination of the agreement—the trend (in Europe in particular) has been, if anything, to maximize the freedom of the individual and to curtail the ability of the corporation to fire without due cause. In between, during the actual term of employment, a whole array of trends is moving our organizations toward greater scope for individual thought and initiative: decentralization, delegation of authority, the flattening and loosening of hierarchical structures, "empowerment," and management by teams. All these trends and more are giving new life and meaning to "freedom" in the employment context.

Remember, in this and all the following examples, my argument is *not* that these values have yet been broadly achieved in the corporate context. It is only that they are now becoming requirements of corporate behavior—and that we have some supporting evidence that they are indeed realistic and realizable expectations.

Dignity and uniqueness of the individual is not an attribute of organizational behavior that comes immediately to mind. Corporate pronouncements that "people are our most important asset" ring hollow to most listeners; and few employees—except perhaps some senior executives—would characterize their standing and treatment as "dignified." But the demand for more considerate treatment of employees as individuals grows as a better-educated workforce requires that its members be treated not as "hands" (the old Industrial Age term) but as "brains" (the new Information Age term).

Indeed, it is the fact that in this new age, knowledge is a new form of capital that reinforces the social pressure on corporations to reorganize work processes, individualize compensation packages, temper managerial authority, and open up the channels of accountability and redress. In the process both organizational efficiency and individual dignity can make gains.

Equality, the third in our array of democratic values, perhaps best illustrates both the potential and the problems of translating these values into practice in the corporate arena. First, there is the matter of definition. Neither in corporate life nor in society at large can we speak of equality as an absolute, if for no other reason than the undeniable fact that individuals are profoundly unequal in their inherent talents and abilities. Rather, we focus on such manifestations of equality as equal treatment under the law and equal opportunity—in particular, equal employment opportunity.

In the United States, the transition in our social agenda from equal voting rights and equal political representation to equal employment opportunity began in the mid-1960s. Since then, there has been a rapid succession of legislative and regulatory initiatives; affirmative-action programs have been mandated and implemented; and the forbidden classes of discrimination have been steadily extended—such as race, sex, national origin, age, religion, sexual orientation, and physical and mental handicaps. We have evidently had no difficulty in translating the principles of this political and philosophical concept into the economic arena. But, thirty years later, despite widespread evidence of progress, the gap between aspiration and reality is far from being closed; affirmative action is itself under attack as a form of discrimination; and the debate between equality and equity has been joined.

The lessons from this segment of history are twofold. First, corporations can and will move toward more democratic practices, but only slowly and following a shift in national mood or priorities: Only as society's values change does corporate social behavior change. Second, progress does not follow a straight line, but zigzags following some kind of social dialectic, from thesis ("the way things are now") to antithesis ("the way they might be") to synthesis ("the first steps toward change"), which then becomes the new thesis. It should come as no surprise, therefore, that we have to measure change over decades rather than years.

Turning now to *pluralism,* we see that in a democracy a system of checks and balances is essential to guard against concentration of power in any one institution, whether within government or between government and other institutions. For the corporation, the countervailing force rests in the hands of a wide variety of internal and external constituencies. Externally, restraint comes from the requirements of regulatory and other government agencies, monitoring by special interest groups, strategies of competitors, and the power of public opinion and the legal system itself. These constraints have over time grown fairly consistently. Internally (that is, within the corporate system itself), the picture has been more mixed. The power of unions, for example, has been in decline for the past twenty years or so, but the power of institutional investors such as the California Public Employees' Retirement System (Calpers) and Teachers Insurance and Annuity Association/College Retirement Equities Fund (TIAA/CREF) has grown markedly and become more proactive. Equally significant however is the ongoing transformation of large hierarchical organizations, in which power and decision making is centralized in a few hands, into more diffused, heterarchical structures with widely decentralized power.[6]

There is a sense, too, in which the corporate equivalent of *justice and the rule of law* becomes a factor in this pluralistic system. Obviously, in its pure and original sense, "equal treatment under the law" is a political concept. Yet even here there is room for corporate application. Any company should have a set of clear, well-thought-out, and well-communicated policies that govern internal relationships—codes of ethics governing standards of corporate conduct are but one example—and that are perceived to be both equitable in intent and equitably enforced. And there should be some form of redress of grievances, whether through external arbitration or by the establishment of an internal ombudsman, to act as a balance against the potential abuse of executive power.

Finally, *the consent of the governed* translates from the political to the corporate arena as the willing commitment of members of all constituencies to the corporate venture. While money or the prospect of profit can buy the work of employees, the involvement of suppliers and dealers, and the capital of investors, experience shows that the vital contributions of innovation, initiative, and commitment cannot be bought. This is particularly true at a time when knowledge is becoming the new form of capital—when strategic success is increasingly dependent on alliances with other companies—when management by command is slowly giving way to management by persuasion as the demand for greater democracy in all our institutions gathers momentum.

The purpose of this litany of values is not to argue that they are already incorporated in the corporate scheme of things, and that "all's well with the world." Manifestly, that is not the case. Rather, my purpose has been to argue that a wide range of values beyond the purely economic—including some we have thought of as solely political in nature—can and should infuse corporate policies and action. This point follows logically from the definition of the corporation as a purposeful social institution, one in which profit-seeking plays a critical but not exclusive role.

IN SUMMARY

The end, one might say, is the beginning. Rethinking the mission of the corporation is the starting point for complying with the new rules. It is a crucial beginning because it sets the tone and motive for every act that follows. Serving a social purpose, whether it is as mundane as producing better home laundries or as elevating as improved education or a cleaner environment, can create an organization with vastly different values from one whose aim is to maximize profit and shareholder value. But it is only a beginning, for this mission has to be carried out in the real world, day in, day out. Ultimately, social legitimacy is earned not by fancy words, but by good deeds.

Some corporations have already shown the way in this regard. The examples I have cited may still be the exceptions; and maybe no one of them has the perfect answer. But they do demonstrate that it is possible to comply with the new rule—to be socially responsive and profitably competitive at the same time.

NOTES

1. Arie de Geuss, *The Living Company: Survival in a Turbulent Business Environment* (Boston: Harvard Business School Press, 1997).

2. Ian Wilson, "Realizing the Power of Strategic Vision," *Long Range Planning* 25, no. 5 (October 1992): 18–28.

3. Andrew Campbell, "Stakeholders: The Case in Favour," *Long Range Planning* 30, no. 3 (June 1997): 446–449.

4. John Kay, "The Root of the Matter," *Financial Times*, July 22–23, 1995.

5. John Kay, "Shareholders Aren't Everything," *Fortune*, February 17, 1997, pp. 133–134.

6. See the next chapter for a fuller discussion of this point.

— 4 —

Governance:
Opening up the Corporation

New rule: The corporation must be thought of, managed, and governed more as a community of stakeholders, and less as the property of investors.

The power shift has brought two key issues in its train: a heightened concern with the "business of government" and a corresponding questioning of the "government of business." We are currently in the midst of a prolonged public debate about the proper role of government in this new global Information Age and in particular about how to make government more efficient, more user-friendly, and more businesslike. At the same time, with the growth in size and global reach of large corporations, we are more concerned and critical about the way power is exercised in and by the corporation and about the adequacy of the checks and balances in the corporate governance process.

I define "governance" in the broadest possible terms, not restricting it, as many do, to questions concerning the role and responsibilities of the board of directors, important though that element is. Governance revolves around such questions as, "Who decides what, and how? How do we ensure accountability for these decisions? What checks and balances are in place to curb abuses of power? What provisions are made to ensure due process and the redress of legitimate grievances?" It covers the division of power and decision making among multiple constituencies, including management and directors, as well as questions about constituency rights and responsibilities.

THE FUTURE IMPORTANCE
OF CORPORATE GOVERNANCE

Developments in the corporate world will be roughly equivalent to the political movement toward more open and democratic systems. I do not expect corporations to become fully democratic institutions within the time frame that we are considering. But in both the corporate and the political worlds, there is a strong drive toward broader diffusion of power, giving more people a say in key decisions, clarifying and strengthening lines of accountability, and placing greater emphasis on due process.

Every one of the new formative forces discussed in Chapter 2 works to heighten the future importance of the governance issue. For instance, clearly the privatization and deregulation associated with the *power shift* places potentially greater power and more responsibility in the hands of corporate management. But this comes with the expectation of more responsible self-regulation and self-restraint in the exercise of this power as a quid pro quo for the relaxation of some of the external restraints of governmental regulation. And a skeptical public is likely to want some evidence of the existence of a governance system that at least reflects some of the key principles of democratic rule. *Globalization* multiplies the number and diversity of stakeholder interests that the corporation must factor into its decisions. *Economic restructuring* assuredly increases the concerns of all those—employees, communities, suppliers, and distributors—affected by management's decisions regarding mergers, acquisitions, downsizing, and refocusing. Finally, *information technology* is rapidly and radically binding corporations and their strategic partners (customers, suppliers, dealers, and distributors) into tightly meshed networks that amount to de facto "communities of interest"—so different from yesterday's largely independent entities that were linked by looser and more transient dealings. The freer flow of information into and out of the corporation that these new technologies make possible also serve to heighten the surveillance of corporate performance by outsiders—institutional investors, money managers, interest groups, and the press.

The combined effect of all these forces will inevitably change the way in which stakeholders perceive their interests and their links to the corporation. We might expect this issue to rank higher on corporate and public agendas in the *Transformation* and *Turbulence* scenarios, though for quite different reasons. In the *Transformation* scenario, for instance, the impetus would come primarily from within the corporation. Focusing on both legitimacy and competitive success, corporations would seek to redefine consensus management to mean building a strong, dynamic coalition of all stakeholder interests, responding to their various claims for a say in key decisions, and so maximizing their contributions to corporate success. In *Turbulence*, by contrast, widespread anger about economic distress and perceptions of corporate mismanagement could lead to a populist-style restructuring of boards of directors that stipulates a membership more representative of diverse interests and that mandates even greater disclosure and prenotification of major moves than currently exists.

Whichever future finally evolves, the general outlines of a new governance paradigm are already apparent (see Box 4.1). No doubt new proposals and

BOX 4.1

Changes in the Corporate Governance Paradigm

The "Industrial Age Paradigm"	The "New Rules Paradigm"
Basic Premises	*Basic Premises*
Accountability to shareowners	Accountability to stakeholders
Maximizing profit to increase shareowner value	Balancing interests in order to earn the right to perpetuate the business
Role and Responsibilities of the board of directors	*Role and Responsibilities of the board of directors*
Paramount duty to represent shareowner interests	Ensure that all stakeholder interests are served
Hire, monitor, and (if necessary) remove management (largely reactive role)	Act as strategic resource, adding value to strategic decisions (proactive role)
Composition–structure of board	*Composition–structure of board*
Nominated by management	Nominated by board
Majority of insiders and "connected" outsiders	Clear majority of true independents
Actions taken by board as a whole	Strong role of board committees
Chairmanship held by CEO	Chairman and CEO separate
Open-ended membership	Term limits
Predominantly national membership	Increasingly international representation
Management structure–style	*Management structure–style*
Hierarchical	Heterarchical
Command and control	Leadership and consensus
Management of internal operations	Growing emphasis on "alliances"
"Transactions-based" dealings with stakeholders	"Relationships-based" dealings with stakeholders
Information–disclosure	*Information–disclosure*
Board reliance on management reports	Direct access to corporate sources and outside assistance
Public disclosure is largely financial, restricted to legal requirements	Public disclosure is comprehensive and audited—the foundation for trust
Due process–redress of grievances	*Due process–redress of grievances*
Reliance on arbitration, union grievance procedures	Establishment of ombudsman to deal with all stakeholder grievances

new ideas will surface in the next ten years, but they are likely to reinforce the existing thrust of a movement already underway: to open up the corporation; to make it more quickly responsive to the claims of stakeholders; to insist on broader and more explicit accountability; and to strengthen the existing checks and balances in the system.

GOVERNANCE AND PLURALISM

A fundamental question that now confronts corporation at this stage is the following: "Under the new rules, what are managers and boards of directors accountable for, and to whom are they accountable?" Given the power of the past and future forces that we have examined, it seems clear that we are moving toward a more pluralistic model of corporate governance. In the Industrial Age paradigm, there was a clear-cut singularity of purpose and responsibility to shareowners for the profitable operation of the company and the creation of shareowner value. The new rules, however, place more emphasis on the plurality of executives' and directors' responsibilities to all stakeholders for all aspects of corporate performance.

This view, I should point out, is still not widely accepted in the United States. Even in Europe and Japan where there has traditionally been a greater commitment to employees and communities, the impact of corporate restructuring and global competition has had the effect of calling into question the ability of corporations to discharge these responsibilities as fully as they have in the past. In its 1997 "Statement on Corporate Governance." The Business Roundtable acknowledges that "a number of states have enacted statutes that specifically authorize directors to take into account the interests of constituencies other than stockholders, and a very limited number of state statutes actually require consideration of other constituencies." But the Roundtable stands by its view that "the paramount duty of management and of boards of directors is to the corporation's stockholders" and adheres to the instrumental view that "the interests of other stakeholders are relevant as a derivative of the duty to stockholders."[1]

However, as we saw in the previous chapter, the new rules insist on recognizing the plurality of stakeholder interests, not as a matter of ideology, but as a matter of fact—a fact that managers have to deal with every day. Without repeating all the arguments in the shareowner versus stakeholder debate, it seems clear that corporate governance must also face up to the implications of this fact. *Governance, in other words, must be designed to clarify and strengthen the lines of corporate responsibility and accountability to all its stakeholders.*

Does this then mean that, for instance, the composition of the board of directors should be changed to mirror this plurality of interests? All the indicators of the future that we have examined would seem to give a "yes"—and a "no"—response to this question. No, it is not necessary, and it is probably impractical, to stipulate in the articles of incorporation that other stakeholders should be directly and specifically represented on the board. But yes, it is important that the board be composed of directors who individually and collectively recognize their responsibility for ensuring that the corporation is managed (in Lem Boulware's words) "in the balanced best interests" of all stakeholders.

Waiting for governments to act on measures to broaden board representation would be time consuming, cumbersome, and in the end probably unproductive. Which stakeholders should be represented on the board? How should they be elected? To whom would they be accountable, and how? A regulatory approach to such governance questions—something that would most likely happen in a *Turbulence* or *Reregulation* scenario—would probably, like most regulations, end up being either meaningless or a straitjacket. It is easy enough to enumerate the standard categories of stakeholders, but the fact remains that they vary in range and importance from one corporation to another. I agree with The Business Roundtable that "good corporate governance is not a 'one size fits all' proposition, and a wide diversity of approaches . . . should be expected and is entirely appropriate."[2] Stipulations that some board positions should "belong" to certain constituencies—that, for instance, there should be a consumer representative or an environmental advocate—would be misplaced and divisive. What is really needed is an assurance that directors collectively possess all the expertise, experience, and perspectives needed to evaluate all the different facets of corporate performance.

A far preferable approach would be for individual corporations to take the initiative to ensure that these broader responsibilities are reflected in corporate decision making. As long ago as the early 1970s, General Electric picked up the "early warning signals" of this impending change in corporate governance and in 1972 moved toward a restructuring of its board of directors that among other things recognized that the board has a role in addressing issues of corporate responsibility beyond the immediate interests of investors. Because these issues involve the place of the corporation in the larger society and its acceptance in that society, they are very much within the province of the board. In describing this new approach at the time, I wrote,

A board composed of members of diverse background and experience is peculiarly fitted to this role. Free of day-to-day operating pressures, sensitive to currents of opinion and to large trends in society and government, able to rely on the collective wisdom of talented individuals, a board can provide the crucial qualities of judgment and perspective. But the directors must be chosen for their ability to contribute on the broad range of issues that the board must deal with, and not simply because they speak for some special interest group.[3]

In assessing the utility of such an approach, we should remember that it is only one part of a broader ongoing transformation of the board's role. In the old Industrial Age paradigm, directors played a largely reactive role in monitoring and auditing management's performance; firing CEOs was an almost unheard of event, and even hiring new ones was often a mere formality of anointing a preselected successor. Under the new paradigm, however, directors are becoming far more active and involved in decision making. It is not a matter of usurping managerial responsibilities, but rather—as more enlightened CEOs are beginning to recognize—of adding value as they bring their experience and differing perspectives to bear on the strategic issues facing the company. In an article in the *Harvard Business Review*, John Pound argued that "just as a democratic political system cannot work without involved citizens, corporate governance cannot work without the informed involvement of the three critical groups"—directors, managers, and major shareholders. Involving outsiders reduces the danger of insularity in managerial decisions and, he asserted, "can mitigate the behavior problems that cause companies to cling to bad decisions."[4] In such a context, it becomes more feasible to argue that directors have a key role to play in attending to the social responsibilities of the corporation.

Even so, this is not a perfect solution, and certainly it will not satisfy the purists. But it is, I submit, feasible, and preferable to straitjacket regulation. Indeed, to paraphrase Winston Churchill's appraisal of democracy, it may be the worst form of governance "except all those other forms which have been tried from time to time." Such an approach is capable of changing the calculus by which corporate decisions are made and so of influencing their performance. And it is the realities of performance rather than the niceties of form that weigh most heavily with the public.

There are, however, a number of further conditions that must be satisfied for this approach to be workable, most notably the need to ensure that the board is truly independent and that there is a clear approach to giving a public accounting of the discharge of their responsibilities.

STRENGTHENING THE BOARD'S GOVERNING POWER

The board of directors will continue to be a key pillar in the corporate governance system; but it will have to change its style and role. For the most part, it has worked effectively in the past in discharging the duties then expected of it. But over the past ten years, a series of major corporate crises has shown all too clearly some strains and defects in the system. We have seen, for instance, the inadequacies of adhering to a largely reactive role and of delegating too much and too trustingly to management in the crises that engulfed such supposedly strong companies as General Motors, IBM, Westinghouse, American Express, AT&T, and Sears, Roebuck. The warning signs were there for all to see in every case, but directors were reluctant to break the implicit bond of trust in management until disaster stared them in the face. Even under the old paradigm of the primacy of shareowner interests, changing conditions were manifestly signaling the need for stronger, more active participation by directors. With the advent of new rules and the addition of new responsibilities, the case for change becomes even clearer.

What, then, needs to be done? First, we need to acknowledge that the board of directors is separate from the management of the company: It is the corporate governing body, and has separate and specific obligations to the owners and, I argue, to the public and other stakeholders. This separation demands that the board should be truly independent—not just a collection of "management's pet rocks," as Ross Perot once disparagingly described them. This independence begins with a stipulation that a substantial majority of directors are outsiders, not company executives. From a governance point of view, insiders are essentially pointless, for they cannot provide independent insight about the company's or management's activities.

Three questions immediately arise: Who is an "insider"? Who is an "outsider"? And, what is meant by "a substantial majority"? Clearly, current company managers are insiders; but even retired executives should be considered inside directors because of their close involvement with the company's past strategies and culture.[5] Directors who are also officers of firms that provide significant services to the company, such as law, accounting, or consulting, could also pose conflict-of-interest problems and, some would argue (as GM does), should be considered inside members. Ideally perhaps, the company's chief executive officer would be the only insider on the board, as is the case at Campbell Soup, Colgate Palmolive, and Merck. But it is not necessary to impose such a tight interpretation of the intent of the new rules. As with fine art, the public may not be able to define exactly what they mean by "independence," but they know it when they see it. Most certainly, however, the definition cannot be stretched to cover such boards as those at H. J. Heinz Company or Archer Daniels Midland.

A second move toward strengthening the board's powers would be to separate the role of chairman from that of chief executive officer, assigning the chairmanship to an outside director. This practice is already fairly common in Europe and was one of the key recommendations of the Cadbury Report on corporate governance in the United Kingdom. It is not yet, however, the norm in the United States, although Benjamin Rosen, the venture capitalist, is chairman of Compaq Computer, and for a brief period, John G. Smale, retired chairman of Procter & Gamble, acted as nonexecutive chairman of General Motors. The key argument in favor of such a move is that the board should be free to set its own agenda and that, since setting the agenda is a function of the chairmanship, this role properly belongs to an outsider to ensure the board has a free rein in exercising its oversight responsibilities. Such a division of responsibilities is also an expression of democratic processes, as the *Financial Times* noted when it called the action by the British Petroleum board several years ago, in ousting Robert Horton from the joint positions, "a triumph for corporate democracy."[6]

The counterargument—that this arrangement would be divisive and hamstring the CEO's ability to manage the company—is based on the misperception that power is a zero-sum game. This is not the case. As John Smale has noted, "In theory, there is no transfer of power, even if some seems to be implied by the process. Boards have always had the same responsibilities. The only difference is in how they have executed them."[7] Strong boards should be a source of strength and not a threat to management.

Another option to this clear-cut separation of roles is to create the role of lead director, selected by the independent directors. This individual would work with the CEO–chairman in setting the board agendas and chair periodic meetings of the independent directors. While falling short of the neatness of the other arrangement, this does have the merit of increasing the independent voice in board governance and provides a quick way for assuming a leadership role in any emergency. However, it is critical for directors to have a clear understanding as to when and how nonexecutive leadership of the board would be assumed. As The Business Roundtable statement noted, "In some boards, the presence of one strong figure might provide the natural leader. In other circumstances, there could be an understanding that leadership would fall to the committee chair responsible for the subject matter that gave rise to the need. In still others, it could be the responsibility of the committee chairs to recommend whether non-executive leadership is required, and if so, in what form."[8]

The expanded use of board committees has proven to be a third route to strengthening the board's governing power. Many companies have already proven that a board can be much more effective and probing if it uses specialized committees to do the necessary preparatory work before the issue is brought before the whole board. This was, indeed, an essential factor in General Electric's restructuring of its board as early as 1972. In the period immediately preceding this restructuring, two factors had become increasingly evident. One was the trend toward demands for greater public accountability. The second was the fact that large companies were entering a period in which they were being caught up in many more diverse crosscurrents than they used to be. Added to the basic problems of running the business and competing effectively on a worldwide basis were a host of new challenges—social, environmental, political, and technological.

In essence, GE's restructuring of its board of directors was a response to those two factors by trying to strengthen the board's approach to them. Formerly, the approach was for the board as a whole to tackle almost all areas of concern at its monthly meetings. The revised structure sought to put much greater emphasis on the committees by enlarging their number and expanding their responsibility. Much of the board's work was to be considered first in committees preparatory to the full board sessions.

Initially, five committees were established: Operations, Audit and Finance, Technology and Science, Management Development and Compensation, and Public Issues (now renamed Public Responsibilities). Subsequently, the Audit and Finance Committee was divided into two separate committees; and, in 1978, a new Nominating Committee was formed to concentrate on board succession and organization. Each committee is chaired by an outside director, and three (Nominating, Audit, and Management Development and Compensation) are made up entirely of outside directors.

The precise details of this restructuring are less important than the fact that it occurred as it did and when it did. The value of early warning and early action—being alert to changing conditions in competition, the market, and society, and being prepared to adapt to new requirements—is obvious. It enabled General Electric to steer clear of the problems and acrimony that have surrounded this topic for the past twenty years. And it is a lesson that still has significance as corporations continue to adapt to the next phases of governance reform.

A fourth and critical precondition for board independence is access to information. Independent judgment and independent sources of information go hand in hand. It is hard to see how outside directors can bring the full weight of their experience and judgment to bear on critical issues, particularly those with broad public and social impacts, if they are always and completely dependent on the CEO–chairman for their information. That is why it has been suggested that nonexecutive directors should be given funds to hire staff and pay outside experts to conduct independent studies and audits. The Campbell Soup board, for instance, hired its own investment banker and legal counsel to appraise a proposed change of strategy for the company. And outside directors at General Motors can call on managers below the CEO at any time, although they make it a practice to do so only with the CEO's knowledge.

These and other measures (see Box 4.2) are all aimed at strengthening and opening up the corporate governance system by ensuring that the board is capable of making informed and independent judgments on *all* the key elements of corporate performance. Directors have always had a legal and statutory obligation to the shareowners. They are now being required to assume a de facto (not yet a de jure) responsibility to the public and other stakeholders in the company. It is, of course, not sufficient that directors and corporations recognize this responsibility. It is not even sufficient that they bring performance into line with these new societal expectations. There must also be (and be seen to be) a clear public accounting and auditing of this performance.

BOX 4.2

"Best Practices" of Corporate Boards

A review of management and financial publications, as well as corporate annual reports and proxy statements, brings to light a variety of additional measures that have been adopted in an effort to strengthen the independence, effectiveness, and governance powers of boards of directors. Prominent among these measures are the following:

- Evaluate performance of the chief executive officer annually in meetings of independent directors.
- Link the CEO's pay to specific performance goals.

- Review and approve long-range strategy and one-year operating plans.
- Have a governance committee that regularly assesses the performance of the board and individual directors.
- Pay retainer fees to directors in common stock.
- Require each director to own a significant amount of common stock.
- Require directors to retire at seventy years of age.
- Place the entire board up for election every year.
- Place limits on the number of other boards on which directors can serve.
- Ensure that the audit, compensation, and nominating committees are composed entirely of independent directors.
- Ban directors who directly or indirectly draw consulting, legal, or other fees from the company.
- Ban interlocking directorships.

EXPANDING DISCLOSURE AND ACCOUNTABILITY

Just as the quarterly and annual reports are published to provide an accounting to shareowners and institutional investors of a company's financial condition, so are we moving toward more detailed and explicit reporting of corporate performance across the whole spectrum of activities. We sometimes refer to these activities as "social" or "nonfinancial" areas, but this terminology misleadingly suggests that they are secondary, less important activities. It masks the fact that activities such as environmental protection, health and safety, equal employment opportunity, employee training, and community relations are now considered integral elements of corporate operations and can have profound financial implications, both positive and negative.

The fact of the matter is that, under the new rules, society is more and more inclined to judge a company *as a whole*. Certainly, the public places a high value on excellent products, courteous service, satisfying jobs, and increased dividends; but this does not mean that they will be forgiving of toxic pollution, overseas sweat shops, antitrust violations, or ethical lapses. This holistic approach to evaluating a company's behavior is a reflection of a whole array of diverse but related forces. Societal values have become more demanding; regulatory requirements have broadened; and public interest groups have grown in number and influence.

A central factor in this new Information Age is that information on almost any topic becomes almost instantly widely and freely available. Attempts to stem this flow, whether from Tiananmen Square, the Pentagon, or the tobacco companies, have universally failed. This is a fact of life with which corporations are having to grapple. Where a repressive Communist government has failed, there is little chance that corporations, with their looser discipline and more porous boundaries, will succeed. Whether from internal whistle blowers or from governments, the press or institutional investors, auditors or interest groups, information will find its way out.

What is emerging, slowly but surely, is a system of corporate disclosure and accountability that will eventually be

- *Comprehensive*: It will be designed to cover both financial and competitive performance and what we now term the "social aspects of business."
- *Understandable*: It must be phrased in terms that are both interesting and intelligible to the concerned lay person. One of the lessons from the failed experiments in social audits, as described in Chapter 1, is that, quite apart from the difficulty of placing a financial evaluation on these social activities, ordinary prose is more appropriate—and more descriptive—than financial calculations for such a report.
- *Standardized*: Although uniformity of reporting is an elusive and probably unattainable goal, some measure of standardization is desirable. Just as financial accounting has developed its conventions as to how expenses, depreciation, and revenues should be reported, so social accounting will have to establish some commonly accepted ground rules governing reports of other corporate domains.
- *Audited*: For this accounting to earn broad credibility, it must be reviewed and certified by an independent professional body in the same way that financial accounts are at present.
- *Available*: The results of the audit must be publicly available and accessible to any concerned stakeholder. Since it is clearly impossible to maintain a register of all stakeholders in the same way that there is a register of shareowners, there cannot be a routine distribution of these reports, but their availability, including being on-line, must be publicized and well known.

We are already farther along the road to such a system than many people or companies recognize. A great deal of information about corporate social performance is in the hands of government regulators (OSHA, EPA, EEOC, CPSC, SEC, FCC, FTC—the regulatory alphabet soup goes on and on), and much of this is publicly available through the Freedom of Information Act. But the new rules require more than that a company should comply with existing regulations: *That* is taken as a given. It is not enough that the company should be law abiding. It is what is done voluntarily that becomes the basis for societal judgment.

Nowadays most corporations include in their annual reports a section describing their efforts in environmental protection, equal employment opportunity, community relations, and philanthropy. But some have gone beyond this, publishing separate social reports that are as detailed in their way as the financial statements. General Motors is a particularly noteworthy example of such reporting, notable for the continuity, detail, and consistency of its efforts. Starting as early as 1971, the corporation convened a conference with prominent educators and representatives of foundations and investment institutions "to explain the progress General Motors has made in a number of areas of public concern and to obtain the participants' thoughts as to the Corporation's activities and goals in these areas."[9] The topics covered in this initial venture included automobile emissions, industrial pollution, urban transportation, minority opportunities, and automotive safety. And, following the conference, the company published the executive presentations together with summaries of points raised in the discussion periods. Over the years, the reports have become more detailed and focused on environmental, health, and safety affairs. The 1996 report, for example, covers

- GM's environmental policies, organization, and management.
- Materials policy and voluntary materials reduction programs.
- Releases to the environment and voluntary toxic emissions reduction.
- Waste management.
- Use of energy and voluntary greenhouse gas reduction programs.
- Workplace health and safety.
- Emergency response and public disclosure.
- Product stewardship.
- Supplier relationships.
- Health, safety, and environmental audits.

Significantly, the document asserts that "performance counts and this report *demonstrates our accountability to all of GM's wide-ranging constituencies*" (emphasis added), thus acknowledging that GM's accountability is not to shareowners alone.[10]

Looking ahead, we can see that perhaps the two most difficult and controversial attributes of such a broad disclosure and accountability system will be standardization and auditing. Resistance, even among corporate leaders, to these proposals will likely be as strong in the future as it has in the past to every other proposal for disclosure of corporate information. Thus, even Intel Corporation, which has a strong and well-publicized record on environmental, health, and safety affairs, opposes the adoption of standardized guidelines with the argument that this "would divert the Company's time, money and effort away from environmental programs that currently are developed and implemented by the Company."[11] General Motors notes that its environmental "audit documents are confidential and not available to the public," although its annual health and safety self-audits are conducted jointly with the United Automobile Workers Union, which maintains independent oversight of the program.

Yet even in these two areas, substantial progress has already been made. Take for example the work of the Coalition for Environmentally Responsible

Economies (CERES) and its efforts to formalize and standardize environmental accounting. CERES is a coalition made up of hundreds of institutional investors, fifteen of the largest environmental groups, and almost sixty endorsing companies who support the CERES principles (see Appendix C) as a guideline for environmental responsibility. Among the endorsing companies are nine Fortune 500 companies, including General Motors, Bank of America, Sun Company, Bethlehem Steel, and Polaroid. In addition to expanding the number of endorsing companies, CERES is moving toward the development of a detailed environmental report that is sufficiently standardized so that it can be audited and rated. Bob Massie, the executive director of CERES, is convinced that sometime within the next ten years it will be possible for anyone, from small investors to pension-fund managers, to log onto the Internet, navigate to a corporate web site, and pull up a detailed standardized report on the environmental performance of every company listed on U.S. stock exchanges. Professional environmental auditors will assess companies according to a body of Generally Accepted Environmental Accounting Principles. And commercial and investment banks will respond favorably to those firms with excellent records of performance, driving down their cost of capital.

The CERES effort is by no means unique. It mirrors, for example, the far broader efforts of the International Standards Organization (ISO), which recognized the need in a global economy for harmonizing national standards through publishing ISO9000, covering quality standards, and ISO14000 on environmental management. ISO's aim is not to enforce uniformity, but to specify the essential elements that a good quality- or environmental-management system must contain if it is to earn general recognition. Many countries, including the United States, India, France, Japan, and Australia, have endorsed the ISO standards and reissued them as their own, including provisions for external assurance of company compliance with the standards.

Another more recent example, designed to piggyback on the ISO quality-auditing system, is Social Accountability 8000. This is an initiative of the Council for Economic Priorities (CEP), a New York public-interest group, but it has already gained the support of a broad spectrum of U.S. and other companies, including Avon Products, Sainsbury's, Toys 'R' Us, Otto Verand (which owns Eddie Bauer), labor and human-rights groups, and, most significantly, accounting firms KPMG-Peat Marwick and SGS-ICS. Although the effort was sparked by the public and political debate in the United States over companies' use of offshore sweatshops, even its initial agenda goes beyond this issue to start the development of common labor standards for the global economy. Thus the proposed standards contain provisions for safe working conditions, respect for workers' rights to organize, payment of wages sufficient to meet workers' basic needs, and a ban on child and forced labor and on regularly requiring more than forty-eight-hour weeks. As with ISO9000, companies that want to comply with these standards can apply for certification by an outside auditor.

All these efforts fall short of the complete disclosure and accountability system outlined above, but they are all steps taken in the same general direction. And the movement is likely to gain increasing momentum, not from government regulations as in the past, but from millions of consumers and concerned citizens worldwide who will come to expect compliance with such standards and who will demand information on which to base their judgments.

"Sunlight," Justice Louis Brandeis once wrote, "is the best disinfectant." In an increasingly democratic society—and that is the direction in which most societies are currently moving—"sunlight," in the form of public access to information on the workings of all societal institutions, is the most direct, least intrusive route to ensuring accountability and the alignment of institutional goals with societal values. This is a truth that corporations must learn to accept. In the past, the emphasis was on minimum disclosure and the *privacy* of the private corporation. In a more open future, one in which their performance is more widely and critically appraised, corporations will have to recognize that increased disclosure is not only the price they must pay for reduced regulatory oversight. It is also (and more positively) a way in which they can build more trusting relationships with the multiple stakeholders on whom their success will depend.

DIFFUSING AUTHORITY AND RESPONSIBILITY

It is not only in the relationship between the board and senior management that the corporate governance system is changing. Changes are also under way in the structure and culture of the organization. From the point of view of governance, two of these changes are of particular significance. One is the structural change from hierarchy to heterarchy; the other, the shift from transactions to relationships as the basis for dealings with stakeholders. Both have profound impacts on the distribution, extent, and calculus of decision-making responsibility in the corporation.

First, take the move away from hierarchical structure and what this means for the governance of the corporation. One way of appreciating the extent and significance of this change is to consider the different images or paradigms that we use to convey our understanding of the true meaning of organizational structure. For instance, the image that we used to represent the old industrial model was the pyramid. This was the paradigm that was virtually universal in the 1950s and 1960s and is still very much extant today. It was the way we viewed General Motors and Charlie ("Engine") Wilson, U.S. Steel and Roger Blough, and AT&T and H. I. Romnes. The mental image that we carried with us accurately conveyed the reality of a rigidly structured organization, with authority tightly focused in one individual or a small group at the top, with successive layers of lower management arrayed in hierarchical fashion, progressively broader in numbers but narrower in authority, until we came to the lowest level (and we used this demeaning term)—the workers who actually performed the real work of the organization. Even in supposedly decentralized companies, this image held good as the model for the major divisions of the corporation. Overall, the paradigm stressed the industrial equivalent of the divine right of kings, channeled power very circumspectly, restricted public accountability, and stressed the literal as well as the figurative dependence of the organization on decisions by a few.

About midway through the 1960s, a new paradigm started to emerge, largely as the result of the "human-resource" movement led by individuals like Abraham Maslow and Douglas McGregor. The new image was the circle, and it underscored a radically different perception of the internal relationships within a corporation. Now the CEO (or business unit head) was placed at the center, rather than at the top, of the organization; the company was not, literally and figuratively, so dependent on this one individual, whose primary function was no longer that of making all the decisions, but rather of supplying the vision and leadership that provided a centripetal force, a central dynamic, to give cohesion and drive to the organization. Without this, centrifugal forces would take over, and the organization would fractionate. This was, in many respects, a more realistic, as well as less hierarchical, view of what was actually happening in the real world. Another commendable and accurate quality of this paradigm was the fact that it positioned the workers, not at the lowest level, but at the perimeter, the true cutting edge of the organization. The impact of this new paradigm was obviously profound in its effects on the way we thought about such matters as manager–employee relationships, the nature of authority, organizational structure, and culture. Purely from a governance point of view, the impact was, therefore, at the micro level, on bringing nonmanagerial employees into the decision-making loop, promoting teamwork, and making union relations less confrontational. Perhaps, however, its major contribution was that it set the stage for the next paradigm shift.

This third paradigm, the one that accords most closely with the intent of the new rules, is more complex and more laden with implications, not merely for governance, but also for strategy and stakeholder relations. The new image is that of a network (see Figure 4.1), a complex interconnection of nodes (each of them a circle) bound together, not by a chain of command, but by a shared purpose. While the new image appropriately suggests the critical importance of the networking technologies of computers and communications, technology has been an enabler rather than the driver. Many of the changes embodied in this model have been required by changing business conditions (for example, globalization and economic restructuring) and strategic requirements. Technology has simply made it possible to make them more smoothly and more completely. This is the model of the new General Electric and the

Figure 4.1
The New Organizational Paradigm: A "Network of Relationships"

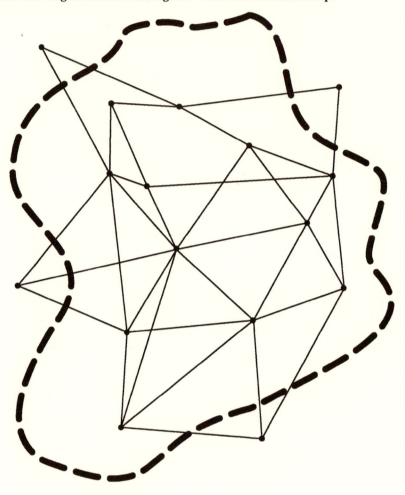

Key:

〜 "Traditional boundary" of the corporation

• Organizational center

"boundaryless corporation" under Jack Welch and of many of the start-up companies in Silicon Valley.

From a governance and management point of view, the most obvious characteristic of this paradigm is that it is heterarchical and polycentric, rather than hierarchical and centralized. Decision-making authority and responsibility is widely diffused throughout the organization, far more so even than in the supposedly decentralized organizations of the past. Why has this come about? Primarily because the speed and complexities of today's business environment require a corresponding speed and flexibility in corporate response and decision making; and this would simply not be possible, even with the new technologies, if the old hierarchical system were still in place. The position of chief executive officer still exists, but it is one more nearly of "first among equals," and its leadership function has changed (as we shall see in Chapter 10).

Another fascinating characteristic of the new paradigm is the fact that some of the nodes appear to lie outside what we have traditionally thought of as the boundaries of the corporation. As suggested in Figure 4.1, these are the joint ventures, alliances, and other forms of strategic "bonding"—linkages with customers, suppliers, distributors, and even competitors—that are reshaping the modern corporation. To serve customers more rapidly and efficiently (on *their* terms), corporations are linking customers' ordering systems with their own inventory control and production systems. To improve product quality and facilitate "just-in-time" delivery of parts and components, suppliers are being linked to design and production systems and even establishing operations in the corporate plants and offices. To penetrate new markets or develop new technologies, alliances are being formed with other companies, even competitors. Prime examples of this new model are Dell Computer and Cisco Systems. Michael Dell's direct business model, selling direct to the customer and building products to order, depends on "virtual integration" and "stitching together a business with partners who are treated as if they're inside the company."[12] At Cisco, the network is pervasive, central to nearly everything. It seamlessly links Cisco to its customers, prospects, business partners, suppliers, and employees.

The character of management—the culture of the corporation—is thus changing dramatically. In addition to their traditional responsibility for managing internal operations, executives now find themselves managing a range of diverse "alliances" with customers, suppliers, distributors, and even competitors. The range of stakeholders is broadening all the time, and the nature of their relationship with the corporation continues to evolve. As a general observation, we might say that the linkage between many stakeholders and the corporation is shifting from a transaction basis to a relationship basis. By this I mean that in the past the relationship between the corporation and its customers, suppliers, dealers, and distributors was largely defined by a series of arms-length transactions, each more or less an end in itself. Now, in many cases, the relationship is closer and more intricate as portions of their operations become interwoven in seamless fashion. In his book, *The Loyalty Effect*, management consultant Frederick Reichheld demonstrated the benefits that companies can gain from fostering these longer, more intimate, and more stable relationships. Old customers do more business and give more referrals than do new customers; reducing turnover among suppliers reduces overhead costs and maintains position on the learning curve; and retaining the commitment of employees keeps their collective knowledge and experience within the corporation and makes for more harmonious relationships.[13]

From the point of view of governance, the importance of these developments is twofold. First, stakeholder interests are becoming more frequently and more closely related to routine corporate operations. Second, in the new heterarchical organization, responsibility and authority for decision making on matters of major concern to the corporation is now widely diffused. As a result, concern for stakeholder interests is no longer just a matter for top management; it is being driven down into and throughout the organization.

FORMALIZING DUE PROCESS

Inevitably, disputes arise over the way stakeholders are treated—disputes over unethical behavior, defective products, abuses of power, discriminatory treatment of employees, or the way in which stakeholder interests are balanced. One mark of a truly democratic institution is the way in which it provides within its walls a system of due process for an objective examination and resolution of these disputes.

Until relatively recently, few corporations had any way of dealing with such disputes other than through face-to-face negotiations between the parties involved. Failing to come to resolution, complainants had no choice but to turn to an external third party: arbitration, the courts, a regulatory agency or interest group, or union grievance procedures. Only now is there a growing recognition that there is a third and in many ways better route to follow: reliance on a corporate ombudsman.

Ombudsmen are common in universities, hospitals, and government agencies, but still relatively rare in the corporate world. However, a series of external and internal developments has come to increase companies' interest in responding more positively to this aspect of governance. In the late 1970s, for example, the then-growing consumer revolt against product and service defects led a number of companies such as Chrysler and General Electric to establish consumer ombudsman offices with powers to resolve legitimate consumer complaints, even overruling previous management decisions. Then in the late 1980s, a spate of ethical crises aroused executive concern and led some U.S. corporations to appoint ethics officers, usually senior managers with long experience, to provide an internal channel for reviewing employee complaints and protecting whistle blowers.[14] Most recently, in 1991, publication of the new federal sentencing guidelines, which give milder penalties to companies with antifraud programs, has given further impetus to this movement, more than doubling membership in the nonprofit Ombudsman Association to 165. Beyond these individual company efforts, there has been a growing number of industry-wide programs such as the Canadian Banking Ombudsman, an independent organization for providing impartial resolution of complaints about banking services, with a dozen participating banks.

These examples are just straws in the wind. But they all indicate a wind blowing in the same direction—a growing recognition that the new rules of governance require greater corporate willingness to admit that mistakes of judgment and abuses of power will occur even in the best of organizations and that the best way to deal with them is openly, directly, and internally.

IN SUMMARY

One of the problems we encounter in any discussion of corporate governance lies in the vocabulary we use. We refer to the *private* corporation (even if it is publicly owned) and the *private* sector in order to distinguish them from the *public* sector of government. This is a legitimate and discriminating use of the word, but we have tended to go on from there to draw some not-so-legitimate deductions. For instance, exaggerated emphasis on the *privacy* of information, and on its sole accountability to the *private* investors who are its shareowners has grown up around the corporation. This flies in the face of the facts: The corporation is clearly a very public enterprise, serving (as we have noted) a public purpose, and depending on public (and consumer) approbation for its legitimacy. These facts, reinforced by the changing trends we have reviewed, are leading to a change in public perceptions and to a rewriting of the rules of governance.

The new rules emphasize concepts that we have, until now, associated more closely with the public domain: pluralism, checks and balances, openness, accountability, and due process. Whether in moves to strengthen the role and independence of the board of directors, to create more open and less hierarchical organizations, or to increase public disclosure and accountability, there is a common purpose: to govern and manage the corporation for what it is— a true community of stakeholders, not simply the property of shareowners.

NOTES

1. The Business Roundtable, "Statement on Corporate Governance" (Washington, D.C.: The Business Roundtable, 1997), 3.

2. Ibid., 4.

3. Ian Wilson, "One Company's Experience with Restructuring the Governing Board," *Journal of Contemporary Business* 8, no. 1 (April 1979): 71–81.

4. John Pound, "The Promise of the Governed Corporation," *Harvard Business Review* 73, no. 2 (March–April 1995): 89–98.

5. General Electric has a long history of requiring that CEOs step down from the company board on their retirement—for a different reason: to give the new CEO greater freedom of action without feeling that a predecessor was "looking over his shoulder."

6. David Lascelles, "A Classic Coup for Democracy," *Financial Times*, June 27–28, 1992.

7. John Smale, Contribution to a Perspectives article, "Redraw the Line between Board and the CEO," *Harvard Business Review* 73, no. 2 (March–April 1995): 154ff.

8. The Business Roundtable, "Statement on Corporate Governance" (Washington, D.C.: The Business Roundtable, 1997), 13.

9. General Motors Corporation, *Progress in Areas of Public Concern* (Detroit: General Motors Corporation, 1971).

10. General Motors Corporation, *Environmental, Health & Safety Report* (Detroit: General Motors Corporation, 1996).

11. Intel Corporation's response to stockholder proposal #3 in 1998 proxy statement.

12. John Magretta, "The Power of Virtual Integration: An Interview with Michael Dell," *Harvard Business Review* 76, no. 2 (March–April 1998).

13. Frederick F. Reichheld, *The Loyalty Effect* (Boston: Harvard Business School Press, 1996).

14. See also Chapter 9.

— 5 —

Equity:
Increasing Fairness in the System

New rule: The corporation must strive to achieve greater perceived fairness in the distribution of economic wealth and in its treatment of all stakeholder interests.

"We hold these truths to be self-evident, that all men are created equal" proclaimed the United States in its Declaration of Independence. Thirteen years later, at the storming of the Bastille, the rallying cry of the French Revolution echoed through the streets of Paris: "Liberté, égalité, fraternité!" Less rousing perhaps, but just as influential, the concept of fair play has been woven into just about every aspect of British life, from cricket to parliamentary procedures. So, with these historical precedents, we should expect that, in a world that is steadily democratizing, the values of equality, fairness, and justice will appreciate in the social and political arena. And, as we have learned from past experience, these values will in time inevitably find their way into the economic arena and influence the standards by which we judge corporations.

However, it is *equity rather than equality* that I believe will be the goal of this new rule. Economic equality has been a chimera that has eluded most societies that have pursued it; and it has failed miserably to promote wealth and prosperity in the few cases where it has been attained or approximated. Equity, on the other hand, is a more robust, and far more widely accepted, goal. By equity, I mean fairness—fairness in the opening up of economic opportunity, and fairness in the way people are treated by the corporation, fairness in the way the economic pie is divided.[1]

FRAMING THE ISSUE

Equity, or fairness, is fast becoming a key social issue, due in part to a reaction against the imbalances arising from recent economic restructurings, and in part to a continuing rise in democratic populism. There is a widespread perception that the 1980s were a decade of *inequity*, one in which there were massive differences in the way in which the pain and the gain resulting from economic restructurings were distributed. The pain of layoffs and declining living standards has been heavily concentrated in the ranks of old-line manufacturing workers and middle managers; the gains, in compensation, status, and security, have been almost exclusively confined to senior executives, financial brokers, and the new technological elite. It is a pattern that we have seen before. As Ron Chernow, the author of *Titan*, a biography of John D. Rockefeller, noted in a *Fortune* interview, "There are striking parallels between the late 19th and late 20th centuries. You have an extraordinary number of new industries created by technological innovation. Whenever this happens, people roll up gigantic fortunes, which forces government to redefine the nature of business and government. It creates tensions between the haves and have-nots. It calls into question the legitimacy of wealth and the functioning of the systems."[2]

In the United States, where the differences have been perhaps the most marked and are still growing, the pressure for change has so far been held in check. Competition, weakened union bargaining power, and the threat of layoffs have combined to restrain wage and salary demands in many industries and moderate the voices of protest. And those who have prospered have had little incentive to add "fairness" to their social agenda. It is also true that, even among those who have seen little increase in wage or salary, there are many who have invested in the stock market where the ebullient rise in share prices has aligned their interests with those of entrepreneurs like Bill Gates, if not with CEOs of more traditional corporations.

It takes little imagination, however, to see that this situation can easily change, regardless of which way the future develops. If economic growth continues, as it would in the *Transformation* and (to a lesser extent) *Reregulation* scenarios, the bargaining power of employees would be enhanced, and market forces would dictate some narrowing of the income gap. Or, if we encounter a period of economic turbulence, as we would in either the *Neomercantilism* or *Turbulence* scenarios, then populist pressure would make economic fairness a much higher priority in the public agenda. There is little chance, therefore, that this issue will disappear.

For corporations, a perplexing problem is the elusiveness of the challenge that this issue poses. While the general intent of the new rule is clear, the devil is in the details; and the details of public and stakeholder expectations are constantly shifting. To start with, there is the slipperiness of the very concept of "fairness." It is much easier to define equality, in both practical and philosophical terms: We may differ as to its desirability and how to achieve it, but we can agree on what we are talking about. Equity, however, lies very much in the mind of the beholder: What is "fair" is almost inevitably a matter of personal value judgment. Indeed, it is perceptions and personal definitions, quite as much as facts, that are at the core of the issue.

Equity pervades every aspect of and every relationship within corporate performance. At its fullest expression, the new rule seeks to ensure fairness as between one group of employees and another, between one group of stakeholders and another, and between one country and another. However, to illustrate the theme and focus this chapter, it is helpful to concentrate on just three aspects of this new rule: equity and executive compensation; equity and diversity; and equity and global employment standards.

EQUITY AND EXECUTIVE COMPENSATION

Perhaps the most egregious—certainly the most publicized and controversial—perceived inequity in recent years has been the developing compensation gap in the United States between the highest and lowest levels in the corporate hierarchy. As Figure 5.1 makes clear, the rapid expansion in this gap was a product of the 1980s. For at least fifteen years, from 1965 to 1980, the CEO and production-worker pay indexes grew almost exactly in parallel, maintaining the pay differential that had been established in the post–World War II years. Then, starting in 1980, a gap emerged, widened in 1982 (even though this was a recession year), and exploded in the remaining years of the decade.

The question then arises, Why? What was so different about the 1980s that triggered this sudden divergence of established trends? Two characteristics of this period immediately come to mind. First, this was the "decade of the deal," a period in which quick financial returns reigned supreme. Junk bonds, LBOs (leveraged buyouts), and hostile takeovers became part of the new vocabulary of Wall Street. In the process financial rewards became associated more with deals, and with those able to negotiate such deals, than with sustained performance. It was not only the investment bankers and lawyers—the Michael Milkens and Carl Icahns—who gained from their role in such deals. Many CEOs and other senior executives were able to reap substantial benefits in many ways—through direct participation in LBOs, through persuading their boards of directors that the "going rate" for executive pay had now escalated, or through negotiating "golden parachutes" to protect them against hostile takeovers.

A second more substantial and longer-lasting factor was the fact that this was a time when U.S. corporations finally came to grips with their need to become globally competitive and to adjust to rapidly restructuring markets and industries. This was a task that required more of CEOs than "run-of-the-mill" management skills: It demanded vision, leadership, a commitment to needed restructuring, and persistence. Experience has shown that surprisingly few executives possessed all these qualities. For every Jack Welch (GE), Lou

Figure 5.1
The Exploding Pay Gap: Product of the 1980s

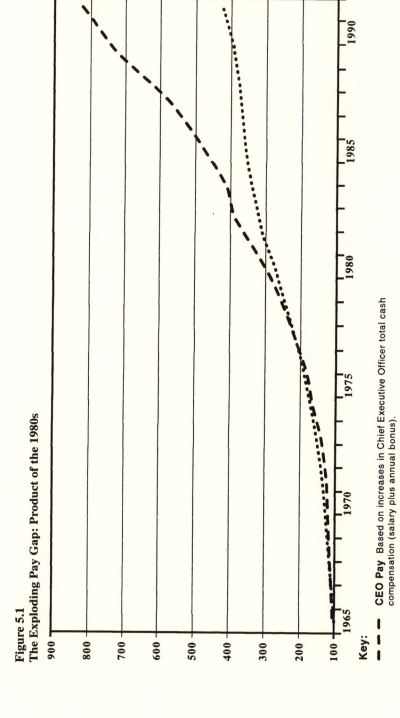

Key:

— — CEO Pay Based on increases in Chief Executive Officer total cash compensation (salary plus annual bonus).

•••••• Production Workers' Pay Based on increases in average hourly wage paid to nonsupervisory manufacturing employees.

Source: Sibson & Company, "Chief Executive Officer and Production Worker Pay, 1965–1991," Princeton, N.J., 1991; Bureau of Labor Statistics, Washington, D.C.

Gerstner (IBM), and Robert Goizueta (Coca-Cola), there were a multitude of John Akerses (IBM), Robert Allans (AT&T), and Robert Stempels (GM). What happened then was what always happens when there is a shortage of supply: The market bids up the price of the needed commodity to meet the growing demand. However, as the pay of star performers escalated, the second- and third-tier executives demanded and, in favorable economic conditions, obtained substantial increases. As a result, there has been a constant ratcheting up of executive pay to its present highly visible and much criticized levels.

And there can be little doubt that this issue is now reaching critical proportions. The evidence is found far more widely than simply in the epithets of public reaction: "shameful," "absurd," "obscene," and/or "totally unjustifiable." Critics as well informed as Graef Crystal, the compensation consultant, have fueled this outrage by showing how often there is a lack of congruence between high levels of executive pay and improved corporate performance. Institutional investors like the State of Wisconsin Investment Board are using their financial clout to press for reforms, particularly in reining in the unrestricted grant of stock options. *The Wall Street Journal, Business Week,* and *Financial Times* all conduct regular surveys of executive and boardroom pay, highlighting abuses and running editorials to the effect that "there is a crucial difference between high pay and too much pay." Even some executives are expressing misgivings about the operation of the compensation system. In a *Business Week*–Harris Poll, for instance, 47 percent of executives—a dangerously high percentage—said that they thought the compensation of top officers of large U.S. companies was too high.[3] The warning signs of trouble are there for all to see.

The situation and the danger of public reaction is even more grave than Figure 5.1 would indicate, because this chart includes only *cash compensation* (salary plus annual bonus). It does not take into account the role of stock options which can escalate executive pay to almost incredible heights. Consider, for example, the top ten earners for 1997 noted in Table 5.1.

Clearly, the up-front cash payments are only the beginning of the story. Indeed, while the salary and bonus for the average CEO actually fell from 1996 levels (to $2.2 million from $2.3 million), the *total* compensation package—including the exercise of options, long-term incentive plans, and perks—increased to $7.8 million—a gain of 35 percent or more than thirteen times the 2.6 percent raise that the average blue-collar worker earned. In sum, *the average CEO's total pay in 1997 was 325 times that of the average factory worker.* Such a multiple is beyond the public's comprehension. Corporations may try to rationalize such figures, arguing that the CEO has, by his or her leadership, contributed infinitely more than this to shareowner value in the company and so deserves this differential. But the public's emotional reaction resists such a rationalization.

Table 5.1
Top-Paid Chief Executives, 1997

		Long-Term Compensation	
Name and Company	**1997 Salary and Bonus**	**Thousands of Dollars**	**As Percentage of Total Pay**
Sanford Weil, Travelers Group	7,453	223,272	96.8
Roberto Goizueta, Coca-Cola	4,052	107,781	96.4
Robert Scrushy, Healthsouth	13,399	93,391	87.5
Ray Irani, Occidental Petroleum	3,849	97,657	96.2
Eugene Isenberg, Nabors Industries	1,675	82,872	98.0
Joseph Costello, Cadence Design Systems	584	66,258	99.1
Andrew Grove, Intel	3,255	48,958	93.8
Charles McCall, HBO & Co.	1,725	49,684	96.6
Philip Purcell, Morgan Stanley Dean Witter	11,274	39,533	77.8
Robert Shapiro, Monsanto	1,834	47,491	96.3

Sources: Proxy statements, Execucomp by Standard & Poor's Compustat.

The question remains: If 325 is not the "right" (i.e., justifiable) multiple, what *is* the right, or "fair," multiple? Where does equity lie in apportioning rewards across the spectrum of executives and employees? The differing answers that are offered to these questions only serve to underscore the difficulty in putting forward a precise figure that will be widely accepted. Ben & Jerry's, for instance, at one time adhered to Plato's reasoning that the right ratio between top and bottom is five to one. Peter Drucker, on the other hand, has suggested that the right multiple is on the order of twenty; and his reasoning has begun to be accepted by a number of companies such as Herman Miller, the furniture maker. Significantly, too, a multiple of fifteen to twenty seems to be the norm among European and Japanese companies, prompting the public to ask the question, If executives in these economically advanced countries "get by" with more modest compensation, why should U.S. CEOs require fifteen to twenty times more?[4]

It is precisely this difficulty that has led to the filing of proxy statements that, while seeking to establish a cap on executive compensation, have not sought to impose an arbitrary figure. Rather, they have proposed, as the Franklin Research & Development Corporation did to General Electric, that the company should "wrestle with the issue of the rising wage-gap," establish its own cap as a multiple of pay of the lowest paid worker, and then "explain to shareholders . . . the determinations used in order to determine the appropriate cap."[5] A reading of the history of this issue suggests that over time, this gap will indeed be narrowed, not by legislation or litigation, but rather through market forces, social and investor pressures, and heightened management sensitivity to the nuances of equity as a desirable corporate value.

The prospects for a substantial narrowing of the gap are in fact quite good. As we have seen, it was the proliferating use of stock options, originally introduced with the commendable objective of linking executive and shareowner interests by rewarding CEOs if they drove up stock prices, that has accounted for the overwhelming majority of executive pay increases. And it is likely to be through greater moderation and rationality in the allocation and exercise of options that some measure of equity and balance is restored to the compensation field.

The pressure for greater moderation in the allocation of executive options comes from many sides—liberals and consumer groups, institutional investors, and the business press. Even *The Wall Street Journal* has criticized the practice: "Options . . . exacerbate capitalism's worst tendencies: the fixation on stock price at the expense of long-term planning, the obsession with personal gain over corporate loyalty, the widened gap between income groups."[6]

At least three key reforms are needed to achieve this objective:

1. *Eliminate (or greatly restrict) the use of "repricing" and "reloading"— two practices that have proved most inequitable to other shareowners and distorted the original purposes of the compensation system.* With repricing, executives are able to exchange existing options for new ones at a lower price when the stock falls. Clearly, this is a luxury that the average shareowner does not enjoy and is designed to set executives apart as a privileged class. *Business Week* characterized it as "the equivalent of heading for the lifeboats while everyone else goes down with the ship."[7] This is an obvious distortion of the original purpose of options and has drawn the fire of the State of Wisconsin Investment Board, TIAA-CREF, and other institutional investors. With reloading, an executive's options, instead of disappearing when exercised, are automatically replenished from the options pool. This encourages executives to lock in profits earlier and takes some of the risk out of the pay process (the risk that the system was supposed to encourage in the first place). Although the reload is always for fewer options than the original grant and executives must "buy" those options by tendering shares they already own, it allows them a hedge that ordinary shareowners do not have. This, too, is a practice that many institutional investors oppose because of its potential for abuse and its absence of restrictions. Both repricing and reloading are representative of the convoluted games that some executives and compensation committees of boards of directors play in an effort to circumvent tax and accounting restrictions. And both draw the suspicion and anger of professional investors and general public alike.

2. *Strengthen the link between pay and performance by raising the standards that must be met before options pay off.* There is no question that standard stock-options plans as they are practiced today set the bar too low and reward even mediocre CEOs for substandard performance. Now there is a movement, led by both investor groups and some tough-minded companies, to raise the bar. The Council of Institutional Investors, representing more than one-hudred pension plans with assets of over $1 trillion, has gone on record in favor of indexing option grants, making their value contingent on a company outperforming the market or a peer group of companies. For shareowners, these premium-priced options championed by Monsanto, Colgate-Palmolive, and Transamerica are much more equitable. Monsanto, for instance, has adopted a premium-priced plan covering Robert Shapiro, the company's CEO, and thirty-one other executives, which stipulates that the stock price must rise by 50 percent over three years before their options are profitable.

3. *Make stock options available to all (or most) employees.* According to a survey by William M. Mercer, Inc., the employee-relations consulting firm, about one-third of the 350 largest companies have set aside grants for broad-based options plans—although only 10 percent have so far given options to half or more of their employees. Furthermore, the National Center for Employee Ownership estimates that 15 thousand U.S. companies have broad employee ownership, most of them (approximately 10 thousand) through employee stock ownership plans (ESOPs), which enjoy special tax breaks under federal law.

It is predictable that a distinguishing characteristic of twenty-first-century capitalism will be growing ownership by employees. ESOP participants alone already number nine million and control on average 10 percent to 15 percent of the stock in their companies. Whether this leads to employees becoming a new force in corporate governance remains an unanswered question. But, regardless of this, such a move has a triple advantage: It breaks down corporate class barriers, reinforces efforts to push responsibility and authority down into the organization, and instills a greater sense of fairness in the way the corporate system operates and is perceived.

Because equity is such a nebulous concept—so hard to define with any precision as to its meaning in any given context—it is difficult to say where the pendulum of public opinion and corporate behavior on this issue will come to rest. All one can say with any degree of certainty is that the next swing will be in the direction of a reduced differential between executive and employee pay—one that is more rational, less convoluted, more defensible—and more "equitable."

EQUITY AND DIVERSITY

Unlike the compensation issue, on which public opinion is sending clear and unequivocal signals as to its expectations, this issue of equity and diversity places the corporation at "ground zero" between two conflicting forces. On the one hand, there is a persistent demand for greater fairness in the treatment of all employees—a "more level playing field" in employment and compensation practices, a lowering of the discrimination barriers between one class of employees and others, and a more democratic community. On the other hand, there is a growing reaction against the conduct and consequences of affirmative-action programs that were originally put in place to correct the discriminatory practices of the past. Determining what is "equitable" (or what the public perceives to be equitable) in these circumstances is therefore particularly difficult.

There can be little doubt that "affirmative action" is in trouble. The assault on it in Congress, in the courts, and at the grassroots level, is gathering momentum, and the charges are multiplying:

- "Affirmative action is now directed toward so many classes—ethnic minorities, women, the elderly, homosexuals, the handicapped and so on—that it has become an impassable tangle of legislation and litigation."
- "Affirmative action programs simply don't work—or benefit only those who need them least."
- "They are themselves discriminatory, most especially against white males."
- "They demean those whom they are supposed to benefit by setting lower standards for them."
- "Quotas and 'set-asides'—in jobs, promotions, or contracts—are especially pernicious."
- "The original noble aims of equal opportunity have been lost or distorted."

This does not mean that the issue will disappear. Indeed, corporations should assume that the objectives of "affirmative action," by whatever name it is called, will remain high on the social agenda. Even if the current political and popular reaction leads to the dismantling of most explicit quota and set-aside programs, there will still remain on the books an array of statutes allowing individuals to sue for discriminatory behavior on the part of employers. In the United States, for example, these statutes would include, at the federal level, the Equal Pay Act of 1963, Title VII of the 1964 Civil Rights Act, the Age Discrimination in Employment Act of 1967, and the Americans with Disabilities Act of 1990; and most states and many cities have civil-rights laws of their own. This fact alone, together with the existence of interest groups intent on publicizing discriminatory behavior and supporting individual law suits, guarantees that equal employment opportunity will remain a critical requirement of corporate behavior.

But there is an additional, more positive, reason for corporations to be concerned with this issue. Multiculturalism is fast becoming a critical fact of life for societies, companies, and other institutions. Not only is the workforce in many countries becoming more diverse, as more and more women and others previously excluded or discriminated against join the ranks of the employed—

and some in management. Globalization is also a factor, multiplying the diversity of cultures, consumers and markets, as well as workforces, with which many companies now have to deal. Accommodating this fact is therefore not only a matter of complying with the law or avoiding lawsuits: It is a matter of recognizing how much the world has changed at home and abroad and that corporate behavior must change as well to take advantage of these new opportunities.

Diversity has become a strategic imperative for corporations, and the term has already entered the corporate vocabulary. Although this has been thought of largely as an American phenomenon, the issue transcends national boundaries. Many of the fundamental principles remain the same even though the specific issues differ. In other countries, issues other than race are at the heart of diversity and discrimination. In Europe and Asia, for example, the biggest diversity challenges revolve around gender, class, education, language, and religion. If there were any question about the global reach of the women's movement, for instance, one need only consider the attention and significance given to the International Conference on Population and Development in Cairo in 1994 and the Fourth World Conference on Women in Beijing the following year. Both represented milestones in the movement toward policies that will ensure women's equal participation in societies around the world.

The goal is no longer integration per se, as it was when the issue was predominantly a racial one, but equality in an open, pluralistic society. This suggests that any action, whether by government or by the private sector, that is directed at this problem should aim for

- A true equality of opportunity, overcoming the historical legacy of obvious inequalities and discrimination.
- An openness of society which gives maximum freedom to individual choice.
- A pluralism which values cultural diversity rather than homogeneity.
- An equitable and proportionate sharing of power.

However unexceptionable these basic concepts may be, there will obviously be room for debate and controversy on some of the implications for action. For example, any program designed to redress the imbalances caused by previous discrimination will almost certainly, as we have seen with affirmative action, encounter charges of "reverse discrimination" or "preferential treatment." This backlash can only be mitigated if it is made clear that the "preferential treatment" is designed only to put people on an equal footing and stops at the *preparation* stage. The same standards of performance and discipline must be expected of all employees; to apply a double standard would only establish a new form of discrimination.

A critical examination of the diversity programs of some of the leaders in this field—Avon, Bank of America, Pitney Bowes (see Box 5.1), and Xerox—

BOX 5.1

Pitney Bowes's Diversity Program

Pitney Bowes has a broad diversity program that touches just about every one of its 32 thousand employees. Although the company has a long history of commitment to equal employment opportunity, the current program picked up speed in 1987 with the formation of a women's resource group and a minority resource group. These groups determined that more should be done to ensure an inclusive work environment, and the company created a formal diversity task force in 1992. As a result the company established the Diversity Strategic Planning Process, which focuses on five general areas for progress:

1. Communications and training.
2. Employee development and profiles.
3. Work–life balance.
4. Business diversity.
5. Community relations.

Specific objectives are to be achieved over a three-year period. Each business unit is now required to develop a diversity plan, reviewed each year by the CEO, with specific goals for representation, recruitment, and employee development and a focus on minority and female inclusion. Importantly, senior managers are regularly evaluated on their diversity results, and this performance is reflected in their pay and promotion.

The company also engages in a number of external diversity initiatives. One is an active minority and women suppliers program, which spent more than $52 million (7.7 percent of discretionary expenditures) on services and materials purchased from these suppliers in 1997. It also creates special alliances and has affinity programs with a number of national organizations.

Overall, the company's workforce is now 38 percent minority and 37.6 percent female. Women represent 41 percent of those reporting directly to the CEO.

underscores the fact that there are a number of critical requirements to ensure that these programs are workable, effective—and equitable:

1. *Diversity planning should be an integral part of strategic planning.* Strategic planning is something that most corporations understand and take seri-

ously, so linking diversity planning (as an element of human-resource planning) to this process helps to gain management attention. It also underscores the fact that corporate action on this front is not just a matter of "social responsibility": It is a matter of business necessity.

2. *Senior management must make a strong and visible commitment to the program.* This is true with any systemic change in a corporation, but particularly true when the change can be perceived as peripheral to the "real business of business." It is often the case that it is not until the organization understands that senior management wants action that action will in fact occur. It also helps when the ranks of top management include women or minority men like Kenneth Chenault, president and heir apparent at American Express; Carly Fiorina, chief executive officer at Hewlett-Packard; Rebecca Mark, vice chairman of the energy company, Enron; Sari Baldauf of the Finnish company Nokia, where she heads up development of the company's Third Generation cell phones; and Eiko Kono, president of the Japanese publishing firm, Recruit.

3. *The program must be as complex and comprehensive as the problem itself.* As the problem is systemic, so the program that addresses it must take a systems approach and a long view; nothing less will suffice. Every branch of the human-resource system must be involved: recruiting, skills development, job placement, mentoring, job rotation, and promotion, along with diversity-training programs for managers to help change attitudes and behavior.

4. *Goal setting is critical.* Setting policy and direction is not enough. For progress to occur, targets must be set and progress toward them measured. There is an important and valid distinction, which the public seems to recognize, between setting targets and establishing quotas or set-asides; targets are more flexible and less restrictive and so fit more comfortably with concepts of fairness and openness.

5. *Managers must be measured and rewarded in part on the basis of their diversity performance.* Measurement is important, not only at an organizational level to determine progress (or the lack of it) toward the attainment of goals, but also on an individual level to help motivate managers to adhere to the new values of inclusion and equity. A portion of an executive's salary should therefore be tied to his or her performance in promoting diversity. The cynic or the ethicist might criticize this practice as "bribing people to do the right thing." It is most certainly true that it is better to do the right thing simply because it is right, rather than because you will be rewarded for doing it. However, the larger point here is that measurement of managerial and executive performance is a healthy and needed activity. And it is better that the measurement take into account *all* the needed aspects of performance, including diversity and equity, rather than focusing only on sales and profit. In fact, it is not unreasonable to argue that inclusion in the measurement system is a good indicator that a new element is now an accepted part of managerial performance.

EQUITY AND GLOBAL EMPLOYMENT STANDARDS

In discussing the effects of globalization (Chapter 2), we note that it raises troubling questions about its uneven impact on national economies and about the integrity and consistency of corporate employment and compensation standards on a global basis. There are—and will be for the foreseeable future—fundamental differences between countries in their living standards, their work conditions, and societal expectations—differences that stem from their underlying economic and social development rather than from corporate action or inaction. The question, however, is how long these differences will endure and what role the corporation should play in their narrowing. In what is fast becoming "one world," the global corporation must move with integrity and consistency, despite the differences it encounters from country to country. For the corporation, this is an economic issue, a political and social issue, and an ethical issue.

It is an economic issue because it impacts the costs and competitive positioning of the corporation. A company decides to build plants overseas for one or both of two main reasons: to serve the local or regional markets more efficiently or to take advantage of lower labor costs, fewer union restrictions, or less onerous workplace regulations. The question then becomes, "How far should the company push the competitive advantage that substandard wages or workplace requirements might provide?" Even a purely economic calculus would suggest that the advantage should not be pushed to its limit, in part because of the desirability of hiring a better qualified labor force, and in part because this extreme advantage is likely to be transitory as global economic trends narrow the gap.

From a sociopolitical point of view, the corporation has to deal with the expectations and requirements of both the host country and its home country. Host countries for the most part welcome the boost to their economic development that corporate infusions of capital, technology, and know-how can provide. However, these countries are now more sophisticated and discriminating and are aware of what it takes to be successful in the global economy. As a result, governments of developing countries are starting to promote more than basic low-cost manufacturing, requiring a proportion of management and higher caliber jobs for native-born employees, skills training, and the establishment of research facilities. The price of entry into new markets is thus being raised. At the same time, home countries, fearful of the wholesale transfer of manufacturing employment to developing countries, are pressuring corporations to adhere to higher wage and employment standards in their global operations. Political, union, and public pressure is building on corporations to raise their level of performance on four issues: substandard wages; child labor; the use of forced (prison) labor; and hazardous working conditions.

The spirit of the times is changing and with it the model of desired corporate behavior. For example, when the International Labor Organization (ILO) attempted to address the problem of child labor in the 1970s, it received scant support from the world community. But by 1998 the ILO was well on its way to approving a ban, not only on abusive forms of child labor, but on the use of forced labor and hazardous working conditions. This time the U.S. decision to support the ban and encourage its trading partners to do so was part of a larger effort to link foreign trade with worker rights and work standards. The ban is thus likely to be a first step toward broader global workplace standards.

Another sign of the times is the experience of two major sporting goods manufacturers. Adidas-Salomon AG had to face embarrassing charges that some of the soccer balls it made to commemorate the 1998 World Cup were sewn by political prisoners at Chinese labor camps. The possibility that prison labor may have been used has become both a commercially and ethically sensitive issue. Adidas's main rival, Nike, saw sales fall off appreciably amid media reports that its products were made in Asian factories with poor labor conditions. The San Francisco public interest group, Global Exchange, relentlessly attacked Nike for paying substandard wages even by Third World standards. After years of pressure to correct these conditions, Nike's CEO, Philip Knight, decided to revamp the company's labor policies, pledging to raise the minimum worker age, increase wage levels, increase workplace health standards by substituting water-based solvents for toluene, and let human rights groups monitor its overseas plants. Nike also agreed to publish summaries of the groups' conclusions and recommendations and use U.S. health and safety standards.

Toy maker Mattel has taken a more proactive stance in publishing a code of conduct for its production facilities and contract manufacturers and developing an independent audit and monitoring system to ensure adherence to the code. Mattel has said that no one under the age of sixteen is allowed to work in a facility that produces its products: As CEO Jill Barad put it, "Simply stated, Mattel creates products for children around the world—not jobs." The code also sets minimum working hours and wage standards, renounces the use of forced labor, and bans discrimination and dangerous working conditions.

What is being asked of corporations? What will be accepted as "equitable behavior" in this domain? If we set aside the extreme positions of those who oppose virtually all multinational operations, the agenda boils down to renunciation of child and prison labor; payment of wage levels above the national minimum; adequate training programs; and health and safety standards that will, over time, move toward those in developed countries. In other words, corporate behavior should be "nonexploitative." Corporations should not exploit the lower workplace standards of less developed societies, for the sake of competitive advantage. Rather, they should set a higher standard of pay, hours, safety, health, and training that will lead the local economy and society to a higher level of development. What exactly a "fair" standard should be in all this is left to judgment in each individual case. It cannot be that of a developed country; and it should not be that of the lowest common denominator. Between these two poles lies a vast area within which the corporation must choose to take its stand.

IN SUMMARY

Equity, the capital invested in a business, is a concrete term for executives. It is definable, quantifiable, and measurable. It is therefore something that they are comfortable in handling. But equity, in the sense we are discussing here, is an abstract value for them. It is hard to define, difficult to quantify, and impossible to measure. It is therefore an inherently uncomfortable concept for them. There is an innate, and to some extent understandable, tendency for executives to emphasize what can be measured and to relegate the unmeasurable to the realm of peripheral concerns. Unfortunately for the corporation, these supposedly peripheral issues can be propelled, by events or interest-group pressure, into a position of central importance, with hard, even harsh, consequences for the business. This is a fact whose force Nike came to recognize when sales fell under the impact of a consumer boycott due to Asian working conditions.

We have touched on just three aspects of equity, but the issue is far more pervasive than this limited treatment might suggest. The growing acceptance of the stakeholder concept multiplies the number and diversity of corporate relationships in which equity is a key, if not a central, factor. Balancing the interests of stakeholders inherently involves considerations of fairness in the treatment of one group versus another. In the future, corporations will be called upon, not merely to demonstrate the rationale for differences in treatment, but to account for the fairness of their actions.

NOTES

1. See, for instance, the definitions given in *Webster's New Twentieth Century Dictionary* (2d ed.): "(1) justice, impartiality; the giving or desiring to give to each man his due. . . . (4) in law, . . . resort to general principles of fairness and justice whenever existing law is inadequate."

2. Ron Chernow, "Rockefeller and Gates: Playing Monopoly," *Fortune*, June 22, 1998, pp. 164–166.

3. Keith H. Hammonds, "Are They Worth It?: How Top Executives and the General Public View Executive Pay," *Business Week*, May 12, 1997, pp. 40–41.

4. Executive "perks," which do not appear in these figures, may well play a larger role outside the United States, but do not account for the wide difference in ratios.

5. Share Owner Proposal 7 in the General Electric 1998 Proxy Statement.

6. John Helyar and Joann S. Lublin, "Corporate Coffers Gush with Currency of an Opulent Age," *The Wall Street Journal*, August 10, 1998.

7. Jennifer Reingold, Richard A. Melcher, and Gary McWilliams, "Executive Pay: Stock Options Plus a Bull Market Make a Mockery of Many Attempts to Link Pay to Performance," *Business Week*, April 20, 1998, pp. 64–70.

— 6 —

Environment:
Strategy and Sustainability

New rule: The corporation must integrate the practices of restorative economics and sustainable development into the mainstream of its business strategy.

At their outset, the nineties were heralded as "the decade of the environment." After the three historic environmental disasters of the eighties—the oil spill of the Exxon Valdez, the nuclear meltdown of Chernobyl, and the toxic chemical cloud of Bhopal—the new decade was supposed to usher in an era of global environmental awareness as nations and industries moved toward the policies and practices of "sustainable development." And the start of this new era was to be marked, in 1992, by the United Nations Conference on Environment and Development—the Earth Summit, as it was optimistically called—held, appropriately, in Rio de Janeiro, a bridge between the developed and developing worlds.

In retrospect, the nineties have become the "decade of the Internet" (witness the explosive growth of Web surfing, e-mail, and electronic commerce), or the "decade of restructuring" (changing the contours of economies, industries, and companies), or the "decade of uncertainty" (witness the turmoil in Russia, Asia—and technology)—choose your term. Certainly these are the concerns that attract most executives' attention. In my work with management groups, the environment does not register prominently on their internal radar screens as a breakthrough issue of the future. It is not that they expect any turning back of the environmental clock. Indeed, they assume that regulations will continue to tighten and spread and take pride in reporting, as General Motors does, on their "green" accomplishments. To that extent environmental quality is now a given in the executive suite. Few, however, believe that we might be entering a new phase of the environmental movement, one which will require the writing of new rules of corporate policy and operations. Yet I am convinced that such will be the case.

IMPETUS TOWARD THE NEXT PHASE

The environmental movement has already, in the nearly thirty years of its modern incarnation, passed through a number of phases, each with its particular sphere of emphasis. Phase 1, starting in the early 1970s with the first Earth Day, focused mainly on the issues of clean air and clean water, with secondary emphases on energy efficiency and endangered species. Phase 2, during the late 1970s and early 1980s, targeted the adverse effects of hazardous and toxic substances on human health and safety. "Save our children" replaced "Save the whales" as the rallying cry. Then later in that decade an embryonic phase 3 started to emerge, emphasizing measures aimed at resource conservation and recycling. Now, after a period of regrouping and preparation, we are, I believe, in the early stages of a new phase—one that shifts the emphasis from dealing with local and topical issues to a global and systemic approach.

This is a shift for which the Rio Conference was designed to prepare us. So far the results have been disappointing. Clif Curtis, the Greenpeace coordinator at the conference, gave his discouraging assessment of the lack of progress: "Political will among governments has fallen far short of the mark, and the private sector, with few exceptions, has shown that the environment always loses when it's a question of profits versus doing what's right for the planet. There are some success stories, but there are far too few."[1]

Despite this discouraging, but probably accurate assessment, the Rio Conference did, however, lay the foundation for—and largely legitimize—a broad agenda for environmental, economic, and political change. Among other things, it succeeded in

- Getting high-level, worldwide attention for such major issues as global climate change, biological diversity, deforestation, and ocean pollution.
- Incorporating into international law, through the global warming treaty, the principle that nations must consider the global environmental consequences of internal economic decisions.
- Taking the first steps toward dealing with the critical North–South issue of financing developing countries' programs to implement conference agreements.
- Creating a new U.N. body to oversee member nations' environmental responses and the assistance to be provided by developed countries.

Taken together, these initial steps have greater potential for forcing governments and corporations to change policies and practices than any previous international agreement.

The question then becomes, What will supply the needed impetus to move us from these principles to a new level of action? Conventional wisdom suggests a number of developments that are likely to advance the environmental cause over the next ten to fifteen years, and move corporations toward a more proactive strategy. First is the fact that, as one element in the power shift, there is a developing trend in regulatory policy to make greater use of market-style incentives (such as pollution trading rights) rather than rely exclusively on command-and-control measures. The reasoning is that this approach provides greater flexibility with least-added cost, and corporations have a vested interest in making these experiments work to avert any public and political backlash. There is also a growing recognition that, as writer and businessman Paul Hawken puts it, "Business is the only mechanism on the planet today powerful enough to produce the changes necessary to reverse global environmental and social degradation."[2] This fact alone works toward an expansion of corporate responsibility for the well-being of the larger society.

We can also identify a number of other trends that are likely to come to fruition in this period:

- Increasing consumer antipathy to the environmental window dressing that, in all too many cases, currently passes for "green marketing," and greater support for real efforts to improve the performance and ecological soundness of products.
- The gradual emergence of standardized environmental metrics which will allow companies—and their external stakeholders—to measure progress and act accordingly.
- The growth of already large markets for environmental products, services, and technology, particularly in the Asia–Pacific region and Eastern Europe.

However, these are largely incremental developments, calculated rather to consolidate and expand the gains made over the past thirty years than to inaugurate a new phase of ecological behavior.

A more plausible candidate to be the new motive force is the onset of global warming; and the 1997 Kyoto Conference on this topic was designed to start world preparation for such a development. There is still, however, considerable scientific uncertainty as to the extent, timing, and effects of this phenomenon; and the focus is in any case almost exclusively on energy efficiency and the emission of so-called greenhouse gases. There now appears to be a developing consensus, led by energy companies like Royal Dutch/Shell, that it is prudent to start putting in place energy conservation practices *that make sense in any case, whether or not global warming actually materializes.* But the likely overall effect of such programs is again to expand the reach and scope of existing measures rather than lead to the systemic change in our industrial economies that will, I believe, be the essence of the next phase.

The most likely catalyst for such a change is the globalization of the industrial economy. As a result of the global economic restructuring and the social and political aspirations it has given rise to, the scale of industrial production

seems likely to expand dramatically on a global basis over the next generation, as more and more countries aim for the levels of material prosperity now
enjoyed by the West. As we expand this system, creating an artificial economic system within the natural one, the strain we put upon the environment
grows inexorably. Incipient global warming and ozone depletion may be the
first signs of this strain, but the destructive potential is far more extensive
than this.

While nature is remarkably adaptive and has a great capacity for healing
itself, there are undoubtedly limits to its ability to absorb the total effects of
industrialization, including both the demands that our economies make on
the supply of natural resources and the strain that their detritus puts on the
earth's carrying capacity. The problem is not one of hazardous or toxic materials and processes alone: it is the sheer volume of the inputs and outputs,
regardless of their nature, that can be damaging. This system is clearly not
sustainable. Consider, for instance, just one aspect of the system: the demand
for some key natural resources. Global stocks of some essential raw materials, such as copper, nickel, molybdenum, and petroleum, will drop perilously
low if the less-developed countries increase their consumption to match that
of the already industrialized nations. A study by Robert Frosch and Nicholas
Gallopoulos, leading researchers at General Motors Research Laboratories,
attempted to estimate the full extent of the depletion of natural resources,
assuming that global population reached 10 billion by the year 2030 and that
consumption levels would approximate current U.S. rates. Given those assumptions, they showed that global resources (that is, the total quantities
thought to exist) of petroleum would be reduced to 7 years' consumption;
nickel, to 16 years'; and copper, to 26 years'. Only coal (457 years) and aluminum (407 years) would still be in abundant supply.[3]

Over the long haul, then, the tension between the economic and the natural
systems will ultimately reach a snapping point—if matters are allowed to
continue as they are at present. Of course, some would argue that things never
do remain the same: technology intervenes, societal values and wants change,
and production processes become more efficient. Although these things are
true, we should still have to make conscious choices as to the direction in
which we want our societies and our economies to proceed.

At the moment, the alternatives over the long haul (say, the next fifty to
one-hundred years) would appear to be either to impose some form of limits
to growth, or to change the system—radically. The first alternative is neither
socially attractive nor politically viable. It does not even meet the test of equity, for it would deny the have-nots of the world—individuals and nations
alike—the material prosperity and well-being that is currently enjoyed by the
developed countries. It is, therefore, on the second alternative that this new
rule focuses, monumental though the task will be. We are facing a challenge
and a transition at least as great as that from an agricultural to an industrial
economy. It is nothing less than a creation of a "post-industrial economy," far
beyond the limited definition that Daniel Bell gave to that term.

THE MARRIAGE OF ECOLOGY AND ECONOMY

Over the centuries, but most particularly since the Industrial Revolution, we have allowed two words, "economy" and "ecology," that share a common root (the Greek word "eco-," meaning house) to become polarized as conflicting concepts. We have come to think of economic growth as an unmitigated good and of our ecosystem as a virtually limitless source of resources and a dumping ground for our wastes. And we made the further mistake of thinking of these ecological services—clean air, clean water, pollination, water purification, natural flood control, and nitrogen fixation—as "free goods," something that we did not have to account for in our economic calculations. Later, as the disastrous effects of this line of thinking became clear, we came to believe that we had to choose between further growth and a purer environment. We could not, we felt, have both.

Now we are coming to recognize both the extent of our economic dependence on the ecosystem, and the fact that its services, far from being free, come at a cost that escalates as our demands on them grow. Robert Costanza, an ecological economist at the University of Maryland, has estimated that the dollar value of the world's ecosystem services—that is, the cost we could incur if we had to replace them with manmade substitutes—is in the range of $16 to $64 trillion a year, with an average of $33 trillion.[4] This compares with $18 trillion for the total of our global output of goods and services.

This dichotomy of values is not a fault that can be attributed solely to capitalism or the large corporation. Until recently, communism and consumers, small businesses and governments, education and religions ("Go forth and multiply, and *subdue the earth*"), and developed and developing nations, have all been guilty of the same mistake. Now that we are, however, starting to recognize the magnitude of the problem, it is to the large corporation that the public looks for action, if not for leadership. Leadership in the movement toward the harmonization of economy and ecology must be shared. Research by the scientific community and public education by interest groups and schools, government policies, and corporate initiatives all have a role to play. But Hawken is right: "Business is the only mechanism . . . powerful enough to produce the changes necessary."

What is the ultimate objective of this marriage of ecology and economy? Hawken himself suggests that it is "restorative economics," the adoption of an economic system of production and distribution designed to "reverse global environmental and social degradation." A more widely used term is "sustainable development," a recognition that "corporations must not compromise the ability of future generations to sustain themselves." This is the central concept of the principles adopted by CERES, the Coalition for Environmentally Responsible Economies (see Appendix C), and of a report prepared for the Rio Conference by the Business Council for Sustainable Development.

Led by the Swiss industrialist, Stephan Schmidheiny, the council, made up of fifty CEOs of major corporations, worked for a year to develop guidelines for corporate action in a report significantly titled, "Changing Course." Among the issues it covered were extending market pricing to the environment, reducing energy consumption, managing the innovation process, technology cooperation, sustainable agriculture and forestry, and the role of business in developing countries. A central thesis of their work was that industry can sometimes benefit from judicious government action—provided that executives recognize that they can gain commercial advantage through anticipating environmental regulations rather than merely complying with them. Well-run companies often benefit from carefully designed, consistently applied environmental policies, because they can meet the higher standards, while their less efficient or less imaginative competitors cannot.

However, while the report does an excellent job of presenting the seriousness and urgency of the problem, it does not come to grips with the deeper, systemwide measures that will be needed to remedy an inherent defect in our current approach to industrialization. Ultimately, I believe, we shall have to face the need for a fundamental redesign of our industrial processes to follow the principles of a living ecosystem, thus bringing the industrial and natural systems into balance.

TOWARD AN INDUSTRIAL ECOSYSTEM[5]

In the mid-1990s, Jean Marc Bruel, the president of Rhone-Poulenc, went rafting on the Colorado River. "We traveled for three days, sleeping on the beaches at night," he recalls. "Each morning, we cleared away every vestige of our stay. The experience helped me understand that garbage is here forever, and that if we want to enjoy our world with the same pleasure in the future, we have to be respectful of the environment."

This personal anecdote can be interpreted as a statement of the ultimate goal for an industrial ecosystem: We should design and operate the world's economic system in such a way that its operations should leave no vestigial trace of their existence on the global ecosystem. (In this section I shall use the terms "economic system" and "industrial system" more or less interchangeably because, while it is our industrial system—the manufacture, use, and disposal of "things," rather than the delivery of services—that stands most in need of reform, the redesign of which I speak will necessarily affect the totality of our economic system.) This is, of course, a goal that we can only approximate in the foreseeable future. The structures of our industrial system will necessarily remain. But we can perhaps envision the possibility of zero emissions and zero wastes. Where we have difficulty is in imagining a zero input of nonrenewable natural resources.

Literally interpreted, such a goal may not be attainable, but it should be the star by which we steer our actions. Even to approach such an objective, we shall have to design a number of salient characteristics into such a system.

First, the system will have to be *global*. We cannot, for long or with impunity, make distinctions between one area of the world and another; all are now inextricably intertwined. Both the globalization of industrialization and the global flows of our ecosystem require that *all* parts of our industrial system, wherever they are located, subscribe to the same principles and requirements. That is why it becomes so essential for the already-developed nations to recognize the need, not merely to reform their own systems, but also to extend assistance (with finance and technology) to the newly industrializing nations in their efforts at simultaneously growing their economies and meeting the new ecological standards.

Second, our approach to this redesign must be truly *systemic*; that is, it must deal with the system as a whole, not just with its discrete parts, and it must do so in at least two ways. The industrial ecosystem that we construct will deal with the complex meshing and interactions of the various parts (individual companies and other players) of the system, not just with the internal operations of the individual parts. As we shall see in the Kalundborg example, when properly designed, the industrial ecosystem as a whole can be in better overall balance with the natural system than any one of its parts. However, the approach must also be systemic *within* each part, integrating all the phases of the business into an ecologically harmonious whole.

Third, the system must abandon the linear mode of its existing processes. In place of the "mine–manufacture–use–discard" sequence, we must put in a closed-loop, cyclical system. In this way our economic system will mimic and cooperate with, rather than fight and subdue, the natural system which endlessly circulates and transforms materials and operates almost entirely on ambient solar energy.

Dr. Karl-Henrik Robert, a Swedish cancer researcher, applied his knowledge of cellular biology to developing an understanding of a general requirement for production in the cycles of both nature and society: Waste products must be recruited to photosynthesis, or recycled within society, or stored away into final deposits. From this understanding he developed four "nonnegotiable" conditions for a truly sustainable industrial system:

1. *Drastic reduction in the use of stored mineral deposits.* Sustainability requires that their use should not exceed nature's sedimentation process and so effectively puts an end to new mining.

2. *Phaseout of persistent nonnatural compounds.* If the use of such molecules exceeds the slow processes by which nature destroys them, Robert argues, the principle of conservation of matter and the tendency of entropy to increase will cause molecular garbage to accumulate in the biosphere.

3. *Preservation of the physical conditions of nature's diversity and capacity for primary production.* This entails sustainable agriculture and forestry, conservation of water supplies, and restrictions on urban expansion.

4. *Reduction in the use of energy and materials* to within the capacity of the ecosystem to process garbage into new resources.

Viewed through the prism of our current thinking and technology, such a system would appear to be, inevitably, a limited-growth model. Most certainly, it would limit inputs of energy and new materials and outputs of wastes. *However, it need not necessarily limit overall economic activity and growth.* It may be difficult for us to believe this, but it is almost certainly true. I believe that our difficulty in accepting this possibility is due to the fact that our thinking and expectations are still rooted in the old "throughput" paradigm; we have not yet fully assessed the possibilities for the new paradigm.

We might get a better perspective on the future if we looked back at our recent past. In the thirty or so years of the modern environmental movement, we have vastly raised the ecological standards that our industrial system must meet. Yet there has been no appreciable slowing of our economies due to that fact. Overall, economic growth rates have been more powerfully affected by traditional economic factors—the size and skill of the labor force, productivity, the cost of capital, technology, trade, inflation rates, and so on—than by the new environmental conditions we have stipulated for our economic system. Our misperception that there is an inevitable tradeoff between ecology and the economy stems from the fact that we focus our attention solely on the immediate costs of environmental regulation without considering the subsequent countervailing effects of competition and innovation. In a seminal article, "Green *and* Competitive," Michael Porter and Claas van der Linde argued that *"properly designed environmental standards can trigger innovations . . .* and the net result is not only dramatically lower environmental impact, but also lower costs, better product quality, and enhanced global competitiveness" (emphasis added).[6] Viewed in this light, the inevitability of a tradeoff diminishes; and the possibility of a true blending of ecology and economy becomes more feasible.

SOME FIRST STEPS

Far off though the prospect of creating such a new industrial system may be, we can get some sense of the direction and the possibilities of the future by looking at the first steps that are already being taken on the long journey toward this distant goal.

One of the most instructive examples of an industrial ecosystem is centered on the town of Kalundborg in Denmark. The key elements in this system are Asnaes, the largest coal-fired electric power generating plant in Denmark; an oil refinery belonging to Statoil, the Norwegian state-owned Statoil; a Novo Nordisk biotechnology production plant; the Gyproc plasterboard plant; the Finnish company Kemira's sulfuric acid plant; as well as cement manufacturers, local horticulture and agriculture, and the district heating system of the town of Kalundborg. All of these players participate in and benefit from a symbiotic relationship that is grounded in ecological principles. The refinery provides excess gas to the plasterboard factory; the power station provides steam to the city for district heating, as well as to the biotechnology company and the refinery; the sludge from the fish farms and the biotechnology company's fermentation operations goes to farmers for fertilizer; hot water from the power plant is provided to local fish farms; a cement company uses the power plant's desulphurized ash; and the power plant harvests its stack gas (normally an air pollutant) with calcium carbonate, making gypsum, which it sells to the plasterboard factory.

This illustration of the emergent new industrial paradigm gives us a glimmering idea of its promise and possibilities. Crude though it may seem to be in retrospect from, say, the year 2020, it does serve to bring into focus some of the system's essential features: the number and diversity of the players; their symbiotic relationship; the cooperation between public and private sectors; and the emphasis on reducing inputs and wastes. Equally noteworthy is the fact that all these transactions grew out of voluntary negotiations—some for economic reasons and others for environmental considerations—without the pressure of governmental regulations.

Other examples serve to underscore the number and complexity of measures that will be required to develop a fully fledged industrial ecology.

Changing Strategic Focus

A number of companies have elected to make environmental principles central, not merely to their processes, but to the strategic focus of their business. The Body Shop in the United Kingdom and Sebastian International of the United States, both beauty-products retailers, have positioned themselves as environmentally friendly companies, using all-natural ingredients in their products. Denmark's Novo Nordisk is emerging as a pioneer in "green chemistry," trying to find natural solutions to industrial problems. With help from biotechnology, Novo has developed more than forty enzymes for everything from stonewashing jeans to ripening apples more quickly, substituting more benign elements for synthetic chemicals.

Probably no company has gone further toward this goal than Ecover, the small Belgian firm that is challenging Procter & Gamble, Unilever, and other packaged goods giants in the market for cleaning materials. Its products—everything from laundry powder and dishwashing detergent to shampoos and car wax—use only natural soaps and renewable raw materials: vegetable extracts, sugar derivatives, and natural oils. And to make them, the company has built what is perhaps the world's most ecological factory, one which operates with zero emissions. As Gunter Pauli, Ecover's CEO, expressed it, "We are not just selling products or building a company. *We are creating a system. We want to create a totally open economic system and a totally closed environmental system*" (emphasis added).[7]

Improving "Metabolic Efficiency"

For the industrial system as a whole to achieve the desired balance with the natural system, we must dramatically improve the efficiency with which its component parts use materials and energy. Porter and van der Linde refer to this as "resource productivity" and suggest that this concept, rather than pollution control per se, should frame our approach to environmental improvement. We can think of it as improving the metabolic efficiency of our industrial system, not merely in transforming materials and energy into products in the manufacturing process by eliminating waste, defects, and stored materials, but throughout the system, by reducing packaging, making distribution more efficient, improving the performance of products, and reclaiming reusable materials from discarded products. At each stage there is currently a cost—to manufacturers, users, distributors or society; and therefore, at each stage, there is the potential for savings and an enhancement of efficiency.

Studies by the Management Institute for Environment and Business show that the cost of compliance with environmental regulations can be minimized, if not completely offset, through innovation that delivers competitive benefits. Even in the chemical industry, which has arguably the greatest exposure to regulatory costs, resource productivity produces surprisingly high returns. For example, a study of 181 waste prevention activities at twenty-nine chemical plants found that innovative changes in process more than offset costs. Indeed, only one resulted in a cost increase; and, of seventy activities that registered a change in product yield, sixty-eight reported increases. Leaders in the industry are well aware of this potential. At DuPont, company policy has evolved from "meet all laws and regulations" to "meet the public's expectations" to "the goal is zero" for all waste emissions. Dow Chemical's "Waste Reduction Always Pays" program and 3M's so-called 3P program—"Pollution Prevention Pays"—take a similar approach, reasoning that pollution is waste, and waste should be eliminated. Dow's latest ethylene plant in Alberta, Canada, is 20 percent more energy efficient than the previous one and did not take longer or cost more to design and build. And, since its introduction in 1975, the 3P program has reduced 3M's annual releases of air, water, sludge, and municipal solid-waste pollutants from the company's operations by one-half million tons, while yielding a 50 percent reduction in pollution per unit of production and $500 million in savings to the company.

Reducing Greenhouse Gases

The majority of oil companies and many other corporations strongly objected to the agreement reached at the 1997 Kyoto Conference to reduce greenhouse gas emissions in industrialized countries by 5 percent from their 1990 levels between 2008 and 2012. Breaking ranks with other oil producers, however, Sir John Browne of BP Amoco announced that his company would set a firm overall target to cut these emissions by 10 percent of their 1990 levels by 2010 and pledged that his company would undertake the cuts "in transparent ways so the reductions can be measured and verified by outside observers." This commitment sets up a whole new set of expectations for other companies in that industry, and pledges the company to do more than the Kyoto protocol requires, regardless of whether or not it is ever ratified.

One way BP Amoco has begun to reduce emissions is by cutting the number of pumping stations on the Trans-Alaska pipeline and by reducing flaring (the burning of waste gas). Future reductions will come from technological advances, more efficient energy use, and less flaring. Interestingly, a key feature of this program is its use of emission trading rights among units of the company—a system developed by the Environmental Defense Fund. An initial trading program would involve twelve of BP Amoco's ninety divisions, accounting for about a quarter of the company's emissions.

Environmental Monitoring

Our knowledge of the workings of ecological systems is still pathetically limited, so if we are to ensure the sustainable operation of our industrial operations within the natural system, we shall have to engage in major and continuing research. One example of the willingness of some major corporations to have a more open mind and take a fresh look at potential problems is the formation of the Pew Center on Global Climate Change, which counts American Electric Power (AEP), Enron, Boeing, 3M, Lockheed Martin, and United Technologies as founding members. As Dale E. Heydlauff, AEP's environmental chief, observed, "It is no longer possible to say there is not a problem."

One critical area of needed research is the development of a monitoring capability that will alert us to changes in the stress levels in the environment. A pioneering effort at integrating environmental, technical, and management data is Johnson & Johnson's (J&J) Emergency Information Systems/Chemicals (EIC/S), which allows the company to map its facilities and their operations in great detail, down to the floor plans of individual buildings and the location of regulated chemicals.

These maps extend beyond J&J facilities to the surrounding communities and can even broaden out to show the country and its regional location. The system collects meteorological data in real time and can use this to plot the predicted dispersion plumes of any airborne chemicals, displaying them on the local area maps. To help local authorities deal with any hazardous emergencies, J&J has donated the EIC/S software, together with personal computers, to local emergency-management teams, so that they, as well as the company, are informed and better equipped to deal with problems quickly as they occur.

Auditing and Disclosure

In the summer of 1998 Royal Dutch/Shell published its first externally verified environmental audit, covering the local impact of Shell's worldwide operations. "What most companies are willing to pay for is data at the head office," Cor Herkstrotter, Shell's chairman at the time, said. "What we and Shell decided was that this was not enough: we need to go to the heart of the company. . . . We must show people that we mean what we say." As a result, a team of 150 auditors from Price Waterhouse and KPMG visited about thirty sites of their own choosing to provide independent verification of management claims.

Environmental accounting of this sort can benefit companies in two ways. First, it can focus internal attention on the need for savings in the use of energy and other materials. By one estimate, a good environmental performance can add as much as 5 percent to net profits. Shell is, for example, seeking markets near its refineries for gas which it otherwise has to flare off. Second, institutional investors are anxious to protect themselves against accusations that they hold stakes in "dirty" industries. The cleaner the bill of health, especially if certified by an independent auditor, the better the chances for a company's share price.

THE CORPORATION AND PUBLIC POLICY

Clearly a systemic transformation of this magnitude cannot be achieved by corporate leadership and action alone. Notwithstanding the power shift's transfer of responsibilities from the public to the private sector, governments will necessarily be called upon to play a major role. Some of the critical issues on which public policy initiatives will be required are

- Population control, ultimately to achieve zero population growth on a global basis.
- International agreements on the "new rules of the game" regarding ecological behavior (e.g., standards and goals with respect to climate change, biodiversity).
- Financial and technological aid from the developed to developing countries to assist in the development of ecologically sound industrialization.
- Reform of environmental regulations to conform to the requirements of the new paradigm (e.g., to encourage risk taking and experimentation and foster continuous improvement, rather than locking in on "best available technology"), make greater use of "market pricing" and tradable pollution permits.[8]
- Development of a new national economic scorecard (e.g., "net national welfare" rather than "gross national product") to provide a better accounting for environmental costs and benefits.

However, just because these issues will be resolved mainly in the public arena does not mean that corporations have no role to play. Indeed, the resolution of each one of these issues requires some contribution from corporations for the simple reason that they have some self-interest in the outcome. The following list describes the corporate role in light of public policy and sustainable development:

Public Policy Initiatives	**Corporate Role**
Population control: Continued public-policy emphasis on reducing high	Supportive statements, recognizing that new market growth depends more on

birth rates in developing countries will be essential for attaining global sustainable development.

International agreements: Follow-up treaties will be required to implement Rio and Kyoto agreements on global issues (e.g., climate change, bio-diversity, ocean pollution) setting firm targets, establishing new rules, and agreeing on environmental taxes.

North–South aid: If developing countries are to conform to global environmental standards while increasing industrialization, developed countries will have to increase financial–technological aid.

Regulatory reform: To encourage innovation and "resource productivity," a new paradigm of regulation and enforcement will be required.

New economic–ecological "scorecard": "Gross national product" will have to be replaced as a measure of economic progress in order to account for environmental impacts.

economic development than on sheer numbers of consumers.

Active participation in debates, lobbying to ensure uniformity–consistency of regulations on a global basis, and promotion of "best practices" in regulation and taxation.

Supportive statements on financial aid (to help ensure global consistency) and promotion of technology diffusion through corporate global operations–marketing.

Active participation in debates, lobbying to promote realistic deadlines, flexible technological solutions, "market pricing" of pollution, use of "pollution permits," and reduced uncertainty in enforcement.

Supportive statements–testimony based on corporate efforts to measure–audit environmental versus economic impacts.

The extent of the corporate contribution varies, of course, with the competence and credibility that a company can bring to discussion of the issue. On population control, for instance, there is little in the way of new reasoning that the typical corporation (except those in the health-care arena perhaps) can contribute; and so its role can best be described as reactive but supportive of government initiatives. At the other extreme, regulatory reform is an area of direct corporate involvement and experience; so, in this area, the corporate role can—and should—be more proactive, positive, and involved.

The trouble is that corporate political involvement suffers from a suspect and unfortunate history. There are few professions that have a more negative public reputation than that of the corporate lobbyist; corporate political contributions are perceived as little more than bribery; and corporate positions on issues are assumed to be negative and conditioned solely by self-interest. Disengaging from this history and these perceptions will not be easy, but it would be in both the public and corporate interest. Public policy would gain, for instance, from greater openness and objectivity in the assessment of new technologies and corporate experience in tackling problems "on the firing line." Corporations would most surely gain from greater uniformity and rationality, and less uncertainty, in the framing and enforcement of regulatory policies.

In an earlier period (the 1970s) and on different issues (corporate taxes, trade policy, and regulatory reform), Reginald ("Reg") Jones, then CEO of General Electric and cochairman of The Business Roundtable, proved the soundness and viability of this approach. In his dealings with Congress and the executive branch, he insisted on meticulous research to back up his statements and on as much objectivity as he could muster in the positions he took. In all his testimony he took the long view at the junction of national and corporate interests. As a result, he was trusted by politicians of both parties: The "white papers" he used to support his positions were accepted—and used—by the politicians with confidence that the data were not doctored or biased, and the policies he advocated were truly in the national interest. As a result, many of the positions he advocated were adopted as public policy; and both the nation and the corporate sector were the gainers.

On environmental policy, too, the major critical requirement for a corporation to succeed in this role is credibility. Credibility will rest on the public's perceptions of the adequacy and sincerity of a company's environmental performance and on its judgment as to the objectivity of the positions the company takes. If the company's commitment to sustainable growth, for instance, is perceived to be more show than substance, the backlash—to the company's reputation and to the policies it is espousing—will be substantial. But credible performance provides the needed sound foundation for advocacy; and prudent advocacy can benefit both the corporation and society.

IN SUMMARY

A systemic change of these proportions will, no doubt, take decades rather than years to accomplish. So the time frame within which we might expect to see this new rule fully implemented is vastly different from those of the other rules. Predicting outcomes thus becomes particularly speculative. One major uncertainty stems from our current lack of hard knowledge about the workings of the global climate and ecological systems, and so our inability to determine if, when, and how soon they might force our hand. Other uncertainties are captured in the structure of the scenarios we considered earlier: the degree of international harmony; the rate at which industrialization spreads in the developing world; the availability of resources from economic growth; the openness of individual and societal values to a shift in the balance between economic and environmental priorities; and the willingness and ability of corporations to change their marketing, technological, and manufacturing practices.

Nevertheless, we can speculate as to how sustainable development might evolve in these various scenarios. In the *Transformation* scenario, for instance, we might expect the greatest progress and the smoothest transition toward this goal, since virtually all the trends support it. Global economic growth increases the need for a new approach to industrialization, but provides both the resources and the technology to achieve it; the climate of international cooperation makes possible greater coordination of environmental policies and goals and a higher level of North–South aid; greater ecological consciousness, certainly in the developed economies, supports the political will to make the needed policy changes; and, above all, corporate innovation and experiments gradually lead the way to a new "industrial ecosystem." These trends would be in motion even in the absence of a global ecological crisis; and, should such a crisis develop, the world would be better equipped, economically, technologically, and psychologically, to deal with it.

In the *Neomercantilism* scenario, however, the picture would be significantly more mixed. With a volatile economic climate, both public policy and corporate priorities would be more focused on traditional economic problems (inflation–deflation, trade, restructuring, and the like). And governments would be less cooperative and more protective of their national economic interests in their international relations. In such a climate, environmental problems would tend to be dealt with on an ad hoc, national or regional (rather than global) basis, and new regulations would be introduced cautiously so as not to impair the competitiveness of domestic corporations. Progress toward the new industrial paradigm would be almost wholly restricted to the already developed economies, while newly industrializing nations struggle to gain their economic footing. A slowing in the pace of global industrialization might delay the advent of an ecological crisis, but would most surely worsen social and political conditions in the developing world.

In both the *Reregulation* and *Turbulence* scenarios, increased industrialization intensifies environmental problems and with corporations unable or unwilling to take corrective action, the public turns again to governments for action. In both cases the next steps in environmental restoration are dictated by regulation rather than by corporate initiative. The difference between them lies in the timing and resources available for these moves. In the *Turbulence* scenario, corporate, government, and public attention is focused almost exclusively on dealing with serious economic problems, so that little new action is taken on the environmental front until the problem reaches virtually crisis proportions. In *Reregulation*, public concern over new findings of ecological problems is the trigger, forcing government—and corporate—action in advance of the crisis.

But however the future evolves—with corporate leadership, or by government fiat; and with or without a deepening of our ecological problems—the agenda required to implement this new rule is awesome. It calls for nothing less than a redesign and rebuilding of our industrial infrastructure over the next few decades.

But the starting point for this change is a radical shift in the corporate mindset—a shift from static, reactive thinking that sees environmental regulations only as costs, to flexible, proactive thinking that sees them as a challenge to innovation and a prompting to resource productivity. It is not merely a matter of timing—proactive or reactive. It is also a matter of perception. We saw the truth of this observation some thirty years, albeit on a smaller scale, when public policy moved to establish goals for automobile fuel consumption. Confronted with this challenge, Detroit hired lawyers to oppose or change the regulations, while the Germans and Japanese hired engineers to develop more fuel-efficient cars. This failure cost the U.S. automobile manufacturers dearly, as they saw their market share decline drastically. We can only hope that this is a lesson that we shall not have to learn again.

NOTES

1. Quoted in "UNCED and Undone," *Greenpeace Quarterly* (Summer 1997): 4–10.
2. Paul Hawken, "The Ecology of Commerce," *Inc.* (April 1992): 93–100.
3. Robert A. Frosch and Nicholas E. Gallopoulos, "Strategies for Manufacturing," *Scientific American*, a special edition on "Managing Planet Earth" 261, no. 3 (September 1989): 144–152.
4. Robert Costanza et al., "The Value of the World's Ecosystem Services and Natural Capital," *Nature*, May 15, 1997, pp. 253–259.
5. For a fuller treatment of this subject, see Hardin B. C. Tibbs's admirable article, "Industrial Ecology: An Environmental Agenda for Industry," *Whole Earth Review* (Winter 1992): 4–19.
6. Michael E. Porter and Claas van der Linde, "Green *and* Competitive: Ending the Stalemate," *Harvard Business Review* 73, no. 5 (September–October 1995): 120–134.
7. "Gunter Pauli Cleans Up," *Fast Company* (November 1993): 63ff.
8. As Porter and van der Linde note in their article (see Note 6), "Just as bad regulation can damage competitiveness, good regulation can enhance it."

— 7 —

Employment: The New Contract

New rule: The corporation must rewrite the social contract of work to reflect the values of the new workforce and increase both the effectiveness and loyalty of employees and the corporation.

Throughout history, work has been the primary means by which individuals have defined themselves in terms of their relationship to society. Today, most people, when asked to describe themselves, start by saying what they *do*. In part, this stems from their reticence and inability to describe their personality and character. But more significantly it reflects the important role that work plays in their lives, not only as the source of income and livelihood, but also as an expression of their abilities and as an opportunity to contribute to a larger whole, and ultimately the well-being of society.

As the nature of work has evolved, so too has our concept of what work means to us, of what we want to put into it, and what we want to get out of it. We are currently passing through a new phase of redefining "work"—a phase that happens to coincide with a restructuring of work and the work environment in the corporation. This convergence provides both the setting and the impetus for rewriting the social contract of work.

THE CHANGING MEANING OF WORK

At a primitive stage of human history, work—mainly hunting and gathering— was accepted as an inevitable part of life. It was not perceived as good or bad, but simply necessary, as a prerequisite for survival. At a later stage, as people settled in agricultural and urban communities, they conceived of work as a social duty, as part of the contract between the individual and the community. The individual contributed labor in serving society's needs and received in return a measure of protection, security, and social life. Still later, there evolved the concept of work as a religious duty, when many sought to work "for the greater glory of God." Associated with this was the Calvinist doctrine of work as redemption: Work redeemed the sinner, Adam—and Eve—and the fall from Eden. It is a belief that still finds expression, even in today's society, in phrases like "idle hands make mischief."

As late as the mid-1960s, the work environment in the United States was still imbued with the spirit of the Protestant work ethic. This ethic held to four beliefs:

- Work is hard—it is done "in the sweat of thy face"—and leisure is a luxury that few can afford.
- Work is unavoidable. This is not quite the same as the original concept of "work as necessity," but rather sees work as the only socially commendable, and hence unavoidable, route to well-being and advancement in a democratic, but materialistic, society.
- Work deals essentially with "things." This is a view that has its roots in the concept of *homo faber*, man the maker, and in the then true observation that manufacturing was the real driver of the economy. Services were largely perceived as fringe activities, incapable of creating "real" economic value.
- Work is a duty one owes to society, to one's family, and to one's self-respect.

It was this concept of work as duty that made for quiet conformity and what, by today's standards, we would consider a tranquil work environment. To be sure, unions were stronger then, and strikes were more frequent than they are now, but they involved just the blue-collar workforce and lacked the violence of the thirties. This was, above all, the age of the "organization man," not merely in the sense of mindless conformity that William H. Whyte lambasted, but also in terms of a lasting relationship that bound employee and company together.

THE MAKING—AND BREAKING—
OF THE CONTRACT

It was this work ethic—and the relative economic stability that most nations then enjoyed—that made possible the employment contract of those times. The contract went something like this: "Give us your full attention and best efforts, show up on time, obey orders, keep your nose clean, and don't question authority—and we will take care of you and your family." Annual salary and wage increases were the norm; work standards were prescribed, and promotion was heavily influenced by seniority; there was health-care insurance for the employee and the family; and, with pensions well established, this caring extended beyond retirement. Career-long employment was assumed, though not (literally) guaranteed, so that it was quite normal to refer to oneself as "a GM guy" or "a Ma Bell alum."

Now, of course, that contract has been torn up—by the corporation, most would say. And certainly the restructurings and wholesale downsizings of recent years has provided ample evidence of corporate brutality and disregard for considerations of loyalty. However, it is worth noting that the initial move to modify, if not reject, the contract's terms came in the early 1970s from the employees' side. At that time it was clear that a major shift in the makeup of the labor force was already underway. Traditional blue-collar operatives, the source of union strength, were a declining percentage of the labor force. Their place was being taken by the rapidly growing population of managerial, professional, and technical employees, whose ranks were then being swelled by the first waves of the baby-boom generation with their new values and cocky attitude (see Chapter 1). To them, the old employment contract did not seem such a good bargain, especially at a time when the economy was growing and employment opportunities abounded. Organizational conformity was anathema and job security a much lower priority for them than it was for the unionized workforce. In a report to General Electric management at the time, I wrote, "Today's young managers, professional and technical workers believe that they owe more loyalty to their profession—and to their own self-development—than to the company they happen to be with at any particular time."

Of course, in the end, job security died—for everyone—in the 1980s. Restructuring, downsizing, delayering, and outsourcing did violence to the contract and to employees'—and society's—expectations. Studies by the Hay Group underscore the impact of these restructurings on employee morale, as concern over job security, which rose sharply in the eighties, continued to increase in the nineties. By 1998, only about one-half of the workforce gave their companies a favorable rating on this score. In the United States, the work contract became, in the words of Anthony P. Carnevale, chairman of the National Commission on Employment Policy, "the sound of one hand clapping." Employees were called upon for greater productivity, flexibility, and speed, but no guarantee was given that high performance would be rewarded or even that the employee would keep a job. Even in Japan the long tradition of lifelong employment has been eroded. Forced to reduce payrolls in order to regain competitiveness, but reluctant to face the public criticism that would come from massive layoffs, Japanese corporations turned to hiring short-term contract employees for whom there is no job security.

There is now virtually no possibility of a return to the old version of the work contract. The pressures of global competition and technological change alone make that inconceivable. And we should not shed too many tears over its passing, for the comfortable existence that it made possible had its shadow side. It was no coincidence that this form of paternalistic welfare went hand in hand with complacency, conformity, inflexibility, and avoidance of risk—attributes that certainly have no place in organizations grappling with the problems of adapting to revolutionary change and that are also the antithesis of the qualities that individuals need for their own self-development and advancement in this age.

However, the present situation cannot long continue unchanged. A contract as one-sided as the present one in many companies is fundamentally unstable: Sooner or later employees will reject it. Indeed, the most surprising thing about the current arrangement is that there has not been a more outspoken reaction against it already. The sense of dissatisfaction, although latent, is widespread. In his book, *White Collar Blues*, Charles Heckscher, a professor at Rutgers University, found that middle managers at large corporations undergoing major restructurings still retained a surprisingly high degree of commitment to their work but had little confidence that their loyalty would be repaid.[1] Fear is a powerful motivator. Faced with the likely alternative of no job at all, employees have muted their outrage and kept their complaints for the anonymity of survey findings. But the situation remains potentially explosive, whichever way the job situation turns. If the economy grows and the unemployment threat diminishes (as in the *Transformation* scenario), then bargaining power would shift from employer to employees, and the terms of the contract would be rewritten in more equitable fashion. If growth stalls and joblessness remains a major threat (as it would in the *Turbulence* and, to some extent, *Neomercantilism* scenarios), then a resort to political remedies would become virtually inevitable.

But people are, as we have seen, leery of government "solutions" to economic problems. Unemployment compensation is welcomed as a cushion in the event of layoffs; but few would consider that a total solution to the problem of employment. The once popular notion of government as "employer of the last resort" has long since fallen out of favor, a victim of its image as a "make-work" program with little or no economic utility. In fact, of all the public-policy measures in this field, only government-funded training and retraining programs attract any appreciable measure of public support.

So, with an unsustainable current situation, no possible return to the old contract, and no public enthusiasm for government-sponsored programs, the search is on for a "middle way"—a contract which acknowledges that job security can no longer be guaranteed, but which addresses both organizational needs and employee concerns and aspirations.

THE SHAPING OF A NEW CONTRACT

The broad outlines of the new contract are being shaped by the major formative forces of our times (see Chapter 2). Thus, the power shift gives impetus to greater "democratization" of the workplace. Restructuring and globalization heighten concerns about job security and the need for new skills. Globalization increases awareness of the need for, and value of, diversity in the workforce. And technology creates the network paradigm of the new organization (see Chapter 4). And some aspects of the new rules relating to governance and equity contribute to a definition of the primary values that this contract should espouse. But there are still other trends we should look to for further clues as to the nature and terms of the new contract.

The most significant of these trends is the emergence of a new philosophy or concept of work. It has been clear for some time now that the old Protestant work ethic no longer represented the predominant value system of the workforce. What has not been clear is exactly what is taking its place. To the despair of the older, more autocratic generation of managers, the young Generation X employees seem to take the point of view that work is a hobby for which you happen to get paid—or even that work should be fun. While there is a great deal of anecdotal evidence to support such a view of intergenerational conflict on this issue, it does not get to the fundamental nature of what is happening and why.

I believe that a better perspective on what is happening and what the new work ethic is likely to be can be gained by viewing work in the light of Maslow's hierarchy of needs (see Box 7.1). Abraham Maslow developed the theory that human needs can be arranged in a hierarchy of five levels, from the most basic physiological needs for food, clothing, and shelter, to the highest needs for self-expression and self-actualization. He further postulated that there was a natural tendency to move up the hierarchy: As one level of needs was satisfied, an individual would tend to move to the next level, and these needs would then become the prime motivators of behavior. Other things being equal, this upward movement is the normal pattern, and regression to a lower level occurs only when a threat develops to the continued satisfaction of these lower needs.

There is also a *rough* correlation between these needs levels and levels of education and family income. For instance, those who are still operating at the basic level of physiological needs tend to be predominantly those with (at best) only some high school education and a family income at or below the poverty level; while those motivated by ego needs tend to be college graduates and enjoy middle-class salaries.

As far as work and the work ethic is concerned, I would suggest that historically there has been a comparable progression up the hierarchy. Thus, it was when most of humankind were hunters and gatherers, motivated by basic physiological needs, that work was perceived as a basic necessity—no more, no less. Later, as communities began to form, and social needs became the main motivator of behavior, the concept of work as a social duty took shape, finally taking on the trappings of the Protestant work ethic (although it was much more widely dispersed than this particular religious connotation would suggest). Now growing percentages of the population in developed societies

BOX 7.1

Maslow's Hierarchy of Needs

The late Abraham Maslow, of Brandeis University, postulated that all men and women share certain basic needs which can be arranged in a hierarchy of five levels, from the most fundamental physiological needs to the needs of intellectual and spiritual fulfillment. The five levels are

1. *Physiological needs*—the basic needs for survival: food, clothing, shelter, rest.
2. *Safety or security needs*—the need to keep and protect what has been gained and to stabilize the situation for the future.
3. *Social needs*—the need for belonging, for sharing and association, and for giving and receiving friendship and love.
4. *Ego needs*—the needs that relate to self-esteem (self-confidence, independence, achievement, competence, and knowledge) and reputation (status, recognition, appreciation, and the respect of one's peers).
5. *Self-fulfillment needs*—the need for growth, self-development, and self-actualization.

A number of observations should be made about the significance and operation of this hierarchy:

- The hierarchy is arranged in terms of importance to living, proceeding from the "lowest" level (survival) to the "highest" (self-actualization).
- At each level, *needs determine values and behavior.*
- A satisfied need is not a motivator of behavior—for example, once hunger has been satisfied, it no longer has much motivating force.
- A higher-level need includes, as integral parts, all lower-level needs (e.g., ego needs assume that survival, security, and social needs continue to be met).
- There is a *rough* correlation between needs level and levels of income and education—except in the case of self-actualization, which does not appear to correlate with income—as the following table illustrates:

Maslow's Needs Level	Family Income (in 1998 $)	Education
5	???	College graduate
4	Over $50,000	College graduate
3	$25,000–$49,999	Some college
2	$15,000–$24,999	High school graduate
1	Under $15,000	Some high school

are college graduates, enjoying middle-class status and salaries; and the center of gravity in most workforces is moving rapidly toward the managerial, professional, and technical sector. Both of these trends are indicators that ego needs and self-fulfillment needs are becoming the key motivators of the values and behavior of a major—and highly influential—segment of our societies and workforces.

Thus, a new concept of work as self-fulfillment or self-actualization is a fact with which the new social contract on work and employment will have to come to terms. This view of work is the antithesis of organizational preeminence, uniformity, and stability that undergirded the old work contract. But it is not as anarchic and egocentric as first appearances and critics might suggest. To be sure, the blending of organizational and individual interests demands greater creativity and a more individualistic approach on the part of management, but the payoff can be great, as Cisco Systems, GE, and Hewlett-Packard have proven.

Paralleling and reinforcing this trend is another: a shift in the nature and source of capital. Until recently, we have thought of capital exclusively in financial terms; and indeed the very term "capitalism" reinforces in our minds the notion that financial capital and the owners of it (investors) are the real foundation and drivers of the system. Now, however, executives are starting to talk of knowledge as "the key strategic resource" and "knowledge management" as the new source of competitive advantage. In this way, capitalism—whose primary foundation has shifted over the centuries from land to natural resources to financial capital and now to knowledge—is being redefined, this time to include and emphasize employees as the source of this new capital. It is therefore not too far-fetched to think of employees as "the new capitalists."

In an insightful pair of articles in *Fortune*, Thomas Stewart expressed it this way: "It's more accurate—and more useful—to think of employees in a new way: not as assets but investors. Shareholders invest money in our companies; employees invest time, energy, and intelligence."[2] Although we might think that this concept applies only to those whom Peter Drucker calls "the knowledge workers"—those who bring brains rather than brawn to their work—Stewart rightly reminds us that "increasingly, we are *all* expected to be knowledge workers" (emphasis added). Ideas that contribute to improved productivity or better customer service, for instance, are being sought from blue- and white-collar workers alike, whether through Dana Corporation's extensive suggestion system or GE's "Work-Out sessions," the corporate equivalent of town meetings to identify and agree on better ways of doing things. If this is so, then the importance of employees as key stakeholders in the corporation is another fact that the new work contract must recognize.

Finally, we should briefly note a third force that has a bearing on the new work contract: the growing segmentation of work and the workforce. At one time there was for the most part a simple dichotomy in the workforce: One was either employed in a full-time job, or one was unemployed, with little in the way of possibilities in between. Now there is much greater diversity, both in the composition and values of the workforce and in the way that jobs are "packaged." It is not only the greater racial and sexual diversity among corporate employees that is the factor here, though that most surely contributes significantly to this segmentation. The other factor is the growth in what we might term "the contingent workforce." Whether from personal choice, family needs, or corporate restructuring, more and more individuals are now employed in part-time, shared-time, or temporary contract or other nontraditional arrangements. In the United States alone, there are some 28 million temporary workers, representing over 20 percent of the workforce; and there are estimates that within the next ten years as much as one-half of the workforce will be engaged in such nontraditional jobs. This trend is spreading globally—already two-thirds of European companies and one-half of Japanese companies use temporary workers—and seems likely to be a permanent feature on the economic landscape of global restructuring.

Each of these three trends—the new concept of work as self-fulfillment, the emergence of employees as the new capitalists, and the growing segmentation of work and the workforce—underscore the need for a new social contract between corporations and employees. They also converge on identifying some of the key elements that this contract must contain.

ELEMENTS OF THE NEW CONTRACT

There are two overarching issues that the new contract must confront—one quantitative, the other qualitative. The quantitative issue can be summed up in straightforward terms—creating the right *number* of jobs; the qualitative one, in the more complex requirements of structuring the right *type* of work arrangements and work climate. Let us examine each one in turn.

The issue of job creation is a worldwide one because, for the next ten years at least, we face the likely challenge, not of overall labor shortage, but of a global labor surplus. The root causes of this issue differ from one region to another:

• In the major industrialized economies, projected increases in the available workforce are relatively moderate. However, the continuing process of corporate restructuring continues to chip away at the established employment base, heightening social and employee concerns over job security. While it is true that employment opportunities will open up in the new growth areas of the economy, it is also true that we operate in a *global* labor market in which production facilities can be relocated or service tasks can migrate electronically, being performed as easily in India as in Indiana.

• In the developing and newly industrializing economies, the problem is mainly demographic: providing jobs for the huge wave of teenagers who will be flooding into the labor market. Even with robust economic growth rates and a reasonable degree of stability, this would be a daunting task.

On no issue more than this one is there a greater potential for conflict between employee and societal expectations on the one hand and corporate needs for restructuring and competitive flexibility on the other. People want a greater sense of security and caring; corporations need efficiency and "right-sizing" in the face of insistent competition. There is now general acknowledgment of the fact that absolute job security and lifetime employment can no longer be guaranteed. But there is an equally widespread demand that corporations manage their operations in a way that makes for less severe and dramatic dislocations. The challenge for corporate leadership is to minimize the frequency and impact of layoffs and ease the transition costs for employees and communities when adjustments become inevitable.

The possibilities for a positive response to this challenge are fortunately all around us. Eighteen of *Fortune's* 100 Best Employers, including Amgen, FedEx, Herman Miller, and Steelcase, have an explicit no-layoffs policy. Nucor, the steel company, manages downturns in its business by moving to four-day work-weeks: Employees lose pay, but keep their jobs. Southwest Airlines, that maverick in the airlines industry, avoids job cuts by sticking to its low-cost strategy through good times and bad. And when Pinnacle Brands lost a major portion of its trading-card business during the 1994 baseball strike, it turned to employees to come up with ideas for new products and cost cutting. As a result, sales jumped 80 percent in two years, and no jobs were lost. In each of these cases, there was an evident conviction that workforce stability is not only good for employees but sound operating policy, which gives the company a competitive advantage.

When layoffs become inevitable, companies can still help employees weather the transition. While *employment* cannot literally be guaranteed by any one company, there is much that can be done to help ensure *employability*. Indeed, this is a fundamental characteristic and essential clause of the new contract: the corporation has a responsibility, as well as a self-interest, in providing the time and the resources for employees' self-development. Training and retraining, continuous learning, and acquiring new skills all help both the company—to innovate and grow—and the employee—to develop, remain marketable, and be prepared for the new jobs that will be created in expanding industries. "Companies owe it to their employees always to upgrade their skills," said John A. Blanchard III, CEO of Deluxe Corporation. And, when the company announced that it would have to close more than half of its check-printing plants, Blanchard stretched the shutdowns over two years and increased company funding for education from $2,000 to $7,500 per worker annually.

Difficult though it may be for the corporation to deliver on promises of job creation and job security, the real challenge is presented by the qualitative aspects of the new contract. Here we are dealing largely with intangibles and idiosyncrasies—work values, personal goals and motivation, work–family balance, and culture. But it is in this domain that the new contract differs most markedly from the old; and it is here that the struggle for the hearts and minds of the new workforce will be won or lost.

In contrast to the phrasing of the old contract (see the beginning of this chapter), the new contract goes something like this: "Share with us your ideas and creativity, challenge the conventional, develop the novel, help us compete— and we will treat you as an individual, provide you with challenges, opportunities for development and learning new skills, and a community of like-minded individuals (but give no guarantee of career-long employment)." There is a seeming idealism in this phrasing, an emphasis on "buzz phrases," and a dissonance with our everyday experience. This may be true if we look at the past; but, to get a sense of the future, we should rather look at the direction in which leading companies are moving (see, for example, Cisco Systems, Box 7.2).

Consider the statement of Gerhard Schulmeyer, CEO of the European computer maker, Siemens Nixdorf: "The corporation exists insofar as it provides a place where the individual can do what he is good at, at a lower cost than he could do it otherwise." The clear underlying thought in this statement is that the corporation should provide an arena (and a climate) for individual self-expression, in a very practical sense, and that by doing so, both the corporation and the individual will benefit.

Or consider the survey of corporate cultures conducted by the Hay Group which revealed a profound difference between the cultures of ten high-performing companies (Asea Brown Boveri, American Airlines, Bristol-Myers Squibb, Dow Chemical, Intel, J. P. Morgan, Southwest Airlines, 3M, Toyota, and United Parcel Service) and those of average companies. In the high-performing group, the key priorities were teamwork, customer focus, fair treatment of employees, initiative, and innovation. In the average companies the top priorities were minimizing risk, respecting the chain of command, supporting the boss, and making the budget—values that are strikingly reminiscent of the old contract.

Moving from the "cutting-edge" present (as represented by the culture of these high-performing companies) to the future (as represented by the new work ethic) may not, therefore, be such a long or impossible journey. In many ways it will involve the heightening and harmonizing of some current "best practices" rather than any revolutionary movement.

The Customization of Work

An article in *Fortune* exploring the increasing customization of marketing practices began in this way: "A silent revolution is stirring in the way things are made and services are delivered. Companies with millions of customers are starting to build products designed just for you."[3] A similar revolution is also in progress in the way we design work: "Work packages" (responsibili-

BOX 7.2

Cisco Systems: Model for the Future Workplace?

Cisco Systems is not only the global leader in networking equipment for the Internet, with annual revenues of more than $8 billion. It is also often held up as a model for the corporation of the future in a high-tech age, in part because it uses technology not only to develop its products and services but to transform its organization and management practices.

At Cisco, the network is pervasive, externally and internally (although these two dimensions are seamlessly interlinked). It links the company to its customers, enabling Cisco, for instance, to respond electronically to 70 percent of requests for technical support and to account for about one-third of all electronic commerce. It links its wide array of business partners—suppliers, contract manufacturers, and assemblers—into a unified operation that presents a single face to the outside world. The network is also the company's primary tool for recruiting talent, with half of all job applications coming in over the Internet, and for linking employees to a vast array of information ranging from customer contacts to employee benefits.

However, though technology is key, it is not allowed to displace human interaction, and the company is admired for its progressive human-relations policies. Some of the distinguishing characteristics of Cisco's relations with its employees are

- *Retention*: In addition to a no-layoffs policy, Cisco places a high premium on retaining employees in the many companies it acquires. John T. Chambers, the company's CEO, insists that Cisco should measure the success of every acquisition, first by employee retention, then by new product development, and finally by return on investment.

- *Personal touch*: Chambers himself holds regular quarterly meetings open to all employees to review business results and listen to their suggestions. Company executives are expected to spend lots of time coaching, mentoring, and communicating with employees.

- *Telecommuting*: This is the subject of a formal company policy, and about two-thirds of all employees avail themselves of this option. As a result, Cisco has seen productivity improve by up to 25 percent and has saved over $1 million in overhead.

- *Egalitarianism*: This is seen as critical to successful teamwork and morale. "You never ask your team to do something you wouldn't do yourself," says Chambers—who flies coach and has no reserved parking space.

- *Share the wealth*: Stock option plans are open to *all* employees.

ties, working conditions, and pay and benefits) are being tailored to the needs and aspirations of individual employees rather than to corporate norms.

If we find this idea so wild and improbable, I suggest it is because our mindset is still fixed on the old mass production–mass distribution paradigm. What is happening now in the workplace is a reflection of current changes in marketing, organization, and technology, but it is a trend that has been developing for thirty years. Back in the late 1960s General Electric began its first experiments in individual choice in savings plans and other benefits, which was at that time a radical departure from the "one-size-fits-all" approach. The move was seen as a threat by unions and accountants alike, but it suited the values of the emerging workforce, and even then the early computers made the accounting task manageable.

Since then, the mass customization of work has grown vastly more complex and extended the concept of individualization in many directions:

- *Employment patterns*: As we have already noted, it is no longer just a choice between full-time employment and unemployment. There has arisen a bewildering array of alternatives: full time or part time; job sharing; temporary or contract work; or self-employment.

- *Job structure*: Thirty—even fifteen—years ago, jobs were tightly structured, bureaucracy reigned, and "position guides" were able to prescribe in great detail the functions, responsibilities, and measures of accountability for each position in the hierarchy. Now job structure has largely been replaced by an ever-changing series of tasks, dictated in part by the fluid business situation, in part by the capabilities and initiative of the employee, and in part by the composition of ad hoc teams. Position guides might now more aptly be thought of as generic descriptors of "arenas of activity."

- *"Flextime"*: To a growing extent, the standardized work-week is being replaced by flexible, individualized schedules, compressing or expanding work-weeks to meet both business and employee needs. For instance, working three thirteen-hour days may both improve customer service and help an employee attend to family needs. A 1998 survey of more than 1,800 companies by William M. Mercer, a New York consulting firm, found that 61 percent offered flextime, up from 40 percent only five years earlier.

- *"Flexplace"*: No longer does work have to be done in one place—a company location. Telecommuting has expanded rapidly as a viable option. The Mercer survey revealed that one-third of the companies surveyed offered this option, up from only 6 percent in 1993. Hewlett-Packard has more than 4 thousand telecommuters in the United States, and one-fifth of IBM's workforce operates out of home, on the road, and out of shared offices.

- *Pay and benefit packages*: Since GE's early experiments, the notion of a "cafeteria-approach" to benefits has taken hold, providing employees with a wide degree of choice in the mix and level of benefits they select—for example, trading off some vacation time for increased health insurance or balancing increased personal savings with a reduction in pension contributions.

In total, these moves represent substantial progress toward the customization of work. And few companies have gone further than Steelcase, the office furniture manufacturer. The company allows employees to work unconventional hours, gives them a choice of benefits, and offers bonuses for individual hard work and overall company performance. For the corporation, these options stimulate productivity, save money, and help create a progressive image that attracts good workers. For employees, they afford more freedom of choice, stronger motivation, and greater ease in juggling the responsibilities of jobs and families.

This trend to customization parallels the emergence of the concept of work as self-fulfillment, the new work ethic of the growing managerial and professional class. These two trends, meshing in many particulars, reinforce and accelerate one another in rewriting the terms of the work contract. But, more important, a greater impetus toward further customization stems from the fact that it responds to a very much broader societal demand—one that is shared by virtually all employees in many industries and many countries— for greater control over their lives. At a time when many feel that they are at the mercy of forces and institutions much larger than themselves, when "things are in the saddle/And ride mankind," any movement that offers people a choice and the ability to influence conditions in an important part of their everyday lives is sure to be welcomed. So, with psychology and technology both supporting it, this is a trend that seems destined to grow and spread.

Those who see this new ethic as excessive self-absorption will argue, first, that it is socially unacceptable; and, secondly, that it flies in the face of the growing—and, many would argue, commendable—trend toward the "boundaryless organization" and the use of teams. While there can be little argument that a new organizational paradigm is emerging along these lines, there is no reason to suppose that it is on a collision course with the new work ethic. For one thing—even if one takes the Maslovian hierarchy literally—we should note that ego and self-fulfillment needs include the need for peer recognition and respect and presume the continuing importance and satisfaction of social needs. And surveys also support the notion that the new workforce and work ethic are not at odds with cooperation, teamwork, and close relationships. A study by Brian Hall, CEO of Values Technology in Santa Cruz, California, has proved just such a point. In an interesting computer analysis of corporate documents covering the entire history of two long-lived companies (one a midsized financial services company; the other, a large global electronics corporation), Hall has demonstrated that there is "a massive transition" in progress from an emphasis on "tasks" to what he terms a "relationship-first" set of values: Employees want to share attitudes and beliefs as well as work space, to establish relationships—with one another and with the company— as a precondition for work. So the realization of a personal goal of self-fulfillment may, in fact, not be in conflict with, but rather dependent on, a network of satisfying professional relationships which can provide both learning opportunities and peer recognition.

An Empowered Workforce

Empowerment is currently one of the most commonly used phrases in management literature. It is also one of the most abused concepts in practice. After thirty or so years of trying, most companies are long on promises and pronouncement, but short on performance. Why this should be so, after so many well-intentioned efforts, remains puzzling. Chris Argyris, the well-known professor and consultant on organizational behavior, suggests that almost everyone is in some part to blame: "The change programs and practices we employ are full of inner contradictions that cripple innovation, motivation, and drive. . . . Managers love empowerment in theory, but the command-and-control model is what they trust and know best. For their part, employees are often ambivalent—it is great as long as they are not held personally accountable. Even the change professionals often stifle empowerment."[4]

That being so, we might well ask, Why bother? Why don't we just write empowerment off as yet another right-sounding, but in the end largely ineffectual, panacea, as we appear to have done with reengineering and total quality management? The answer is that the basic concepts behind "empowerment"— whatever we might choose to call it—remain valid and important, and merit our continuing efforts to "get it right."

Empowerment should remain the keystone of the new contract first because it is in tune with the growing demand for more "democracy" and greater participation—in all our institutions; second, because it is a correct response to the advent of the new work ethic; and finally, because it supports the changes in organizational performance that are critical for success in this era of global competition and transcendent change. In his efforts to create an empowered workforce at General Electric, for example, Jack Welch has constantly emphasized the importance of what he has termed "soft values for a hard decade"— the values of speed, simplicity, and self-confidence. An organization that embodies these values will not only be one with a high level of trust, morale, commitment, and job satisfaction, it will also perform well. And performance, as Argyris rightly reminds us, is the ultimate goal—the aim is to produce and prosper, and the values that make this performance possible are penultimate. But they are also determinative, for without trust, there can be no risk-taking; without freedom of action, no initiative; without learning, no innovation; and without commitment, no execution.

It is beyond the scope of this chapter to prescribe in detail how empowerment should become a way of life in the corporation;[5] but there are a few caveats that are worth noting here:

- *Empowerment is not for everyone* ("You can't empower all of the people all of the time"): Not only is it unrealistic to expect that you can allow thousands of employees to participate fully in self-governance; but it is also unrealistic to think that everyone *wants* to be empowered. Some individuals can be excellent performers, but don't want the headaches and responsibilities that come with empowerment. And the "customization" of work should allow for them, too.

- *Empowerment is not for every task*: You cannot have empowerment for tasks that have no room for guesswork or flexibility and present little challenge. Empowerment is possible only when individuals *define* the task and the performance goals it should meet. In this regard, empowerment goes beyond and differs from mere delegation: Any task can be delegated, but only some tasks carry within them the potential for generating empowerment.

- *Empowerment is a bottom-up, not a top-down, movement*: Too many efforts to generate empowerment have foundered on the rock of executive prescription: a "program" has been developed, "processes" have been designed, and "change agents" have been designated—all of which has taken on the connotation that "as of now, you are empowered—and here's the way to act!" Empowerment is a much more subtle process, requiring time and patience to take root and produce results—a fact that was described well in General Electric's 1991 Annual Report in reporting on the early results of the company's Work-Out program:

  For a couple of years, we resisted the traditional GE predilection to quantify and measure Work-Out, and, in truth, there was little beyond the anecdotal and atmospheric to report. For a year or so, individual Work-Out environments seemed to just sit there, as one observer noted, like popcorn kernels in a warm pan. The cynics no doubt believed the warmth came only from the hot air of company rhetoric. *But all that time, trust was building, confidence was growing and teams were coming together.* Then, suddenly, things began to pop, here and there, with big ideas, process breakthroughs; and today they roar almost everywhere. (Emphasis in original)

- *Empowerment is more creativity than productivity*: Although it embraces both characteristics, empowerment has more in common with creativity. Productivity is a matter of working faster and smarter, but still is largely conceived as doing the same things in a better way. Those who are skeptical about empowerment argue, therefore, that we are fast approaching the point of diminishing returns, and wonder aloud "how much more juice we can squeeze from this orange." Welch, however, correctly rejects this argument, and insists that the better analogy is that of tapping the limitless springs of human creativity—the ability to conceive of radically different ways of doing things, and of the infinite possibilities of "what might be."

Balancing Work and Life

If there is one phrase that rivals empowerment as a corporate claim to a new approach to the workplace, it is "family-friendly." It, too, is a response to the values and needs of the new workforce and an attempt to retain and motivate key employees. It, too, is "politically correct," for it presumes to align corporations with the new social and political emphasis on family values. And, like empowerment too, it is a claim more honored in the breach than the observance.

However, the problem of balancing the often conflicting claims of work and home is not one confined to families: It is one shared, for instance, by those with elder-care responsibilities, childless couples, and even singles. It is a problem that is reflected in the popular phrase, "Get a life." Important though work is as a way of defining ones's position in society, it is not, for most, the be-all and end-all of existence. Life has other dimensions, and it is becoming increasingly difficult to give them the balanced consideration that individual employees might wish. A 1995 survey at Eli Lilly & Co., often cited as one of the more progressive companies in these matters, showed that little more than one-third of employees felt you could get ahead in your job and still devote sufficient time to your family. In another survey, one employee put it succinctly: "Anyone who thinks that you can have it all—your career and a fulfilling family life—is either naive, dumb or crazy."

Nor is the problem one that is caused entirely by inconsiderate corporations. Certainly, there are managers who regularly schedule meetings at short notice and at odd hours with little consideration for others, and executives who assign promotions to those whose cars are regularly in the company parking lot at 7 A.M. or 7 P.M. But there is more to it than that. Technology is steadily breaking down the barriers of time and place so, left unchecked, the responsibilities of a job can demand attention at any time, anywhere; the globalization of business makes for increased travel and twenty-four-hour business days; and the growing—and commendable—emphasis on "serving customer needs" can mean that, when a customer calls for attention, service is preeminent and personal schedules are secondary and may have to go by the board. Even good corporate intentions can be undermined by business pressures.

The problem is one that many corporations recognize, and there are encouraging signs that something is starting to be done to correct it. Corporations like MBNA (the credit-card issuer), Eli Lilly, Motorola, and Levi Strauss—the ones who regularly rank high in surveys by *Business Week* and Boston College's Center for Work & Family—have started an array of programs and services to help employees deal with the problem: on-site day care, flextime, parental leaves, concierge, valet and shopping services, and limits on travel. And the "customization of work" should ultimately be a major supportive trend.

But the evidence suggests that these programs are still the exception. Several years ago *Business Week* conducted a survey of the benefits and programs offered by 188 major employers to accommodate the problems encountered by their employees in balancing the demands of job and family. Using a "family-friendly" index with a maximum score of six-hundred points, the survey found that these companies averaged a score of only sixty-eight points, and only two companies scored higher than two hundred. And a 1993 study highlighted the "two-career penalty" that hits families in which both husband and wife are employed. This survey, covering 236 male managers who had received MBAs from two large northeastern universities and all of whom were married with children, showed that the men married to nonworking wives earned more and won more promotions than those married to women who worked either part time or full time.

In many ways we have yet to challenge the assumptions underlying the way work is currently organized. But such a rethinking seems necessary. Randall Tobias, Eli Lilly's CEO, has advocated "out-of-the-box" thinking on the subject, adding that "I'm not sure that a lot of corporate America understands." Whatever the outcome of this rethinking may be in terms of specific programs and approaches, one thing seems sure: The key, as MBNA has found out, lies in creating a culture that reinforces the programs and developing a shared mindset, from executives to the rank-and-file, that respect for the individual and fair treatment are paramount values.

IN SUMMARY

We should remember that there are other elements in the new social contract between employees and the corporation beyond those we have discussed in this chapter. For instance, the stakeholder concept of the corporation requires that employees should be considered on an equal footing with shareowners and other stakeholders. The rules of governance require the establishment of an ombudsman position to ensure due process within the corporate walls. And the three major thrusts to promote greater equity between one class and another in the corporation—narrowing the compensation gap between executives and employees; extending the reach of diversity programs; and designing global employment standards—all have an obvious place in defining the terms of the new contract.

Putting it all together, we can identify at least eight clauses in this new contract:

- *Vision and a sense of shared purpose*—something other than profit and shareowner value, to give employees a sense that they are working together toward a common and worthwhile goal.
- *Inspiring leadership*, preferably with the "common touch"—Herb Kelleher, CEO of Southwest Airlines, is everyone's favorite example.
- Serious, persistent, and consistent commitment to *creating an empowered workforce*—recognizing both its potential and its limitations.
- *Customization of "work packages"*—tailoring work responsibilities, schedules, and compensation to individual employee capabilities and needs.
- Creating a climate of *equity, respect, and due process*—to ensure fair treatment.
- *Reducing volatility in employment patterns*—to ease concerns about job security and restructuring.
- *Increasing "employability"*—through major emphasis on continuous learning (training and retraining to acquire new skills).
- *First-rate on-site amenities and services*, from day care to athletic facilities to valet services.

For the most part, these clauses relate to what the psychologist Frederick Herzberg called the "satisfiers" or true motivators of performance. What he called the "dissatisfiers," or hygiene factors—basic pay, work conditions, job security, and safety—are assumed and taken for granted, and so are no longer capable of generating that spark of creativity and action that would take performance to a higher level. No doubt there are still many places in the world where the "dissatisfiers" have yet to be met and are therefore still the primary agenda items of those workforces. But it is to the trend-setting patterns of workforces whose members operate at the higher levels of Maslow's hierarchy that we should look for clues as to the future of the social contract on work and employment.

We are currently facing a crisis in the matter of loyalty in the workplace. This is a malaise that affects both parties to the contract. Despite a relative handful of commendable exceptions, most corporations are more committed to flexibility of management and operations than they are to retaining and motivating employees. And most employees, shaken by the continuing uncertainties of restructuring, and skeptical of management's commitment to employee welfare, are inclined to hold back in their own commitment to their work.

We badly need a "rebirth of loyalty"—not a return to the smothering paternalism and dependency of the 1950s, but a move forward to a more respectful acknowledgement of the needs and contributions of both parties. This, above all, should be the main objective and lasting benefit of rewriting the social contract of work.

NOTES

1. Charles Heckscher, *White Collar Blues: Management Loyalties in an Age of Corporate Restructuring* (New York: Basic Books, 1996).

2. Thomas A. Stewart, "A New Way to Think about Employees," and "Will the Real Capitalist Please Stand Up?" *Fortune*, April 13, 1998, pp. 169–170, and May 11, 1998, pp. 189–190.

3. Erik Schonfeld, "The Customized, Digitized, Have-It-Your-Way Economy," *Fortune*, September 28, 1998, pp. 114ff.

4. Chris Argyris, "Empowerment: The Emperor's New Clothes," *Harvard Business Review* 76, no. 3 (May–June 1998): 98–105.

5. Argyris has a number of pertinent suggestions in his *Harvard Business Review* article (see Note 4).

8

Public–Private Sector Relationships: Redefining Roles

New rule: To ensure the success of the power shift, corporations must work closely with governments to achieve a viable and publicly accepted redefinition of the roles and responsibilities of the public and private sectors.

Two articles, both appearing on the front page of *The New York Times*, illustrate very graphically the dangers that corporations face if they misread public sentiments regarding the power shift or overplay their hands in exploiting the opportunities that economic and political transitions present to them.[1]

One article related the efforts of Goldman, Sachs & Company to become Russia's leading deal maker, helping the government raise money by selling $1.25 billion in bonds and, a few weeks later, arranging a complex deal to exchange short-term debt for long-term debt. Within two months, Russia stopped paying what it owed on much of its debt; and buyers of the bonds Goldman sold held nearly worthless paper. Goldman, Sachs, however, not only escaped the disaster but, in the course of the deals, earned tens of millions of dollars in fees and protected hundreds of millions of dollars it had at stake in Russia. There is nothing inherently wrong in trying to minimize losses, but even bankers interviewed by the authors of the article said that "quickly selling off its own holdings, just after it led investors to buy the same securities, suggests that [Goldman, Sachs] was worried more about the firm's own money than the long-term interests of its client, the Russian government."

In the other article we learned about the problems encountered in implementing Wisconsin's welfare-to-work program, which has attracted national attention and praise from social workers, economists, and corporate executives alike. By one measure, the so-called Wisconsin Works program has been remarkably successful: In one year alone, it reduced welfare rolls by 70 percent. But the writer quoted one observer as saying, "It works despite itself," in the face of bureaucratic confusion and rivalry between public and private agencies. Each of the five private agencies that run the program gets paid a flat fee and serves an exclusive territory, and each therefore has an incentive to withhold services: the less they spend, the more their profits rise.

Though these events played out in widely different fields, they are linked by three common threads. They both deal with the movement of private corporations into arenas that have for the most part been previously reserved for governments. They both raise questions about what was said to be the dominating role of profit in making corporate decisions. And both deal as much with perceptions as with facts: Even though no charges of illegal activity have been raised in either case, the corporate activities were *perceived* to be ill conceived and insensitive, if not immoral.

The importance of such events might be minimal were it not for the fact that the power shift now stands at a critical juncture. After the global surge toward privatization, deregulation, and market systems that occurred during the eighties and early nineties, the problems as well as the benefits of this transition have become more and more apparent. In one country after another, consumers and politicians alike are debating whether to stay the course and proceed with further reforms or to reverse course and seek shelter from the harsh adjustments that this transition demands. That is why it is no exaggeration to state that the power shift—and with it, the private corporation—stands at a point of crisis, in the literal, medical sense: The current situation will not long persist, but will be resolved—one way or the other. It was for that reason that I selected the future of the power shift—success or failure—as one of the two critical axes of uncertainty in describing alternative futures for the corporation (see Chapter 2).

This fact necessarily propels executives into the arena of political debate and a struggle for public opinion. Neither challenge is one that executives have historically welcomed or been well equipped to deal with. H. I. Romnes, the chairman of AT&T in the 1960s, recognized this limitation in corporate capability when he said, "If we in business can say of the bureaucrat that 'he never met a payroll,' it can also be said with equal justice that 'we never carried a precinct.' We have a lot to learn from each other." To succeed in the coming debate, executives will, therefore, have to learn what it takes to "carry a precinct," recognizing that the public (in most countries) has little patience with or belief in the old paradigm of alternatives: swashbuckling capitalism or paternalistic government.

At the heart of the matter is the need for a redefinition of the roles that we want governments and the private sector to play in the future. We seem collectively to sense that the old models are no longer appropriate in the new world; but there is as yet no consensus on what the new model should look like. This is, of course, a vastly complex and multifaceted issue covering not only the relationships between business and government, but also the devolution of power among various levels of government and the role of not-for-profit institutions in providing social services. However, there are three specific issues that are of critical importance to corporations and on whose outcome their actions can exert an important influence:

- The broad question as to the future nature and role of capitalism itself: What changes and limits, if any, will be needed if capitalism is to be the model for economic organization on a global basis?
- The more limited question of the future scope of government regulation: How far can deregulation be pushed in a rapidly changing and globalizing economy?
- Finally, a comparable question concerning the future extent of privatization: How far can the privatization of public services be pushed? Where should we draw the dividing line between core public services and those that can be safely privatized?

THE GLOBAL FUTURE OF CAPITALISM

For a decade after the end of the Cold War and the collapse of communism in the Soviet Union, the spread of capitalism and market-oriented systems appeared to be unstoppable. In rhetoric and in action (though to varying degrees), governments in developing countries, in the former Communist bloc, and in previously socialistic Europe, all echoed the same theme: Markets beat Marxism. Now, however, economic crises in Asia, Russia, and Latin America have prompted second thoughts about the merits of unrestrained global capitalism. Even in Europe, rising unemployment and the financial crises in social programs have led to the election of left-of-center governments in France, Germany, and the United Kingdom. Everywhere, it seems, doubt is in the air.

Broadly speaking, this questioning attitude is prompted by the inevitable volatility and uncertainty—in markets and society alike—that has resulted from the convergence of two of the formative forces discussed earlier: the power shift and globalization. Taken alone, either force would have caused major restructuring of national economies. Taken together, the two have plunged the world into a new—and, in the long term, promising—system of economic organization for which it has been ill prepared. In particular, we have seen social and political concern focused on two criticisms of unrestrained capitalism: the volatile global flows of capital and, as Rodrik noted (see Chapter 2), the inadequacy of social programs to cushion the impact of sometimes abrupt and violent economic adjustments on individuals and communities.

Today it has been estimated that something like one *trillion* dollars are moved around the global financial system *each day*. The financial needs of the world's economies are vast, and capital inflows are needed to jumpstart growth in developing countries. The trouble comes with volatile currency speculations, with sudden and panicky outflows of capital, and with the use of highly leveraged capital from hedge funds leading all too often to overcapacity, profitless sales, and widespread corruption. Financial flows differ from product flows in one important respect: They are not self-regulating. As a result, deregulation is increasingly perceived as an enemy of stability and growth; more and more nations are questioning their commitment to market systems; and a backlash against capitalism is in the making.

The concerns and criticisms come from all points of the economic and political spectrum, expected and unexpected. Thus, it is not surprising to hear India's intensely nationalistic premier, Bihari Vajpayee, proclaim, "The world is paying the price for the dogma of the invisible hand of market forces," or to hear Tony Blair, British prime minister, and German Chancellor Gerhard Schroeder call for greater controls on international capital flows. The Chilean finance minister, Eduardo Aninat Ureta, said that the really worrying aspect of these crises is "the lack of differentiation. . . . We are seeing countries being traded as commodities." But even the president of the New York Federal Reserve, William J. McDonough, was moved to assert that the speculative attacks on Latin countries show that "what we believed is a very rational world financial system can be very irrational." Perhaps the most surprising and damning criticism, however, has come from George Soros, the Hungarian-born financier and prototypical capitalist, whom the Malaysian premier Mahathir Mohamad at one time blamed for his country's financial problems. In a well-publicized article in the February 1997 issue of *Atlantic Monthly*, Soros expressed his grave concern that "unbridled self-interest and laissez-faire policies may destroy capitalism from within."

At the moment there is no clear consensus as to exactly what changes are needed, nor how to implement them. However, some initial guidelines are emerging from the economic and political debate:

- *Recognize that unrestrained freedom can lead to anarchy as well as to prosperity*: The recent explosive growth of global financial markets has not been accompanied by a similar expansion of global regulatory capabilities. If capital is to flow smoothly and efficiently into productive investments, the world needs a strong and clear framework of bank regulation, accounting principles, and bankruptcy proceedings.

- *More disclosure and transparency are absolutely essential in this era of global capital and hedge funds*: Crises such as that which nearly sank Long-Term Capital Management clearly underscore the need for more disclosure of positions—by countries, international agencies, and major players in foreign exchange markets—and improved oversight of all financial institutions, both by private lenders and by government regulators.

- *Rethink the old orthodoxy that currencies should be made freely convertible as quickly as possible*: There is an emerging consensus that capital controls should be removed only *after* a country's financial institutions are strong and sophisticated enough to be able to manage in a turbulent situation.

- *However, do not shackle markets with permanent curbs on capital and currency flows*: As Banco Centrale de Chile head Carlos Massad made clear, "Capital controls aren't a cure. They are prevention. They can't be used to hide external or domestic disequilibrium." It is important to proceed with the further integration of previously closed economies into the free-market system—given the right conditions. *Business Week* editorialized, "We think the solution is more integration, not less; more political reform within each emerging market, not more regulation of the global capital system."[2]

While these are policy decisions that only governments can make and implement, corporations should not sit silently by, nor should they in a reflex reaction protest the strengthening of a global regulatory framework that is so manifestly deficient at present. All corporations—financial institutions most particularly—have a threefold stake in the outcome: a reduction in volatility; the stabilization and expansion of markets; and, above all, the renewal of faith in global capitalism. Volatility is anathema to markets and to corporations: They have a self-interest at least as great as that of governments in the creation of a more stable global financial system. Global consumer and infrastructure markets, so attractive to corporations, have been battered and weakened by devaluations, capital outflows, and the resulting political unrest: A resumption of growth depends heavily on a renewal of confidence and a reduction of speculation. Even the continued acceptance of capitalism as the preferred global model—and of the private corporation as its prototypical expression—will be in doubt if a greater measure of predictability and (some would say) rationality is not reintroduced into the financial system. Most nations are still prepared to buy into free markets and private enterprise—*provided* they have some assurance that their people will benefit if they play by the rules. There is, however, a growing conviction that the rules need modification and strengthening, and an insistence by these nations that they have a hand in modifying and implementing the rules.

The global future of capital thus rests on the successful resolution of two disturbing problems: financial volatility and individual and community hardship resulting from economic restructuring. Both problems call for government action, at the international and the local level. But both also call for some further modification in the way that "gung-ho" capitalism operates.

We would do well to remember that "capitalism," as it operates today in different countries, is not a single model. As Lester Thurow, the MIT economist, sees it, there are at least three major models competing to see which does best for its people:

- *The American model*, which might be described as individualistic, finance, or consumer capitalism. The individual is king, and government exists to keep corporations from harming the consumer. This assumes that they have opposite interests: the corporation wants to maximize short-term profits, while the consumer wants to pay the lowest possible price.

- *The Japanese form*—or what Thurow calls "communitarian capitalism"—where the interests of the entire country or community take precedence over the short-term interests of consumers or shareowners. This model emphasizes close government–industry cooperation, and the government feels no reluctance about intervening in the affairs of companies, or even entire industries, to stimulate investment and ensure cooperation in key fields.
- *The German model* lies somewhere in the middle. The government takes a much smaller policy-setting role, although it owns far more companies than in the other two systems.[3]

In the past forty years each of these models has been hailed as an "economic miracle" and the model of the future: the American model, in the sixties, and now again in the nineties; the Japanese model, in the late seventies and eighties; and the German model, in the sixties and seventies. Each has also been written off as outmoded and out of touch with changing economic and political trends: the American model, in the seventies (in the wake of the oil crisis) and the late eighties; and both the Japanese and German models, in the middle and late nineties. As recently as 1990, Fred Branfman, executive director of Rebuild America, a Washington economic policy center, forthrightly declared a winner: "The American model has been defeated decisively by the Japanese model, but just as in Vietnam we are denying our loss as a nation."

Predicting which model will be the global winner in the next twenty years is likely to produce as embarrassing an error as Branfman's. Indeed, it can be argued that *none* of the existing models as they are currently defined will be the clear winner. For one thing, we have seen how impractical it is to try to transplant any economic system into another culture without some change and adaptation to national values and priorities. Look, for instance, at the many potential sources of tension that exist between the goals of developing countries and those of international private enterprises (Box 8.1). For another, it would really be surprising if *all* the existing models did not undergo some radical modifications in the future as they adapt to changes in the global economic and political environment.

In part, they will all change as they learn from each other, picking, choosing, and adapting elements that have proven successful elsewhere. But, more than this, the main driver of change will be the need for each of the current models to adapt to the emergence of a radically different economic system— global in scope, transformed by technology, and modified by a heightened ecological consciousness.

So, while there will doubtless be some convergence among these three models, as they mimic each other's successes, the greater impetus to change will come from the imperatives of this new system. Rather than give it a name, we should try to focus on its salient characteristics. Capitalism of the future will be

BOX 8.1

Tensions between Developing Countries' and Corporate Goals

Even when developing countries claim to welcome infusions of capital and the entry of multinational corporations into their markets—and even when these corporations recognize that they must adapt to local customs and values—the potential for tension still exists. Consider, for example, the following differences in goals—all rational, but all potential sources of conflict:

Developing Countries' Goals	*Multinational Corporations' Goals*
Promote local ownership	Maintain global standards and efficiency
Increase local control	Minimize cost and complexity of delivering technology and capital
Change payment characteristics and reduce duration of contracts	Receive just returns for risks
Minimize source firm's control over use of technology and capital in user nation	Gain assurance regarding property rights over use of private resources
Separate technology from normal private investments	Provide technology as part of long-term production and market development
Remove restrictive business clauses in investment and technology agreements	Maintain ability to affect the use of capital, technology, and associated products
Minimize proprietary rights of suppliers	Protect rights to profit from private investments
Reduce contract insecurity	Use contracts to create an environment of stability and trust
Encourage transfer of R&D to host country	Maintain control of R&D paid for by the company
Develop products suitable for domestic markets	Gain global economies of scale to lower cost of products to consumers

Source: Murray Weidenbaum and Mark Jensen, *Threats and Opportunities in the International Economy* (St. Louis: Washington University, Center for the Study of American Business, 1990). This table was adapted from the President's Task Force on International Private Enterprise, *The Private Enterprise Guidebook* (Washington, D.C.: U.S. Government Printing Office, 1984).

- *Knowledge based*: As we have seen, corporations already consider knowledge to be the key strategic resource. If this is, indeed, the new form of capital, then "capitalism" takes on a radically different connotation, placing the "knowledge owners" on at least the same level as the "money owners."

- *Entrepreneurial*: This is a return to capitalism's roots, substituting individual initiative, flexibility, and risk taking, even within a corporate structure, for the bureaucratic "corporate capitalism," which is today's prototype.

- *Democratic*: As we noted in the discussion of governance, the new capitalism will reflect a shift in the balance of power—not a total transfer, but a noticeable shift nevertheless—both internally (from centralized authority to diffused empowerment) and externally (from the corporation to its customers, alliance partners, and even suppliers). This broad diffusion of power, combined with the expansion of the system of checks and balances already noted, matches the trend toward political democracy which is a key part of the power shift.

- *Cooperative–competitive*: While global competition will be every bit as fierce as we now know it, cooperation will simultaneously increase. This "two-headed" form of relationship will extend to the corporation's dealings with, for instance, unions—traditional bargaining versus joint approaches to productivity—competitors—traditional competition versus cooperative ventures—and government—traditional "arms-length" dealings versus public–private projects.

- *Socially responsible*: This is perhaps a trite phrase, but it aptly captures the spirit of what some have called "capitalism with a heart and a conscience." Fundamentally, this concept reflects the corporation's growing concern for the interests of *all* stakeholders rather than for those of shareowners alone.

What are we to call this new model? William Halal in his book *The New Capitalism* wrote that "the most useful thing Americans could do is to stop thinking of our economy as 'capitalism' in any form." Instead, he suggested, we should start thinking about "democratic free enterprise" as the new model.[4] "Democratic" and "enterprise" are terms I agree with; but I have trouble with the unfortunate connotations of "free enterprise" and its association with unrestrained capitalism of the past (and sometimes present). It may be better at this stage in history to refer to it simply as the "post-capitalist" era, as Daniel Bell first introduced our new era with the term "post-industrial," and leave it until later to place a more definitive label on the system that actually emerges.

THE LIMITS TO DEREGULATION

The typical knee-jerk reaction of most corporations—certainly those in the United States and Britain—is to welcome any and all deregulation of economic activity and to oppose any and all regulation. Given the clumsy, inefficient, and sometimes counterproductive nature of much government regulation, such a reaction is perhaps understandable. It is not, however, an intelligent or adequate response. Not only does it overlook the fact that *some* regulation, or even some addition to regulation—as, for instance, in the case of the global financial system—can benefit corporations by clarifying the "rules of the game" and moderating volatility and uncertainty. It is also a primary source of public distrust of corporations because for most of the public, government regulation stands as a needed bulwark against corporate abuse.

Even in times of economic expansion, there is a great deal of public skepticism about corporations' motives, especially when it comes to their opposition to legislation that people believe is "in the public interest." For all their railing against governmental bureaucracy, the public still turns to political solutions—if not at the federal level, then locally—as a "court of final redress" for their economic concerns and complaints, whether in consumer protection, occupational safety, or environmental protection. They believe the invisible hand may be fine in delivering "the goods," but it is the very visible hand of regulation that they invoke when things go wrong. And it is corporations' unvarying opposition to *any* regulation that confirms their worst fears.

What is called for, therefore, is a more thoughtful, discriminating, and proactive stance on the part of corporations. The public deserves it; and corporations need it. At present, as new societal concerns appear, develop, and start to move through the political process, corporations typically move slowly through seven stages of response, from initial outrage and rejection to ultimate compliance and assimilation (see Box 8.2). It is particularly in the earlier stages that corporations need to change their attitude and course of action, substituting research for emotion and constructive alternatives for destructive argumentation. This is not, of course, to argue that they should now accept every new proposal unquestioningly. It is, rather, to assert that their questioning should be calmer, more rational, and (if you will) more "businesslike," looking behind the proposal to understand the concerns that led to it and looking forward to examine the possibility of alternative solutions. If they are to be truly influential in the political process, they must follow Romnes's advice and learn how to "carry a precinct." And, despite the cynics, the way to carry precincts depends ultimately on positive positions, not negative attacks.

BOX 8.2

The Stages of Corporate Response

As new societal needs, wants, and expectations develop, corporations tend to progress through a series of seven stages of reaction, from initial outright rejection to ultimate strategic assimilation:

1. *Dismissal:* The initial corporate reaction is to reject the new proposal out of hand, dismissing it as unreasonable and "socialistic." To the extent that there is any corporate response, it is to the effect that the proposal represents the thinking of a "fringe" minority and so should not be taken seriously. Indeed, not every new proposal does take hold of the public's attention

and support, but for those that do, the sequence then moves to the second stage.

2. *Outrage*: As anger follows denial in Elizabeth Kubler Ross's sequence of reactions to the prospect of death, so outrage follows dismissal in this sequence of corporate reactions. As the new proposal starts to attract public support, and interest groups become active, corporations react with angry, rather than reasoned, outbursts. The proposal is not needed, they assert, because the problem it addresses does not exist, or is already being taken care of; and adoption of the proposed measures would undermine the foundations of the free-enterprise system.

3. *Counterattack*: With politicization of the issue and the drafting of legislative proposals, the corporate lobbyists and business associations swing into action, marshaling more detailed and specific arguments against the legislation: For example, its estimated cost would put corporations at a competitive disadvantage in global markets; it is too inflexible in its requirements for implementation; or it is too vague in its standards for compliance. If the issue is broad enough in its sweep, new business coalitions will form and public advertising campaigns will be started to counter the influence of interest groups.

4. *Experimentation*: At the same time that corporate opposition is becoming more organized and vocal, we can also see the early signs of a more positive corporate response. Some companies, blessed with more farsighted leadership and convinced of the inevitability—and basic merits—of the new legislation, start to anticipate the new rules and experiment with their own approaches to a solution. Persuaded, too, that bad regulation is damaging to competitiveness, but the right kind of regulation can enhance it, they try to influence the course of regulation in more positive fashion, sharing the results of their experiments and working with legislators to frame more flexible, less costly regulations.

5. *Compliance*: With legislation enacted and enforcement underway, corporations have no option but to comply with the new requirements. This is, however, also the stage at which the benefits of earlier corporate experimentation start to multiply. "Leaders" continue to develop and refine their approaches to the issue; "followers" learn from leaders; a form of competitive race develops to determine who is the most successful adapter; and a climate more receptive to regulatory reform sets in.

6. "*The PR phase*": As companies start to comply with new regulations, they find that compliance brings public-relations rewards. An image of genuine commitment to the new rules can be an important asset. But any image must be clearly grounded in reality, if it is to last. Accomplishing this grounding means first establishing clear principles and objectives; second, finding objective measures of performance; and third, communicating the results—publicly.

7. *Strategic assimilation*: By this final stage, the corporation has assimilated the new social requirement into its operations and in time has found ways to reduce the initial costs of compliance.

The change must start with a recognition that complete deregulation is no longer feasible, if it ever was. Free-market advocates may insist that government can and should get out of the regulatory business entirely and let competition do the job. New technologies are certainly opening up competition in industries that were once regulated as monopolies, but it turns out that establishing the new competition often requires a regulatory framework to set the new rules of the game. This has been the experience, for example, in the telecommunications and electric utility industries, with agencies continuing to be involved in setting ground rules for competition and directing traffic. Even the auction of the broadcast spectrum, once hailed as the epitome of free-market principles, required a multitude of regulatory decisions to determine how the auction should be conducted, which parts of the spectrum should be allocated to which uses, and whether licenses could be traded.

But that is not the end of it. As Robert Kuttner and other economists constantly remind us, some degree of regulation is also needed for a variety of other reasons, such as the following:

- *Public purposes*—for instance, providing universal access to certain services, such as telephone and electricity in rural areas. Left to its devices, the free market might decide that serving these areas was "uneconomic." But once public policy requires that companies serve all areas, there needs to be some kind of cross-subsidy scheme to pool the cost.

- *Systemic risk*—such as the risk of financial meltdown in global capital markets. The more competition there is, the more fluid the market and the greater the task for regulation to reduce systemic risk.

- *Externalities*—such as air and water pollution. Because air and water have been considered "free goods," the market system has difficulty in accounting for them. It was this area that gave rise to the idea of substituting "market incentive" regulation for "command-and-control" regulation: in effect, "put a price on it and let competition sort it out." The idea, as Charles Schultze, chairman of President Carter's Council of Economic Advisers said, was to harness "the public use of private purposes" by creating economic incentives for companies to install pollution-control mechanisms.

- *Monopolies*—the focus of all antitrust legislation. The recent classic case, of course, was the break-up of AT&T's monopoly which provided the opening for MCI and Sprint to gain a foothold in the long-distance phone service.

In sum, what a more sophisticated and concerned public expects of business in this regard is that it will be more open minded and less ideological in its approach to regulation; more cooperative and less automatically confrontational in its relationship with government; and more concerned with the public interest and less inclined to judge the merits of a proposal solely by its impact on the bottom line. There seems, at the moment, to be an appreciable but fluid majority of public opinion in many countries in favor of deregulation. The way to consolidate and expand that favorable majority is, I suggest, for corporations to heed the examples set by "Hi" Romnes and "Reg" Jones.[5]

THE SCOPE OF PRIVATIZATION

With privatization, the question is, "How far can it reasonably be pushed?" This, in turn, raises two related questions: "Which government activities can be privatized? And are there core public sector services which should always be reserved to the public sector?"

David Osborne, whose book (coauthored with Ted A. Gaebler) *Reinventing Government* revolutionized thinking in this area, answered these questions by asserting that government functions can safely be left to the market if they meet three conditions:

- If the market can provide them: If buyers will purchase the services, and nonpayers can be excluded from enjoying them, then private producers will supply them.
- If they primarily benefit individuals or groups of individuals, rather than society as a whole (if they are "private goods").
- If the community does not care whether everyone has access to them, and if there is no concern about equity or universal access.[6]

Of course, even in these cases, the government may have to regulate the activities and monitor compliance with the regulations: It does not, however, have to own or operate them. Osborne went on to point out that most "steering functions" (policy and regulatory activities) and many compliance functions normally have to remain in public hands because "the public is not comfortable with letting private organizations carry out such functions such as those involving the courts, the police, and tax collection."

In considering the potential scope of privatization, it is useful to distinguish among four related but distinct aspects of the potential transfer of responsibilities from public to private ownership or operation:

1. Economic enterprises.
2. Infrastructure construction and maintenance.
3. Public services, such as garbage collection and public park operations.
4. Human services, such as education, welfare, and emergency services.

Broadly speaking, the further one moves down this list, the more controversial the case for privatization becomes and the more difficult it is to win public support. But the fact remains that private corporations are now operating in each of these four domains, either as a line of business or as a measure of social responsibility. They are thereby increasing their visibility and their exposure to public judgment as to the merits, not only of specific corporations, but of the market system as a whole, in undertaking these new responsibilities. This is therefore a crucial testing point to determine the success or failure of the power shift.

Privatizing economic enterprises such as steel mills, airlines, banks, and railroads is now widely accepted around the world as the best route to increased efficiency and competitiveness. The classic example of a "big bang" approach to such a transfer of ownership was provided by New Zealand, surprisingly under the Labor Party, newly elected in 1984. At that time, the New Zealand government owned and operated about one-eighth of the nation's economy, including the telecommunications industry, all the ports, railroads, and the national airline, several of the largest banks, most of the coal industry, and the only two television channels. The first step was to "corporatize" some of these government entities, and on "Big Bang Day" (April Fools Day, 1987!) nine state-owned enterprises came into being, covering coal, electricity, property management, land forestry, the post office, the postal bank, telecommunications, and air traffic control. Although the government still owned their assets, these entities for the first time faced market pressure, paid taxes, and could no longer draw free capital from the government. Over the next five years, they achieved such astonishing turnarounds that the government decided to take the next step—selling them off—in part to reduce the deficit, but most importantly to achieve even greater efficiencies. By 1995, the Labor government had sold more than twenty organizations, representing more than two-thirds of its commercial assets.

While the case for privatizing such economic enterprises is now widely accepted, there is greater debate, and a wider diversity of responses, with respect to the next two categories: infrastructure construction and maintenance and public services. A major cause of the public's greater reluctance to privatize these operations stems from the fact that they are predominantly "public goods" (thus failing one of Osborne's three criteria for privatization). However, even in these areas, it is remarkable how wide a net some governments have cast in seeking out private companies to provide communal services and operate facilities. Surveys have shown that the services range from garbage collection and building maintenance to data processing and handicapped services; and facilities management, from roads, bridges, and tunnels to office buildings and garages.

Infrastructure development is an issue that is rapidly gaining public and political attention as a key issue in the new economy—both the physical infrastructure (e.g., highways, airports, telecommunications) and the social infrastructure (e.g., education, health care, community development). Whether the problem is one, for developing countries, of building infrastructures or, for developed countries, of rebuilding and renovating them, this issue is taking on greater importance because of its bearing, not only on social welfare, but on national competitiveness in the global economic struggle. In one country after another, the public is starting to recognize that neither the social structure nor the economy can bear the encumbrances of a poorly trained workforce, social unrest, decaying transportation systems, or the lack of an "information superhighway."

The public seems comfortable with the fact that corporations have an obvious and commendable self-interest in upgrading the infrastructure: They are, after all, highly dependent on the quality of the workforce, the stability of communities in which they do business, and the physical systems which support their operations. And, in varying degrees, both the public and government officials also recognize that the private sector has acknowledged contributions of management, technology, and financial resources that can be brought to bear on the task of increasing the effectiveness and efficiency of these public facilities and services. The major concern here is that the profit motive will, in the long run at least, negate or distort these benefits. And, for that reason, they insist on preserving the check of public monitoring and control.

Where the privatization movement encounters the greatest public misgivings and reluctance to change is in the area of human services—those that touch people as individuals rather than as the public as a whole. Even as staunch a conservative intellectual as William Bennett, the former U.S. secretary of education, admitted his concern over "the idolatry of the market" when it is applied to social welfare issues. "Unbridled capitalism," he has written, "may not be a problem for production and for expansion of the economic pie, but it's a problem for . . . the realm of values and human relationships because it distorts things." This is precisely the concern underlying the doubts about the operation of the Wisconsin Works program, as reported in *The New York Times* story mentioned at the beginning of this chapter. The profit motive is seen by many people as, per se, inconsistent with the aims and principles of public-welfare programs.

Nonetheless, experimentation goes on across an amazingly diverse range of services—from child support to Medicaid to welfare-to-work programs—as the following examples illustrate:

- Lockheed Information Management Systems, a division of Lockheed Martin, has won child-support enforcement contracts with the District of Columbia and sixteen states, and contracts in twenty states to convert welfare benefits to a debit card system.
- Maximus, Inc., a $100 million government consulting company, has a contract with California to recruit Medicaid beneficiaries into H.M.O.s, and welfare-to-work contracts in Boston, Fairfax, Virginia, and two California counties.
- Andersen Consulting, the large global consulting firm, has contracts with fourteen states, including child-support enforcement and redesigning the management of child welfare programs.
- America Works has contracts with New York City, Albany, New York, and Indianapolis to provide support services for the first four months on the job, charging a fee for each successful job placement.

In each of these cases, and many others, it is not merely the reputation of the individual company, and the success or failure of a particular program, that is at stake. It is the success or failure of privatization as a principle to guide the redrawing of the boundaries between public and private sector responsibilities.

Education, however, is one point at which societal expectations, governments' revenue problems, and corporate acceptance converge. "Developing an educational system for the twenty-first century" is more than a political slogan. It is an acknowledged social and economic imperative. It is an area of public spending that has suffered from deficit-induced cuts. And it is an area in which the public seems to recognize the appropriateness of corporate leadership and input. Most particularly this is the case with respect to the training and retraining required to keep the workforce up to date and competitive.

Corporate executives, too, single out the quality of education as the most significant social issue affecting their organizations. In a survey of managers in twenty-five countries on six continents, the *Harvard Business Review* found that 77 percent of those executives approved of business taking on a very active role in this field.[7] Signposts already pointing in this direction include company sponsorship of local schools, the "corporatization" of university research programs, and increasing attention to cooperative educational ventures between business and community groups to design and support economic infrastructure developments.

There is a well-established tradition of "in-house" corporate education and training programs, and these are now taking on the trappings of "corporate universities." In the United States, it has been estimated that the number of corporate universities will exceed the number of traditional universities by the year 2010. But this is not exclusively a U.S. phenomenon: It has also taken root strongly in Western Europe. Early in 1999, British Telecommunications (BT) announced plans to establish one of the world's biggest corporate universities in an attempt to "create a workforce with the business and technology skills needed in the new millennium." The academy, with a collegiate structure similar to that of Oxford and Cambridge, will train BT's 125 thousand employees, offering tailor-made degrees and vocational courses.[8]

Corporate contributions of money and equipment to schools, colleges, and universities are by now a well-established tradition, but corporate involvement now is moving beyond its traditional support programs to market-oriented projects like Michael Milken's Knowledge Universe and Chris Whittle's Edison Project, which aim to run schools and offer a spectrum of educational products and services. There is, thus, a reasonable prospect that privatization might move further and faster in education than other areas of human services.

IN SUMMARY

The issues involved in this new rule may appear to have more to do with political philosophy and social policy than they do with corporations' strategy and their standing in public repute. Yet it is no exaggeration to say that the resolution of these issues over the next fifteen or so years—the way that "capitalism" comes to be redefined and practiced; and the extent to which deregulation is advanced, and privatization accepted by the public—will have profound consequences for the corporation. The outcome will be determined by many factors beyond the control of corporations, but their statements and actions—the way in which they apply market principles around the world, their regulatory self-restraint, and their privatization practices—will play a major role in shaping public opinion and the policies it creates.

The risk is that corporations, sensing that the current tide of market forces is with them, will overplay their hand and turn the public against them. Self-restraint is not a typical corporate (or market) virtue: yet, in some measure, that is exactly what is called for in dealing with a public that still has a "Yes, but . . ." attitude to the way in which corporations and the market system operate. Without that self-restraint, there is a real danger of a backlash, whose principal casualty would be a loss of faith in globalization and the market system.

NOTES

1. Joseph Kahn and Timothy L. O'Brien, "For Russia and Its U.S. Bankers, Match Wasn't Made in Heaven," and Jason DeParle, "Wisconsin Welfare Experiment Easy to Say, Not So Easy to Do," both in *The New York Times*, October 18, 1998, p. 1.

2. Bruce Nussbaum, "The Time to Act," *Business Week*, September 14, 1998, pp. 34–37.

3. Lester C. Thurow, *The Future of Capitalism: How Today's Economic Forces Shape Tomorrow's World* (New York: William Morrow & Company, 1996); and *Head to Head: The Coming Economic Battle Among Japan, Europe and America*, also by Thurow (New York: Warner Books, 1993).

4. William E. Halal, *The New Capitalism* (New York: John Wiley & Sons, 1986).

5. See previous references to Romnes (p. 122) and Jones (Chapter 6, p. 100).

6. David Osborne and Ted A. Gaebler, *Reinventing Government: How the Entrepreneurial Spirit Is Transforming the Public Sector* (Reading, Pa.: Perseus Press, 1992).

7. Rosabeth Moss Kanter, "Transcending Business Boundaries: 12,000 World Managers View Change," *Harvard Business Review* 69, no. 3 (May–June 1991): 151–164.

8. Simon Targett, "BT to Establish World-Class University," *Financial Times*, January 19, 1999.

9

Ethics: Elevating Performance

New rule: The corporation must elevate and monitor the level of ethical performance in all its operations in order to build the trust that is the foundation of sound relationships with all stakeholder groups.

Pick up any copy of the *Wall Street Journal* or *The New York Times* and you will come across one or more articles with headlines such as

FTC Files Suit Against Abbott Labs, Charges Price Fixing

S.E.C. Charges Grace and 6 Former Executives With Fraud

German Business Ethics Loses Some Luster

GM Removes 2 Top GMAC Officers in Aftermath of Credit Swindle

DuPont Settles Charges of Withholding Evidence

Day after day, the recitation of unethical or illegal conduct goes on, to the point where many wonder whether we really have made much progress in raising the level of corporations' ethical performance over the past century.

It is not that these lapses have gone unnoticed and uncondemned by corporate executives themselves. The management literature is replete with their writings on the need for high moral standards in business and their condemnation of the failings of fellow executives. I remember that back in the 1950s, Chester Lang, who was at that time vice president of public relations at General Electric, gave a frequently delivered speech on this subject, in the course of which he said that the businessman's credo seemed to be, "Get on; get honors; get honest." Lang himself adhered to a stricter code, but this was his way of wryly acknowledging—and condemning—the frailty of the ethical connection in many of his fellow executives. Their code, he said, was centered on a belief that, at the height of their careers, the first priority had to be "getting on,"—growing the business and making the sale, regardless of any moral cost that might be entailed. It was only later, in the twilight of their business careers, when they were able to coast on past success, that these executives felt they had the "luxury" of behaving ethically. Five years after Lang gave such speeches, the truth of his observation struck home as General Electric, as well as Westinghouse and Allis Chalmers, reeled under the impact of the massive electric-utility antitrust cases.

Of course, such behavior, although all too common, is not the whole story. The executive suite can and does produce such exemplars as Max DePree, the chairman of Herman Miller, whose leadership set a high ethical standard for his fellow employees; and James Burke, the former chief executive officer of Johnson & Johnson, who steered his company through the Tylenol poisoning crisis by adhering to a strict insistence on adhering to the company's credo and on "doing the right thing" by openly acknowledging and dealing with the problem. Indeed, *The Economist*, which is not known for turning a blind eye to corporate malfeasance, has speculated that corporations and consumers alike seem to be moving toward a higher ethical standard in their marketplace dealings. In an article with the intriguing title, "Who Cares, Wins: Nice Firms Often Finish First," the magazine observed editorially that "in many ways economics seems to be moving in the nice guys' direction. . . . A growing number of consumers now base their buying decisions on 'non-commercial' concerns."[1]

The public debate about the state of business's ethical behavior is far from being a new one. Indeed, one can trace the debate back to the Golden Rule and Saint Augustine's writings on what constitutes a "fair price." A legitimate question might, therefore, be "What's *new* about a rule on corporate ethics?" It might appear that everything that can be said on this subject has already been said and that the moral standards of yesterday are still the standards of today. But there *are* new elements in the picture, and they have more to do with raising the bar of public expectations than with any presumed worsening of corporate behavior.

WHAT'S NEW ABOUT CORPORATE ETHICS?

To begin with, consider the fact that we appear to be adopting a broader and deeper definition of what constitutes an ethical issue—a definition that goes far beyond an insistence on honesty and trustworthiness. *The Economist* article cited went on to enumerate some of these new public concerns: "Does a product harm the environment? Was it tested on animals? . . . Was it made in a Surinam sweatshop? If a firm can answer 'No' to all of the above, it can make an ethical killing."

Indeed, there is an ethical core at the heart of each of the new rules. The legitimacy issue, for instance, is based on the presumption that the public standing of a corporation rests fundamentally on the execution of its social purpose—to serve society by providing needed goods and services—rather than on its ability to maximize profit. Legitimacy rests, therefore, on adherence to a moral purpose rather than to an amoral need. The purpose need not be a "highfalutin" one: Indeed, as often as not, it is as mundane as, for instance, meeting personal transportation needs by manufacturing and servicing safe, reliable, and affordable cars. But the moral foundation of serving society's needs—and the responsibilities that come with it—remains.

Governance, too, presents ethical as well as legal and organizational issues. Nothing could be more loaded with moral significance than the questions surrounding the roles and responsibilities of the various stakeholders in the corporate system: What are the rights of stakeholders? How should these rights be protected? Whose values and interests should determine corporate actions? To whom, ultimately, should corporate executives be responsible? How should their accountability be structured? What is the right balance between privacy and disclosure of information? In the corporate as well as the political system, the answer to such questions depends at least as much on value systems as it does on facts.

Equity also rests on a foundation of values as well as facts. Corporations can, for instance, make a logically persuasive case for the level of compensation that they pay their chief executive officers, citing the compensation paid in comparable companies and their need to be competitive in order to retain executive talent. But logic gives way to emotion and considerations of "fairness" when the public and employees make the comparison, not with other executives, but with their own pay. It is simply "not right," they argue, for there to be such an outrageous difference. (Interestingly, this same line of thinking is starting to infect public perceptions of the salaries paid to sports stars who have, up to now, been exempt from such criticism.) Similar arguments between rationalization and morality develop in the areas of diversity and global work standards, two other aspects of equity that we examined. The fact that definitions of equity or fairness are hard to come by and exist more in the mind of the observer than in any dictionary does nothing to reduce the impact of this moral imperative. It only makes the corporation's task that much more difficult to prescribe.

The concept of sustainable development is the product of what is rapidly becoming a new ecological ethic. This is truly a new dimension in human morality. Up to now, ethical questions have focused on issues arising out of the relationships between individuals or between an individual and society. The ecological ethic, however, seeks to redefine the relationship between man and nature, moving from a dynamic of exploitation to one of conservation and harmonization between manmade and natural systems. It also extends the ethical horizon from the present to the future, forcing the present generation to acknowledge its responsibility for holding the earth's resources and environment in custody for future generations.

In employment the ethical quotient is high, as it must be in any aspect of human relationships. Just as a work ethic shapes an individual's behavior and attitude toward work, a corresponding "employment ethic" guides the organizational culture a corporation seeks to develop and the relationships it establishes with employees—as well as those it encourages between employees. Beyond the physical characteristics of the workplace and the practical details of the employment contract (e.g., responsibilities, pay, benefits) lies an array of ethical questions such as, Is the organizational climate one that insists on unconditional honesty, openness, and trust? Or does it tolerate (if not encourage) "cutting corners," "shading the truth," and meeting performance goals at all costs? Is the contract based on respect for the individual as an essential contributor to corporate success, or does it treat employees as resources to be used or discarded as economic conditions dictate? Is there a system of due process to ensure fair treatment and redress of grievances? Because of the closeness of the relationship between employee and employer, ethics play a more important and diverse role than in any other stakeholder relationship.

Finally, in the power shift in public–private sector relationships, there is a paramount ethical issue: It is nothing less than a reformation of the capitalist ethic. As the conservative philosopher and politician William Bennett has noted, this ethic, in its unbridled form, "is a problem for the realm of values and human relationships because it distorts things." If the power shift is to succeed—if deregulation and privatization are to grow—corporations will have to exert more self-restraint and greater self-discipline, substituting self-policing for government regulation and moderating the pursuit of economic gain with stronger ethical restraints.

Beyond the evidence of these new rules, we can see the parallel development of another trend in public consciousness: a greater propensity to expand the scope of corporate liability and hold companies responsible for more and more of the consequences—for individuals and society—of the products and services they sell. The most obvious example is the recent onslaught against the tobacco industry. For thirty years following the first Surgeon General's report on the negative health consequences of smoking, there was a slow build-up of public awareness of the facts, but little change in consumer behavior and a near-total failure of individual lawsuits against the industry. If there was one event that triggered a heightening of public outrage and marked a turning point in the antismoking campaign, it was the image of the industry's CEOs standing before a congressional committee to be sworn in to "tell the truth, the whole truth, and nothing but the truth," and then testifying that they had no evidence or research to support claims of the negative impacts of smoking on human health.

It was the blatant dissonance between this testimony and the accumulating evidence to the contrary, quite as much as the evidence itself, that catalyzed public opinion against the industry and gave the needed impetus for success to the states' lawsuits, claiming reimbursement for the treatment of smoking-related illnesses.

We can now see similar cases, based predominantly on ethical arguments, being built against other industries and companies. The long-running dispute between gun-control advocates and the National Rifle Association over registration and restrictions on firearms is a case in point. More recently, there has been a developing attack on the gaming industry, based on the morally corrupting consequences of gambling and its potential for wrecking individual and family lives. Regardless of how successful these and other campaigns might be in achieving their objectives, a trend is in the making: Corporations should expect to find that their practices and their products are, more and more, subject to moral scrutiny. In retrospect from 2010, it may be only a slight exaggeration to say that ethics are replacing economics as the primary criterion for evaluating corporate performance—not because economic value is unimportant, but because it is taken for granted, and ethical performance is not.

Taken together these pieces of evidence support the argument that there is indeed a new dimension to the public debate about corporate ethics—a broadening of the issues, an intensification of the pressure, and a raising of the standards.

THE "DRIVERS OF CONSCIENCE"

Still a legitimate question remains: Why now? What has happened, or is happening, to cause this heightening of public conscience? The answer lies not in any dramatic reformation—we have not all suddenly become saints—but in a combination of forces, inside and outside the corporation, that make us more questioning, more demanding, and more impatient with the working of all our social institutions—including the corporation.

Start with the fact that each one of the four formative forces of our time poses inescapable moral issues as well as practical problems on the way to realizing the positive potential that they present. To cite just a handful of these issues, the power shift raises new questions about the power, purpose, and responsibilities of the corporation; restructuring forces the issue of "sharing the gain and easing the pain," as we adjust to new economic and political circumstances; globalization compels us to confront issues as diverse as the impacts of trade on social structures and the dilemmas posed by the diversity of ethical codes among nations; and, as the new technologies of computerization, nanotechnology, and bioengineering increase our ability to reshape our organizations, our relationships, and even ourselves, they force us, every step of the way, to answer the pointed question, "Does 'can' imply 'ought'? Should we do it because we can do it?" It should come as little surprise, therefore, that ethical questions have taken on a new urgency as the pace and reach of these forces has increased.

There is also that "lower frustration tolerance" that I have identified (in Chapter 1) as one consequence of our higher levels of affluence and education and as a prime motivator of our growing impatience with all forms of economic hardships, social injustice, and inequity. We have always assumed the worst about corporations' ethical behavior but until recently have done little about it except in the most egregious cases. As recently as the 1960s, whenever a news-breaking story confirmed our worst expectations, we greeted it with a shrug and the resigned comment, what can you expect? We have always been cynical about corporations and their leaders but felt that there was little we could do about it. So long as corporations made the products, provided the jobs, and raised our standard of living, we were, it seemed, prepared to "cut them a lot of slack." This is true no longer. In a highly competitive world, better educated and more affluent consumers have more choices and greater power—power that is amplified, not only through the ballot box, but also through a growing network of interest groups, each monitoring a specific area of corporate performance. Punitive activism, rather than cynical resignation, is now the more likely public response to corporate lapses.

This activism is further reinforced by the widespread availability of information. An errant corporation has fewer places to hide. "The good news is that the Net will make us honest," said Esther Dyson, president and owner of EDventure Holdings and chairman of the Electronic Frontier Foundation. Executives have to understand that they are going to be more visible and more transparent, and they must act accordingly. As Dyson concluded, "You have to start walking the walk, because just talk is going to be disclosed if that's all it is."[2] In the past, the disclosures of corporate wrongdoing have come from the professional muckrakers—the Ida Tarbells and Upton Sinclairs of an earlier age; the Ralph Naders of our times—who researched, accumulated evidence, and then published. Now newspapers and television give much greater coverage to business on a daily basis. Publications like *The Wall Street Journal, Business Week,* and *Fortune* employ investigative reporters with MBAs and business experience to dig into corporate affairs. Equally significant, however, is the opening up of the Internet which, with its countless opportunities for sharing and dissemination of information, provides a readily available outlet for anyone with a grievance—a disgruntled consumer, a wronged employee, or an outraged environmentalist or ethicist. This is a phenomenon of growing impact and relevance: As Rushworth Kidder, the president of the Institute for Global Ethics, has noted, "What I see happening . . . is that every company that has any kind of international activity has attracted around its periphery a bunch of Web sites devoted to exposing everything the company does."[3] The searchlight of growing public scrutiny is perhaps the best guarantee that we have of raising the level of ethical performance in *all* our social institutions—including corporations.

However, not all of what I call the "drivers of conscience" are external forces: There are changes *within* the corporation that move us in the same direction. In the first place, the executives of the future are products of their past—their education, their environment, and their experience: They reflect, in part, the changing social mood and values of our times, because they are themselves part of this scene. This is not to say that they are on the cutting edge of these changes—indeed, their initial reaction is usually to resist them—

but in the end they have little alternative but to accept and to adapt to them. So the executives of today—and tomorrow—bring to their work a far different set of ethical premises from those of their predecessors in the fifties and sixties, for whom equal employment opportunity and an ecological ethic, for example, were virtually unknown concepts. Executives may not be saints, but they are, above all, rational beings: They make their decisions with an acute awareness of the fact that long-term business success depends increasingly on abiding by the ethical standards set by society. Morally, there is still a great difference between doing something because it is right and doing it because it is expedient. But at least the expedience in executive decisions is moving corporations in the right direction.

This movement is being reinforced by a change in the structure of corporate relationships. As I pointed out in Chapter 4, "The linkage between many stakeholders and the corporation is shifting from a transactions basis to a relationships basis. . . . The relationship is closer, more intricate as portions of their operations become interwoven in seamless fashion." This network of relationships is based on business factors—the growing need for speed, simplicity, and efficiency, and the spreading effects of communications technology. But it depends critically on maintaining a high level of trust among managers, employees, customers, suppliers, shareholders, and lenders. Relationships of any sort can work only when they are founded on trust. And trust can exist only in a climate of high ethical performance. If companies slip into shoddy or downright unethical practices, these crucial relationships start to deteriorate rapidly. The effects may not be obvious at first: People may feel badly about their actions, but they rationalize their behavior. Eventually, however, a moral cancer sets in; trust is shattered; relationships deteriorate; and the network effectively disintegrates. Nowhere has the truth of this observation been more forcefully displayed than in the aftermath of Sears Roebuck's guilty plea to a criminal charge of bankruptcy fraud. As Arthur Martinez, Sears's chairman, said at the time, the true costs were incalculable: "We've rebuilt our customers' trust and confidence brick by brick, and now all of that has been bulldozed."[4] Most surely, Martinez, for one, would subscribe to the proposition that the primary force for a higher standard of corporate ethics should be executive insistence rather than external pressure.

The movement toward more persistent and consistent executive attention to the pressing issue of corporate ethics is thus driven equally by the strategic benefits of working relationships based on a high level of mutual trust and by a recognition of the heightened public vulnerability of corporate misdeeds.

THE CODIFICATION OF ETHICS

The best evidence of this heightened attention to ethical performance is to be found in the growing number of corporations that have developed codes of ethics to guide corporate behavior. More than two-thirds of large U.S. corporations now have codes of business ethics; and, according to a 1997 survey by the Institute of Business Ethics in London, 57 percent of large U.K.-based companies have such codes, up from only 18 percent ten years earlier.

As might be expected, there is great diversity in the detail and the quality of these codes. Consider, for example, the following different approaches to this subject.

Texas Instruments (TI) has developed a statement on "The Values and Ethics of TI" which stresses first the qualities on which the company seeks to build its strategic position—the qualities of integrity, innovation, and commitment— and then spells out the ethical foundation of these qualities. For instance, the statement defines integrity as respecting people by "treating others as we want to be treated," and as honesty in "representing ourselves and our intentions truthfully." It then goes on to spell out the key implications of these principles (e.g., "exercising the basic values of respect, dignity, kindness, courtesy and manners in all relationships" and "competing fairly without collusion or collaboration with competitors") and to touch on some of the ethical dilemmas that these principles may present (e.g., although Texas Instrument has an obligation to monitor its business information systems, "we will respect privacy by prohibiting random searches of individual TIers' communications"). Although the statement necessarily deals with generalities, it makes a marked effort to personalize responsibility to protect and enhance the company's reputation so that "each of us can say to ourselves and to others, 'TI is a good company, and one reason is that I am a part of it.'"

One of the best known corporate statements on this subject is Johnson & Johnson's "Credo" (see Box 9.1). In contrast to Texas Instrument's approach, J&J frames its statement in terms of its responsibilities to stakeholders, starting with "customers" (doctors, nurses, and patients), moving on to employees and communities, and—notably—*ending* with the company's responsibility to stockholders, reasoning that "when we operate according to these principles, the stockholders should realize a fair return." When General Robert Wood Johnson first wrote this credo in 1943, the notion of putting customers first and stockholders last was a new approach to management—and, arguably, is still the exception rather than the rule. Over time, the language of the credo has been updated and new areas recognizing the environment and the balance between work and family have been added; but the overall spirit of the document has remained the same. As with any such statement, the credo deals with generalities but, as in the Tylenol crises of 1982 and 1986, it has proven its value in helping management make tough decisions "in the real world."

Activity on ethical codes has spread to professional and industry associations following the pattern set by lawyers (American Bar Association) and doctors (American Medical Association). The American Association of Advertising Agencies (4A), for instance, has had a "Standards of Practice" statement, which it first adopted in 1924, but this statement is limited to condemning advertising that contains false or misleading statements, misrepresents testimonials and price claims, or is offensive to public decency. Far more comprehensive, both

BOX 9.1

Johnson & Johnson: "Our Credo"

We believe that our first responsibility is to the doctors, nurses and patients, to mothers and fathers and all others who use our products and services. In meeting their needs everything we do must be of high quality. We must constantly strive to reduce our costs in order to maintain reasonable prices. Customers' orders must be serviced promptly and accurately. Our suppliers and distributors must have an opportunity to make a fair profit.

We are responsible to our employees, the men and women who work with us throughout the world. Everyone must be considered as an individual. We must respect their dignity and recognize their merit. They must have a sense of security in their jobs. Compensation must be fair and adequate, and working conditions clean, orderly and safe. We must be mindful of ways to help our employees fulfill their family responsibilities. Employees must feel free to make suggestions and complaints. There must be equal opportunity for employment, development and advancement for those qualified. We must provide competent management, and their actions must be just and ethical.

We are responsible to the communities in which we live and work, and to the world community as well. We must be good citizens—support good works and charities, and bear our fair share of taxes. We must encourage civic improvements and better health and education. We must maintain in good order the property we are privileged to use, protecting the environment and natural resources.

Our final responsibility is to our stockholders. Business must make a sound profit. We must experiment with new ideas. Research must be carried on, innovative programs developed and mistakes paid for. New equipment must be purchased, new facilities provided and new products launched. Reserves must be created to provide for adverse times. When we operate according to these principles, the stockholders should realize a fair return.

Source: Johnson & Johnson, "Credo" (New Brunswick, N.J.: Johnson & Johnson, 1998).

in its statement of principles and in its program of implementation, is the Defense Industry Initiative on Business Ethics and Conduct (DII). The DII, which has forty-eight signatory companies (as of February 27, 1998), does not have an overall code of ethics as such, but the first of six principles to which signatory companies must subscribe states that "each company will have and adhere to a written code of business ethics and conduct." The other principles cover the following:

- Training employees concerning their personal responsibilities and the high values expected of them.
- Creating a free and open atmosphere that encourages employees to report violations of the code without fear of retribution.
- A commitment to self-governance by monitoring compliance with federal procurement laws and adopting procedures for voluntary disclosure of violations.
- Accepting a responsibility to other companies in the industry to live by standards of conduct that preserve the integrity of the defense industry.
- Public accountability for commitment to these principles.

Although the DII does not embrace an overall, industrywide code of ethics, it has in its annual reports given illustrations of the types of fundamental principles articulated by member companies in their codes:

Conduct all aspects of company business in an ethical and strictly legal manner, and obey the laws of the U.S. and of all localities, states, and nations where the company does business or seeks to do business.

Employee conduct on behalf of the company with customers, suppliers, the public, and one another must reflect the highest standards of honesty, integrity, and fairness.

Respect the rights of all employees to fair treatment and equal opportunity, free from discrimination or harassment of any type.

Ensure that all financial transactions are handled honestly and recorded accurately.

Protect information that belongs to the company, its customers, suppliers and fellow workers.[5]

Governments, too, have made some initial moves in this arena, driven largely by the globalization of corporate activities and the consequent need for some form of international agreement on common standards of business conduct. For instance, the U.S. Department of Commerce has produced a statement of model business principles intended to serve as a starting point and framework for individual corporate codes. This statement covers principles in five major areas:

1. Safe and healthy workplace.
2. Fair employment practices, including avoidance of discrimination, avoidance of child and forced labor, and respect for the right to organize and bargain collectively.
3. Responsible environmental protection.
4. Compliance with U.S., and local laws promoting good business practices.
5. Maintaining a corporate culture that respects free expression, avoids political coercion in the workplace, and encourages good corporate citizenship.[6]

The U.K. Foreign Office is drawing up a guide aimed mainly at small and medium-sized companies to help them act responsibly abroad. In this effort, it is seeking inputs from business, human rights and environmental groups, and other governments including the United States and Sweden.

Recently the European Parliament has agreed on a code of conduct for multinationals operating in the developing world. This code builds on existing international agreements on corporate behavior, and establishes minimum standards in such areas as labor relations and the treatment of indigenous people. A crucial fact is that it also provides for a system of monitoring corporate performance.

An antibribery convention drawn up by the Organization for Economic Cooperation and Development has also recently come into force that should work toward leveling the playing field. U.S. companies have long felt disadvantaged by the Foreign Corrupt Practices Act which forbids them from bribing foreign officials, while other countries had no such prohibition. The new convention should also mean an end to the widespread practice among OECD governments of allowing companies to treat bribes as tax-deductible expenses.

TRANSLATING CODES INTO ACTION

In the midst of all this activity, two critical questions stand out: How should codes be developed, and what should they cover? And, most important, how effective are they anyway in raising the level of ethical behavior in corporations? The two questions and the answers to them are in fact closely related since the effectiveness of a code depends, in the first instance, on the relevance of the code to the real issues confronting a corporation, and second, on the level of commitment, by executives and employees alike, to that code.

To be truly relevant and to enjoy the widespread commitment of employees, a code must be a product of the company whose values it purports to reflect. Transplants are largely ineffective. The code must address the issues that have the greatest impact on the success and public image of the corporation. It must give specific and realistic guidance to employees who may be confronted with a moral dilemma. And, above all, it must truly reflect "the way things are done around here," for nothing is more damaging to a corporation's reputation than the hypocrisy of lofty statements unmatched by comparable behavior. *Code, culture, and conduct must, in other words, be in complete harmony.*

It is for this reason that codes developed by governments or associations are largely ineffective. They can be a useful starting point, but they are of limited value because of their distance from the firing line. This is a fact that the Defense Industry Initiative recognizes with its insistence that, rather than relying on an industry-imposed code, signatory companies must take responsibility for developing their own codes as one condition for membership in DII. Developing codes in this way has a dual advantage: It heightens the relevance of the code by targeting the issues of greatest impact and significance to the company, and it greatly increases the level of commitment in the organization to living by the terms of the code. Indeed, it is this commitment factor that has led some companies, like the Bank of America in the 1980s, to involve their whole workforce in developing statements of corporate values, reasoning that—despite the difficulties inherent in a companywide effort—the broader the base of involvement, the greater the adherence to the code.

What should codes of ethics cover? As we have seen, there has been and continues to be a steady expansion in the public's definition of what constitutes an ethical issue. As a result, codes of ethics are confronted with a moving target, as Robert Holland, senior fellow at The Wharton School, has documented. Basing his projections on the research of two of his Wharton colleagues (Thomas Dunfee and Thomas Donaldson) and what they call "integrated social contract theory," Holland has developed an estimate of emerging ethical standards for companies operating in global markets (see Box 9.2). He is quick to point out, however, that this list is certain to be in a constant state of flux as conditions change and issues evolve.

Trying to keep a code up to date with changes in the ethical climate would, therefore, be a Sisyphean task. The code would itself be constantly changing, confusing, and, ultimately, unwieldy—and consequently ignored. The solution many companies, like Texas Instrument and Johnson & Johnson, have turned to is a statement of "core values" that provide a reasonably constant underpinning of corporate culture and supplementing this with policy statements on specific issues such as antitrust compliance, bribery, privacy, equal employment opportunity, and environmental protection. Such a combination stresses the permanent importance of core values that should guide every decision and action, while giving the system flexibility to provide the detailed guidance needed to deal with an ever-changing agenda of ethical issues.

BOX 9.2

Global Principles of Business Ethics: A Glimpse of What Might Emerge

Principle	Comment
1. Produce high-quality products and services.	As the years pass, this may be broadened to encompass other aspects of exercising due care by performing work competently and responsibly.
2. Respect the sanctity of contracts.	Stakeholder pressures may also gradually broaden this to the concept of honoring other forms of corporate promises as well.
3. Create and preserve a sense of corporate integrity that makes the firm trustworthy.	This may come to encompass all the aspects of acting in good faith, including not only honoring

	contracts but also avoiding deceit, acting fairly, and living up to the reasonable expectations of other participants in business dealings.
4. Obey applicable laws—usually.	The major exception will probably grow to be avoiding passive compliance with laws in particular localities that conflict with the emerging global ethical standards.
5. Protect proprietary information and respect confidentiality in business transactions.	However societal, pressures will probably work toward limiting this protection to circumstances where such limitation serves some public interest.
6. Respect the environment.	This may include both the avoidance of harm that is disproportionate to the societal benefits being extracted and the remedying of undue damage inflicted on the environment by present and past activities.
7. Respect the rights and liberties of others.	This will include nondiscrimination on the basis of race, sex, or creed.
8. (Later) Respect human well-being.	In particular, this will include concern for all persons harmed by the firm's actions.
9. (Possibly, but still later) Respect the independence of all individuals.	This includes giving them room to make informed judgments concerning their own self-fulfillment.

Source: Robert C. Holland (Philadelphia: University of Pennsylvania, The Wharton School, SEI Center for Advanced Studies in Management, 1996).

But codes are merely a collection of words: They may embody worthy goals, but by themselves they provide no guarantee of performance. At worst, a code of ethics may be little more than a public-relations ploy to deflect public scrutiny and criticism. At best, it can do no more than clarify and communicate the values that the organization wishes to embody and define the parameters within which decisions should be made. A code, therefore, has a limited but nonetheless essential role to play in guiding the ethical performance of a corporation. It is essential for it documents the shared values of the organization and provides a yardstick against which individual and corporate performance can be measured. Without it, there is no unifying force— no anchor—for corporate conduct. But on its own, it is limited and insufficient in its ability to ensure that the desired behavior does in fact occur.

A quick review of corporate experience in this arena shows that translating the words of a code into effective and sustained action involves a lengthy and complex process, including the following key elements.[7]

Executive Leadership

Executives obviously must take the leadership role here, both by the personal example they set and in the organizational provisions they make. More and more companies, for instance, are establishing ethics committees or appointing full-time ethics officers, generally at the corporate vice-presidential level, reporting to the CEO. In recent years the membership of the Ethics Officer Association, based in Massachusetts, has grown dramatically to 560 members, drawn from U.S. and European companies. Providing this top-level focus serves to underscore the seriousness with which a corporation views these issues, as well as to provide a channel for dealing with problems as they arise. When Texas Instruments established a corporate ethics director in 1987, it did so, not because of any immediate problems, but because it wanted a formal focal point to reinforce what it saw as an already strong ethical culture.

However, it is by the personal example that they set that corporate executives can do most to establish and maintain ethical standards. By their words, decisions, and unspoken signals, they do more than any other single influence to set the tone for an organization. Arthur Martinez of Sears underscored the importance of this factor when, in the wake of the company's bankruptcy fraud scandal, he urged his fellow officers to reexamine their own conduct and ask, "Is what I do, the direction I give, the body language I use, creating an environment where something like this could happen? Is my message, 'Make the numbers at any cost'?"[8]

Employee Education

It is not sufficient merely to distribute the code of conduct (and related policy statements), or even to insist on employees' acknowledging in writing receipt of the code and certifying that they understand and will abide by the standards of conduct. There needs also to be strong back-up from orientation (for new employees) and training programs, both in clarifying the code and in assisting employees in identifying and dealing with ethical dilemmas. Hewlett-Packard, for example, devotes considerable time and effort to ensure that all employees are familiar with its standards of business conduct, which cover everything from conflicts of interest and accounting practices to handling confidential information and accepting gratuities. Citicorp developed an ethics board game which teams of employees use to solve hypothetical dilemmas; at General Electric, employees can log onto interactive software on their personal computers to get answers to ethical questions; and Texas Instruments publishes a weekly column on ethics over an international electronic news service.

"Hotlines" and Due Process

Although an ethics officer is charged with responsibility for helping an organization to face up to and resolve its ethical dilemmas, she should not be thought of as some kind of "enforcer." Linking ethics to a punitive image is counterproductive. Rather, the primary emphasis should be on acting as advocate, counselor, or ombudsman—one who can provide a system of due process and a channel for resolving problems before they reach corrupting and disruptive proportions. With this in mind, many ethics offices have turned to confidential telephone "hotlines" as a favorite channel, both for reporting misconduct and for seeking advice. Raytheon and General Dynamics, both of whom established ethics offices in the 1980s, have found that the great majority of inquiries on their hotlines can be resolved on the spot, and only a relatively small number (5 to 10%) require disciplinary action or discussion with senior management.

Audit, Evaluation, and Disclosure

Common sense and standard management practice both point to the need for auditing the degree of compliance with codes of conduct. Annual performance reviews, both of individual compliance and of the adequacy of the code itself, serve to keep ethical behavior as an active issue on the management agenda. For the most part, companies have in the past conducted these audits on an internal basis; but increasingly they are turning to outside auditors—blue-chip law firms, or accounting firms like KPMG Peat Marwick and Arthur Andersen, both of whom have established ethics consulting businesses—to give the results greater public credibility. Certainly that is the new norm following an ethical crisis such as the sexual harassment suit against Mitsubishi Motor Manufacturing of America, when the company asked former Labor Secretary Lynn Martin to review its workplace policies. Disclosure of the results of these audits is also gaining ground—for instance, with the Defense Industry Initiative, which requires its signatory companies to adopt procedures for the voluntary disclosure of any violations of federal procurement laws.

IN SUMMARY

On no issue is there a greater divergence between public perceptions and corporate claims than on the state of ethical behavior in most companies. For cynical members of the public, "corporate ethics" is the ultimate oxymoron. They remain convinced that Gordon Gekko's credo in the film *Wall Street*—"Greed is good; greed works"—is the true guiding principle of business. And when corporate executives start to talk about ethics, the typical reaction is likely to be, "Watch out for your pocketbooks—we're going to be cheated."

The single most frequent trigger of unethical behavior is the corporate conviction that its true and only purpose is profit. All too often, the end is cited to justify the means; and if the means involve some shading of the truth, some cutting of corners, so be it. Even Warren Buffett, the "sage of Omaha," has lamented that "in recent years, probity has eroded." Writing in Berkshire Hathaway's annual report, he lambasted the attitude of many U.S. executives as "a business disgrace" and complained that "many managements purposefully work at manipulating numbers and deceiving investors." And if this is symptomatic of corporate attitudes toward shareowners, supposedly the prime stakeholders in management's view, what are we to suppose that their attitude toward other, "lesser" stakeholders is likely to be?

Elevating the level of ethical behavior in corporations will be a challenge and an imperative of the first order. It involves, as we have seen, a lengthy and complex process. But the starting point surely is clear: It is a recognition of the need for redefining the purpose of the corporation. As long as "maximizing profits" or "increasing shareowner value" is accepted as the primary *purpose*—rather than a key *objective*—of the corporation, there will always be a strong tendency for financial expediency to override moral principle. Unless and until there is such a rethinking of purpose, a fatal flaw in corporate ethical performance will remain.

NOTES

1. "Nice Firms Often Finish First," *The Economist*, May 16, 1992, pp. 19–20.

2. Esther Dyson, "The Net Will Make Us Honest," *Business Week*, March 23, 1998, special advertising section on "Connections: Competitive Strategies for the Age of E-Business."

3. Alison Maitland, "Exporting Better Business Practices," *The Financial Times*, January 26, 1999, p. 12.

4. John McCormick, "The Sorry Side of Sears," *Newsweek*, February 22, 1999, p. 37.

5. Information from the Defense Industry Initiative on Business Ethics and Conduct on the Internet (http://www.dii.org/).

6. Information on U.S. Department of Commerce Model Business Principles on the Internet (http://www.depaul.edu/ethics/principles.html).

7. It is worth noting the similarity between these guidelines and those suggested by the Federal Sentencing Guidelines for Organizations. These guidelines provide for reductions in fines for corporations convicted of criminal misconduct if the company has in place an "effective" compliance program. The seven factors on which the effectiveness of the program is evaluated are

- Established compliance policies and procedures for its employees.
- Assigned high-ranking individuals to oversee the compliance program.
- Took care not to give known wrongdoers positions involving discretionary authority.
- Training provided to all employees on the company's policies and procedures.
- Steps taken to ensure compliance and detection of violations, such as auditing systems, as well as to create a mechanism to which employees feel comfortable reporting concerns.
- Consistent response to detected violations.
- Evaluation and modification of the program to ensure enhanced protection and detection of illegality.

8. John McCormick, "The Sorry Side of Sears," *Newsweek*, February 22, 1999, p. 37.

Part III

THE RESPONSIVE CORPORATION

— 10 —

The Role of Leadership

It is no coincidence that the examples I have cited of corporate responses to the emerging new rules have been set by corporate leaders—both individuals and organizations—who have an ability to see where the future lies and how it might differ from the present, and an ability to translate that vision into needed corporate response. Leadership is, indeed, at the heart of the responsive corporation. As such, it deserves some attention on our part as we move from discussion of the issues posed by the new rules to the agenda of action that the responsive corporation might undertake.

THE NEED FOR LEADERSHIP

In a report that I wrote for SRI International in 1991, I observed that "business, particularly U.S. business, is overmanaged and underled." My thought in offering that observation was that a once commendable belief that good management was essential to corporate success had been distorted into a conviction that *every* organizational problem could be resolved by subjecting it to the objective principles of professional management—planning, organizing, integrating, and measuring. In the process, the less tangible, more human qualities that we associate with democratic leadership had been sadly neglected.

In the intervening years since then, however, the subject of leadership, particularly corporate leadership—its nature, scope, and cultivation—has become a cottage industry with an astonishing output of books, articles, speeches, and seminars (e.g., "How to Accelerate the Development of the Leaders You Will Need"). The evidence is clear that there is a growing recognition that leadership is needed, but lacking.

One might reasonably ask, Why is this? What has happened to make us believe that leadership is needed now more than ever before? Has the character of what we call "leadership" changed in some subtle or obvious way? The short answer is that both the external drivers and the internal needs have changed the need for leadership in a way that has riveted both corporate and public attention.

Forty, or even twenty, years ago, our business horizons were more limited, and the framework of our economic and political decision making was more established and familiar. Most managers, even senior executives, worked comfortably within this framework: They did not have to rethink the basic conditions of doing business. Over the past two decades, however, we have moved increasingly and more rapidly from a condition of relatively predictable, incremental change, such as we had in the 1950s, to a condition of largely uncertain, radical change. The old framework has broken, and we have to start from scratch to develop a new frame of reference.

Looking at it from a management point of view, we can say that one can *manage* incremental change and its impacts; but dealing with uncertainty and radical change requires *leadership*. Or it can be put this way: The changes we have seen have been so pervasive that corporations (and many other organizations, for that matter) are having to rethink, quite radically, their roles, their structures, their strategies, and their relationships. And this rethinking requires the vision, the ability to invent the future, and the setting of new directions that we associate with leadership, rather than the cool competence of management.

With leadership, a company is better equipped to explore and to push the envelope; with management, it is more comfortable preserving stability. But the new challenges—the challenge of the new rules, as well as the challenge of new markets, new competition, and new technology—do not allow us the luxury of stability: They demand that we change, continually and radically, without losing our sense of direction or purpose.

The new emphasis on leadership is needed, too, to counter the widespread and persistent decline in public confidence in virtually all our major social institutions, most particularly in large corporations. For more than thirty years now, since the mid-1960s, opinion polls have tracked this decline and the reasons for it. And, over and over again, the response has shown that the major reason is distrust of corporate leaders: Large segments of the public remain convinced that corporate executives are "impersonal," "ruthless," and have little concern for anything except their companies' profit and their own financial well-being.

The depth of this public distrust is illustrated in the following anecdote. Several times during the 1970s, I had the opportunity of listening to presentations by William H. ("Holly") Whyte, the sociologist and *Fortune* editor. His speech was usually focused on two themes: his well-honed attack on the "organization man"; and the seeming inability of executives to grapple with the implications of the forces that were then roiling U.S. industry—the oil shock, inflation, and Japanese competition. On this latter theme, he would build up to a punch line that went something like this: "It is obvious to everyone that our so-called corporate leaders are as confused as the rest of us. We've always known that they were bastards. Now we can see that they are *dumb* bastards!" It would be easy to argue that this statement was a cheap shot—a demagogic trick. But it worked. Every time I heard him give this speech, the punch line evoked a spontaneous outburst of audience appreciation—a recognition of a shared perception. And I suspect that it would draw the same public reaction today!

The evidence of the need for a change in the character of corporate leadership has been with us for a long time. Only recently, however, have the forces for change gathered sufficient momentum to alter both our definition and practice of leadership.

(RE)DEFINING LEADERSHIP

We are beginning to recognize that there are real and appreciable differences between "leadership" and "management." Asked to encapsulate these differences, I would say that

- Leaders envision the future; managers focus on the present.
- Leaders set an organization's direction to deal with "what will be"; managers run its operations, dealing with "what is."
- Leaders lead people; managers manage "things" (e.g., programs, resources, schedules).
- Leaders seek to develop commitment and motivation; managers rely on controls.
- Leaders emphasize values and relationships; managers emphasize processes and procedures.
- Leaders build the *effectiveness* of an organization ("doing the right things"); managers focus on organizational *efficiency* ("doing things right").
- Leaders emphasize heterarchy and the diffusion of authority and responsibility; managers emphasize hierarchy and the chain of command.
- Leaders take a synoptic view of the corporation's internal and external relationships; managers deal almost exclusively with its internal operations.

There are a number of caveats that should be considered with this list. First, the distinction I make is sharper in this listing than it is in practice. Clearly, leadership and management share some concerns and qualities; but, on balance, each function does tilt in the direction I have indicated. Second, and most important, the lists are not intended as either–or guides to selecting a management style. Certainly I do not suggest that a corporation should embrace leadership because it is a "nobler" activity and neglect management because it is "baser." To succeed in today's demanding environment, a corporation clearly needs both leadership and management.

Nevertheless, the list does accurately reflect the fact that there is a "distinction with a difference" here. And there are strong and demonstrable reasons why, at this point in the corporation's evolution, we should choose to emphasize the development of leadership, because this is the area of greater need.

The question is: What *kind* of leadership? I am not here referring to the obvious fact that there are—and always will be—individual differences in style, from the strongly assertive leadership of a Jack Welch, to the quieter consensus-building style of Sony's Akio Morita, to Robert Greenleaf's concept of the "servant-leader." At a more fundamental level, we seem to be in the process of moving away from our traditional reliance on the leadership of a single individual to a preference for what might be called "group leadership," in which the qualities of leadership are broadly diffused throughout the organization. In part, this movement is a reflection of the broader democratizing trend—a preference, I have said, for being led rather than managed— that is remaking the structure and governance of so many of our societal institutions. In the main, however, this movement is driven by the inescapable fact that it is no longer possible for one individual to have all the answers and make all the decisions. The need for organizational change is now so universal and pervasive that initiative and innovation—leadership—must be available at every level and at many points throughout the corporation.

In a very real sense, the essence of leadership is now *not* the leader, but the *relationship* between the "leader" and the "followers." In his book, *Leadership in the 21st Century*, Joseph Rost points to a shift from the industrial concept of leadership—a leader-centered view—to a paradigm of the post-industrial concept of leadership based on relations among leaders and followers.[1] This new definition of leadership rests on four elements:

1. The relationship is based on influence, and influence is multidirectional—that is, it can move in any direction, not just top-down. This influence is not coercive, so the relationship is based on persuasion rather than authority.[2]

2. Both leaders and followers, as the ones involved in this relationship, are practicing leadership. Rost does not say that all players in this relationship are equal, but all the players can exert influence.

3. There is a commitment to change—substantial change—on the part of both leaders and followers.

4. The changes that are sought reflect both the wishes of the leader and the desires of the followers.

In all this, there is a sense that we are breaking down the previously clear-cut differences between "leader" and "followers." Indeed, these terms may have largely outlived their usefulness in describing organizational relationships. While we may not yet have reached the point at which everyone is a leader, many corporations have set their sights on a comparable objective: "Everyone is a change-agent."

THE FIVE COMPASSES OF LEADERSHIP

Responding to the new rules requires leadership in at least two regards: setting new directions, and communicating values. If we consider the list of contrasting attributes of leadership and management, we can see that neither of these is a particularly strong suit of managers. Indeed, if left to them, the response would almost certainly lack conviction and impetus.

In setting a new direction and maintaining that chosen direction in a turbulent environment, successful leaders need some form of compass in order to negotiate safely through the shoals of changing and conflicting demands. In fact, in meeting the challenges we have outlined above, leaders need not one, but five "inner compasses."

Before going on, I should note that there are obvious difficulties with any analogy, and the compass metaphor is no exception. An ordinary compass seeks out magnetic north and is easily duped or misled by other, nearer magnetic fields. However, if we think in terms of a gyrocompass, the metaphor becomes more appropriate. The gyrocompass always points to true north; relying on its own internal guidance system, it never deviates. The leadership compass must be of this type: internal, consistent, always seeking true north.

The Strategic Compass

Leadership implies setting a direction that others will follow. This direction must not be random or haphazard: It must be guided by some form of strategic sense—an intuitive, entrepreneurial sensing of the "shape of the future"— that uses, but transcends, ordinary logic. It is a unique blending of thinking and feeling, analysis and intuition.

Having a strategic compass is the trait that most markedly sets leadership apart from management. A leader uses this inner compass to help determine what the destination and direction for the company should be; to know when a change of course may be required; and, having established "true north," to keep the organization on course to its destination, whatever zigs and zags a flexible strategy may entail.

Strategy is, importantly, an inclusive, integrating activity—that is, it

- Examines *all* aspects of a company's business.
- Does so in the context of its *total* environment.
- Develops a *comprehensive* vision of the shape and character of the future company.
- Sets an *integrated* strategy to achieve that vision.

There is no artificial division between the economic and the political environment, between competitiveness and social responsibility, or between the local and the global. The corporation is a single entity, embracing all these aspects, and must therefore deal with them in an integrated way. The new rules are too important to be left to the public-relations or community-relations functions to determine what the corporate response should be. Indeed, many, if not most, of the implications of the new rules lie outside the competencies and responsibilities of these functions. The new rules give rise to issues that can only be resolved at the most senior levels of corporate management. The strategy to respond to these issues is as essential a part of overall business strategy as is a marketing strategy or a technology strategy.

The Action Compass

Leadership, almost by definition, implies movement or action: You move an organization from point A to point B. Vision—a sense of strategic direction— is admirable and necessary; but *action* is the end point. So leaders are driven by a strong propensity for action—action by self, and action by others; they are focused on results. Arthur Martinez, CEO of Sears Roebuck, had it right: "If you're unable to galvanize people into action, all the thinking, the analysis, the strategic prioritizing doesn't matter at all."

Of course, managers too are action oriented. The difference lies in Warren Bennis's astute observation that "managers catch and ride the waves: leaders create the waves." In other words, it is the combination of vision and action that marks the true leader. There is this inner compass that always guides the analysis, the strategizing, and the vision toward its ultimate goal—the change of direction, the new impetus, and the realization of the vision.

Certainly, the new rules demand action. No longer will bland executive speeches, ambiguous policy changes, and public-relations programs that seek to deflect rather than deal with the issues suffice. A retrospective glance through the previous chapters will quickly reveal the outlines of a substantial agenda of responsive actions that corporations should undertake.

The Culture Compass

The connection between culture and strategy and the role of leadership in reshaping culture is by now widely accepted in the corporate world. Evidence of the importance of the "culture connection" is all around us. We see it in the many efforts to create a more entrepreneurial climate in large organizations. We see it in the stories of mergers that have failed because of a "culture clash" between the merging companies. And, as always with a new management fad, we see it in the plethora of writings, conferences, and courses on the subject.

Nowhere is the influence of leaders more obvious and pronounced than in shaping the culture of the organizations they lead. With the change in the character of leadership we have just noted, it is no longer accurate to describe a company as the extended shadow of a single individual. However, it is still, without question, true that corporate leaders—at any level—set the tone and character of their organizations. This influence can be benign, as it is when working toward improved teamwork, empowerment, or greater openness; or perverse, as it is when a single-minded emphasis on higher profits can lead to "cutting corners," corruption, or illegal arrangements.

The cultural aspects of leadership are its most significant characteristics. In his *Harvard Business Review* article, "What Makes a Leader?" Daniel Goleman writes that his research has shown that whatever differences there may be in leadership style, "the most effective leaders are alike in one crucial way: they all have a high degree of what has come to be known as *emotional intelligence*" which he defines in terms of self-awareness, self-regulation, motivation, empathy, and social skills. The hallmarks of emotional intelligence exert their influence on the culture of an organization through "trustworthiness and integrity," "building and retaining talent," "cross-cultural sensitivity," "effectiveness in leading change," and "expertise in building and leading teams." Not only do these elements contribute more to excellence in leadership than such obvious factors as IQ, technical and cognitive skills, Goleman's analysis showed that "emotional intelligence played an increasingly important role at the highest levels of the company."[3]

To comply with the new rules, a company must change far more than its policies and practices: It must change its values, its attitudes, and its culture. Governance, for instance, involves far more than restructuring the board of directors or establishing an ombudsman: It is a matter of reperceiving who the corporate stakeholders really are and of acknowledging the need for a broader set of corporate responsibilities and greater openness and accountability. Sustainable development depends even more on a new mindset and a heightened environmental consciousness than it does on new technology and redesigned processes. And, as we have seen, the new rule on legitimacy presumes a changed attitude on the role of profit and a redefinition of corporate purpose. Taken together, these and other implications of the new rules amount to a radical change in corporate culture; and this in turn requires more leadership rather than more management.

The Sociopolitical Compass

If there is one central characteristic of the emerging business environment of the future, it is the predominance of social and political issues with which the corporation must now grapple. To some extent, this has been true for much of the past century as rising societal expectations have been translated into legislated requirements. What makes the current and future situation different is the global reach of the power shift, for what is at stake now is nothing less than the opportunity for the market system and its corporate embodiment to become the global model for the next century.

The challenge demands nothing less than the best of corporate leadership; and leadership requires a highly sensitive social and political compass to negotiate this minefield of potentially explosive issues. It is only a slight exaggeration to say that corporate leaders of the future will have to be "political animals" almost as much as they are business executives. Most assuredly they will have to heed "Hi" Romnes's advice to learn "how to carry a precinct," not of course in its literal sense, but in paying close attention to the mood of public opinion and being flexible and proactive in their dealings with legislative bodies.

This is *not* to suggest that executives should abdicate their responsibilities by keying their decisions to a reading of public-opinion polls. Leadership must find a way between intransigence and weakness, making the inevitably tough decisions only after weighing their impact on the interests of all stakeholders.

The Moral Compass

In light of the new rule on ethical behavior (see Chapter 9), the moral dimension of corporate leadership should be obvious, and little more needs to be added here. But its very obviousness can blind us to the inherent difficulties in making ethical decisions in a corporate context in which multiple interests are involved. There is far more to ethical behavior than being honest and fair. In recent years, more and more questions have been defined as moral issues: Equal opportunity, arms sales, business in South Africa or Myanmar (Burma), animal testing, slave labor in China, bioengineering have all, at one time or another, been brought within this fold.

Suffice it to say here that leadership leads by example, by spelling out the values by which the business will be conducted, and by ensuring that everyone without exception—executives, managers, and employees—is judged by the same standard of unwavering adherence to these values.

LEADERSHIP AND VALUES

A key—perhaps even defining—role for leaders is to act as the formulators, the communicators, and the custodians of the values the corporation lives by. This is not, of course, a new concept: Indeed, one of the best personal statements of leadership values that I have encountered dates back to the early 1980s (see Box 10.1). But it is a role that takes on even greater importance as soon as one defines leadership as an "influence-based relationship" between leader and followers rather than as a leader-centered phenomenon. Creating a culture of shared values then becomes a central feature both of the organization and of the leader's obligations.

An interesting case study in the evolution of the leadership style of one executive is provided by the history of Jack Welch's tenure as CEO of General Electric, a position he has held since 1981. For the first six or so years, he was the aggressive restructurer of the business portfolio and the proponent of downsizing: This was when he earned his nickname "Neutron Jack" ("The buildings are standing; the people are gone."). Then, starting in the late 1980s,

BOX 10.1

Leadership Values

Leadership by example: In every field of human endeavor, people scrutinize the actions of the leader to determine whether he or she is consistent—that the leader practices what he or she preaches. A leader can expect no more from people than that which he or she personally is willing to contribute.

Leadership responsibilities and prerogatives: The higher the position, the greater the responsibilities of the leader. As overall responsibilities increase, so too does the leader's freedom of action and individual prerogatives. The leader uses such prerogatives with discretion because of his or her visibility and the example he or she sets through actions.

Leadership and change: The leader accepts responsibility for accomplishing concrete results in a changing environment. He or she attempts to anticipate external, uncontrollable change, manages resources accordingly, and willingly accepts the consequences that result from such decisions.

Leadership and decision making: Leaders are responsible for decisions that are based on uncertain, imperfect information. They make decisions because they recognize that more opportunities are lost through inaction than action. Leaders also make every effort to eliminate the perception of individual risk because of decisions that prove to be faulty.

Leaders and organizational culture: The leader depends upon the assistance of supportive, professional people whose shared values contribute to organizational effectiveness. The leader therefore seeks to build a system of shared values.

Leadership and people: A leader achieves results through the actions of others and therefore is foremost concerned with managing people effectively. The ideas, concepts, and decisions of the organization invariably are not those of the leader.

Leadership and trust: The leader believes that people are trustworthy and that they possess the desire to perform and contribute. He or she creates an environment that enhances communication—the exchange of ideas, trust, and personal initiative. He or she treats people with respect.

Leadership and control: The leader attempts to keep controls to an absolute minimum. He or she recognizes that centralized decision making stifles individual initiative and results in organizational ineffectiveness.

Leadership and delegation: The leader realizes that organizational performance improves with delegation of authority to the lowest possible level. The leader manages by objectives and results, emphasizing substance (performance) over form (the way to do things).

Leadership and confrontation: The leader readily uses constructive confrontation as a technique to improve performance. He or she is frank and open, seeking win–win solutions to conflict by avoiding either–or solutions.

Source: William R. Wahl, Personal statement of leadership values made when assuming the presidency of AMAX Coal Company, 1985.

he became the culture changer and the advocate of empowerment and the Work-Out program; his theme became "soft values for a hard decade." The change was due, I believe, not to some personality change or a midcareer conversion, but rather to a shift in strategic priorities. For GE to become the company Welch envisioned, the first requirement was to restructure the portfolio and reduce the level of employment to ensure globally competitive costs. Then, and only then, could he focus on the shift to a more "empowered," entrepreneurial culture that had from the beginning been a critical part of his vision.

From the point of view of leadership, two observations are worth noting. First, achieving these two strategic objectives—portfolio restructuring and culture shift—did require, if not a change in leadership style, at least a difference in leadership emphasis. Thus, in terms of the five compasses, it is not unreasonable to say that the task of restructuring called for some tough, clearly defined decisions—sometimes unilateral decisions by Welch himself. Here it would have been the strategic and action compasses that played the major role in making and executing these decisions. However, in the long, open-ended task of changing the culture, "change by edict" ("From now on, you shall be empowered!") was simply not feasible; the more pertinent guidance would come from the culture compass and to some extent the sociopolitical compass. It is to Welch's credit that he was able to make this transition, while still maintaining the integrity of his overall vision.

The second point is the use that leadership makes of values in effecting organizational change. The greater the change, the more important it is to clarify and communicate the new values that should guide strategy, policy, and conduct—starting with the personal conduct of leaders themselves. Consider, for instance, the values that Welch has said GE leaders should embody:

- Create a clear, simple, reality-based, customer-focused vision, and are able to communicate it straightforwardly to all constituencies.
- Understand accountability and commitment and are decisive . . . set and meet aggressive targets . . . always with unyielding integrity.
- Have a passion for excellence. . . . Hate bureaucracy and all the nonsense that comes with it.
- Have the self-confidence to empower others and behave in a boundaryless fashion . . . believe in and are committed to Work-Out [GE's empowerment program] . . . are open to ideas from anywhere.
- Have, or have the capability to develop, global brains and global sensitivity and are comfortable building diverse global teams.
- Stimulate and relish change . . . are not frightened and paralyzed by it. See change as opportunity, not just a threat.
- Have enormous energy and the ability to energize and invigorate others. Understand speed as a competitive advantage and see the total organizational benefits that can be derived from a focus on speed.

The importance that Welch has attached to these leadership values can be judged from his incessant emphasis on them at every opportunity, public and private. He has used his office, as Teddy Roosevelt did the presidency, as the "bully pulpit" to drive home the importance he attaches to this cultural transformation of an old industrial organization.

At every turn he has been aware, too, of the difficulty of the task and of the conflicts it can give rise to. Nowhere is this better illustrated than in his remarks to shareowners in the company's 1991 Annual Report, which are worth quoting at some length:

Over the past several years we've wrestled at all levels of this company with the question of what we are and what we want to be. Out of these discussions, and through our experiences, we've agreed upon a set of values we believe we will need to take this company forward rapidly through the 1990s and beyond.

In our view, leaders, whether on the shop floor or at the tops of our businesses, can be characterized in at least four ways.

The first is one who delivers on commitments—financial or otherwise—and shares the values of our company. His or her future is an easy call. Onward and upward.

The second type of leader is one who does not meet commitment and does not share our values. Not as pleasant a call, but equally easy.

The third is one who misses commitments but shares the values. He or she usually gets a second chance, preferably in a different environment.

Then there's the fourth type—the most difficult for many of us to deal with. That leader delivers on commitment, makes all the numbers, but doesn't share the values we must have. This is the individual who typically forces performance out of people rather than inspires it: the autocrat, the big shot, the tyrant. Too often all of us have looked the other way—tolerated these "Type 4" managers because "they always deliver"—at least in the short term.

And perhaps this type was more acceptable in easier times, but in an environment where we must have every good idea from every man and woman in the organization, we cannot afford management styles that suppress and intimidate. Whether we can convince and help these managers to change—recognizing how difficult that can be— or part company with them if they cannot will be *the ultimate test of our commitment to the transformation of this company and will determine the future of the mutual trust and respect we are building* (emphasis added).

THE CHALLENGE TO LEADERSHIP

Welch was clearly right, I believe, to bracket together "making the numbers" and "sharing the values" as being equally important to taking the company forward. Future success demands a "both/and," rather than an "either–or," approach: You need both the strategic performance and the enabling culture.

Similarly, the new rules' challenge to leadership is not merely to be alert to changes in the social climate, to understand the new obligations that they imply, and to take the initiative in adapting corporate policies and operations to these new requirements. Rather, the challenge is to do all of this while simultaneously coping with the demands of the new competition, new markets, and new technology. The shape and culture of the corporation are being reformed by forces operating on two fronts.

There are two critical and reciprocal truths embedded in that statement. One is that "social responsibility" is not—and, in fact, has not been for some time now—a peripheral matter of community-relations programs, aid to education, and institutional advertising. It is central and strategic to a company's success and profitability: Neglecting or flying in the face of the new rules can have negative effects on the bottom line just as surely as mistimed marketing or a botched product introduction.

The other truth is that a company's strategic planning must deal with the new rules as well as the new competition, new stakeholder expectations as well as new markets and new technology. To succeed over the long term, a corporation needs an environmental strategy, an employment strategy, a governance strategy, an equity strategy—and, yes, an ethics strategy—as well as marketing, production, technology, and financial strategies.

It is the interplay between these two truths that makes leadership—rather than plain, old-fashioned management—the critical ingredient for the next decade. Look back over the differing characteristics of leadership and management that we reviewed at the beginning of this chapter, and you will see the reasons why this should be so. It is leadership, rather than management, that looks at the totality of the corporation's relationships, external as well as internal; that emphasizes "doing the right things"; that builds an organization on people rather than on "things"; and that creates a vision of the future and uses that to capture the imagination and commitment of people.

NOTES

1. Joseph C. Rost, *Leadership in the 21st Century* (Westport, Conn.: Praeger, 1991).

2. Earlier in this century, Mary Parker Follett, one of the pioneers in management, propounded a similar concept. Management decisions, she said, can be more effective, more easily implemented, if they reflect the "law of the situation" rather than the "law of the individual."

3. Daniel Goleman, "What Makes a Leader?" *Harvard Business Review* 76, no. 6 (November–December 1998): 93–102.

— 11 —

Toward a Corporate Agenda

OUTLINING THE AGENDA

Taken together, these new rules, shaped by changing values and global trends, represent a major revision of the terms of what we loosely call "the corporate social charter." The fact that it is as yet a largely unwritten charter in no way diminishes its reality and its power. For one thing, as history has shown us, what start out as unwritten societal expectations will, if not satisfied by corporate actions, quickly turn into written regulations. But, even short of this ultimate power of enforcement, these expectations exert a moral power which corporations ignore at their peril.

Conforming to the substance and the spirit of these rules will require much of corporations—visionary leadership, imaginative responses, sustained effort, and a high tolerance for change and uncertainty—for the agenda of needed response will be as demanding as any challenge that corporations face from competition or new technologies. We can get some sense of the total scope of this agenda by summarizing the potential implications of these new rules as we have examined them in the preceding chapters:[1]

A. *Legitimacy*

1. Review and revise the corporate and business unit mission statements and objectives to ensure that they

   - Reflect the basic social–market purpose that drives the organization.

   - Focus on meeting the needs and wishes of all stakeholders, not just shareowners.

   - Place the profit objectives of the company in the context of the full range of objectives, nonfinancial as well as financial.

2. Develop, communicate, and implement a strategic vision (defined as a coherent and powerful statement of what the company can, and should, be [ten] years hence) that will focus and motivate the organization.[2]

3. Revise the measurement system by which the performance of both managers and business units are measured to incorporate the full range of objectives that the company should meet and to help ensure balanced performance.

4. Communicate these new values and perspectives consistently and continuously throughout the organization, ensuring in particular their inclusion in all manager education programs.

5. Develop community-outreach programs as a long-term social investment to help insure the stability, development, and well-being of communities in which the company does business.

B. *Governance*

1. Ensure that the board of directors collectively possesses all the expertise, experience, and perspective needed to guide and evaluate all the different facets of corporate performance.

2. Strengthen the governance powers of the board by

   • Ensuring that a substantial majority of its members are truly independent outsiders.

   • Separating the roles of chairman and chief executive officer and assigning the chairmanship to an outside director.

   • Strengthening the committee structure of the board.

   • Increasing the board's access to independent studies and audits by enabling them to hire staff and/or outside experts.

3. Develop a culture of public disclosure and accountability, ensuring that information about the company's performance is comprehensive, understandable, standardized, audited, and publicly available.

4. Establish a corporate ombudsman to handle disputes and provide a system of due process for all stakeholders in their dealings with the corporation.

C. *Equity*

1. Develop more equitable compensation policies by

   • Narrowing the CEO–employee compensation gap (reducing the multiple).

   • Eliminating abuses in the executive stock option system (e.g., repricing and reloading).

   • Strengthening the link between pay and performance by raising the standards that must be met before options pay off.

   • Making stock options available to all (or most) employees.

2. Commit to a comprehensive diversity program that will ensure true equality of opportunity in hiring, training, and promotion, and provide the corporation with the human resources it will need to deal with the increasing diversity in its business environment.

3. Design and execute global employment standards—such as hiring, pay, training, work conditions, health and safety—that are equitable (given diverse

economic and social conditions), "nonexploitative," and consistent with the values professed by the corporation.

D. *Environment*

1. Commit the company to the CERES principles (or some comparable set of principles) (see Appendix C).

2. Make environmental principles central to business strategy.

3. Set stretch goals (comparable to DuPont's "the goal is zero" wastes) for key elements of ecologically sound performance, such as

   • The use of recycled materials in production.

   • Increasing energy efficiency in products and processes.

   • Reducing materials intensity of products.

   • Reducing emissions and wastes.

   • Facilitating recycling of products.

4. Monitor and reward managerial performance against goals.

5. Establish independent audits of performance and publish results.

6. Develop linkages with other corporations and institutions to form "industrial ecosystems" (following the Kalundborg example).

7. Promote constructive reform of environmental policies–regulation to encourage flexibility, risk taking, and innovation and foster continuous improvement (rather than locking in on best available technology).

8. Conduct research and monitoring to improve understanding of ecological systems.

E. *Employment*

1. Develop policies and programs to reduce volatility of employment and minimize layoffs and their impacts on employees and communities.

2. Increase emphasis and funding for employee education, training and retraining, to help increase employees' employability.

3. Develop customization of work packages to meet individual employee needs and wants and heighten motivation.

4. Get realistic and consistent about creating an empowered workforce.

5. Promote flexibility in organization and scheduling to enable employees to balance the demands of work and family life.

F. *Public–Private Sector Relationships*

1. Develop executive and staff capabilities to enable the corporation to participate constructively in public debates on issues affecting *either* the corporation specifically and directly *or* the market–enterprise system in general.

2. Adopt a more proactive, less ideological approach to new regulatory proposals (e.g., outline alternative approaches to public concerns, promote market-oriented solutions).

3. As global economic activity increases, acknowledge the need for

   • A global regulatory framework to establish accepted rules of the game (e.g., capital flows, currency trading).

- Adapting free-market principles to local–national cultural differences.

4. Promote privatization responsibly, recognizing social and political limitations to the concept. Undertake careful evaluation of political risks (and corporate flexibility) before agreeing to provide privatized services.

5. Increase level of activity–support for educational programs, inside and outside the corporation.

G. *Ethical Performance*

1. Develop and communicate widely and consistently a code of conduct—a statement of the core values which should guide corporate policies and actions.

2. Implement a comprehensive system (including, e.g., training, hotlines, audit and disclosure mechanisms, due process procedures) to ensure meticulous adherence to the code.

3. Appoint an ethics officer or ethics committee to act as a focal point for monitoring the adequacy and operation of this system.

This listing cannot claim to cover all the possible implications of the new rules: It merely covers the principal ideas we have explored and the precedents that are already being set by leading corporations. Nor is the terse phrasing of the possible actions intended to convey anything more than the barest reference to what the corporate agenda might be. The agenda will take on meaning and conviction only when the management team of a particular corporation has made its selection and put its own imprimatur on the actions to be taken.

GUIDELINES FOR CORPORATE RESPONSE

1. *Establish priorities*: Confronted with the challenge of such a diverse potential agenda, corporations will need to set priorities in mapping out their course of action. No corporation can deal equally and adequately with all challenges at once, nor indeed will every corporation have to put an equal effort into each one of the many changes included in this list. Some companies are, as we have seen, already well advanced in adapting to the new rules, as, for instance, Campbell Soup is on the governance issue or Ecover is in its ecological strategy. But, even after some pruning, the agenda will still require careful planning and selection of priorities to ensure that the corporate responses are appropriate, timely, and coordinated.

One way to ensure that these responses are indeed balanced is to plot them on an "action priorities matrix" (see Figure 11.1), assessing each of the planned responses on two dimensions:

- *Extent of impact*: When implemented, how pervasive will the impacts of the planned action be on the corporate system (e.g., strategies, policies, structure, relationships)? Will the impacts be "program-specific" (i.e., confined to a particular function or activity), major (i.e., having more pervasive effects), or "systemic" (i.e., changing the corporate system in some fundamental way)? This rating will provide some indication of the level of effort required to implement the change, with systemic changes being the most demanding.

- *Timeframe for implementation*: How long will it take for the planned change(s), not just to be introduced, but to take root in the corporate system—two to five years? Five to ten years? More than ten years? This assessment should provide some guidance as to the likely length of time require for full implementation—and the probable need for setting interim goals.

I hasten to say that the plottings I have made on this matrix are for purposes of illustration only; they are, in fact, a composite of scorings developed in management workshops I have conducted at one time or another. In reality, developing a corporate agenda on these issues must be a highly customized exercise: What a company chooses to do is a reflection of its situation, its management values, and its assessment of the imminence and impact of these issues on its business. The scoring must, therefore, reflect the judgments of the executives involved, if the exercise and the action it leads to is to be taken seriously.

2. *Factor the new rules into strategic planning*: This point has been made before, but it is of such central significance to the corporation that it bears a brief repetition. Social performance and strategic performance are now so closely intertwined that planning the corporation's response to the challenges that they present must be integrated into a unified whole. Strategic success in the future will depend on meeting both the economic–competitive *and* the social–political challenges. It follows, therefore, that an environmental or employment or governance strategy is as needed as is a competitive or technology strategy. And all deserve—indeed require—top management attention. It is no longer possible to relegate these social factors to public relations, human resources, or some other function.

3. *Be prepared, and be proactive*: These issues in some form are highly likely to force themselves onto the corporate agenda at some point in the next ten years or so. Thinking through, in advance, the positions that a company should adopt and taking preemptive action when appropriate will always pay off. Remember the dictum developed by GE's Business Environment Studies: "Without a proper business response, the societal expectations of today become the political issues of tomorrow, the legislated requirements of the next day, and the litigated penalties of the day following." The further along that progression of events a corporation moves before action is taken, the less maneuvering room and freedom of choice it will have.

4. *Broaden the environmental monitoring–scanning systems*: In this age of global change and uncertainty, every company should have systems in place for monitoring and tracking critical trends and for giving "early warning" of possible impending change. The tendency is—rightly perhaps—to focus these systems initially on trends in the market, competition, and technology. What is needed here is an extension of these systems to cover the trends and events that will shape and foreshadow the outcome of social and political issues, building a

Figure 11.1
Action Priorities Matrix

	Timeframe for Implementation
10 + years	**5–10 years**
• Develop culture of disclosure and accountability (B3)	• Develop strategic vision to focus and motivate organization (A2)
• Develop linkages to form "industrial ecosystems" (D6)	• Commit to a comprehensive diversity program (C2)
• Conduct research and monitoring to improve understanding of ecological systems (D8)	• Make environmental principles central to strategy (D2)
	• Set "stretch" goals for ecological performance (D3)
	• Get realistic about "empowerment" (E4)
	• Ensure board possesses needed breadth of perspectives (B1)
	• Design and execute global employment standards (C3)
	• Establish independent audits of environmental performance (D5)
	• Promote flexibility to assist work–life balance (E5)
	• Develop political capabilities (F1)
	• Support framework for globalization (F3)
	• Develop community outreach programs (A5)
	• Promote reform of environmental policies, regulations (D7)
	• Customize "work packages" (E3)
	• Promote privatization responsibly (F4)
	• Implement a comprehensive system to ensure adherence to the code of ethics (G2)

Note: The reference cited in parentheses after each item on the matrix (e.g., A1, G2) refers to the items included in the previous section.

Figure 11.1 (*continued*)

2–5 years	Extent of Impact When Implemented
• Revise mission statements to reflect social–market purposes, stakeholder interests (A1) • Communicate values consistently and continuously (A4) • Commit to CERES principles (D1) • Reduce volatility of employment and minimize layoffs (E1)	Systemic
• Revise managerial measurement system to cover full range of objectives (A3) • Strengthen governance powers of board (B2) • Monitor and reward environmental performance (D4) • Adopt proactive approach to regulatory reform (F2)	Major
• Establish corporate ombudsman (B4) • Develop equitable compensation policies (C1) • Increase employee education to help ensure employability (E2) • Increase activity/support for education (F5) • Develop and communicate a code of conduct (G1) • Appoint an ethics officer (G3)	Program-specific

warning system of leading indicators that will alert the corporation to the prospect of a heightening of public concerns and the emergence of new demands.

It is often forgotten that there is a great deal of intelligence *inside* the organization that should be tapped. This is a point that is not lost, for instance, on Charles Holliday, DuPont's CEO. He holds a biweekly phone conference with twenty top managers around the globe to stay abreast of changes in customers, competitors, local economies, and politics. The sessions aren't just for Holliday's benefit: they are largely for the others: "By hearing the answers simultaneously from their peers, they broaden their perspective of the global landscape."[3]

5. *Consider the broader implications of corporate actions*: Earlier, I made the assertion that "the next decade will be a critical testing time for democracy, market systems, and (by extension) the private corporation." The point I want to make here is that the actions (or inaction) of a single corporation often have far-reaching implications—for other corporations, and for the cause of deregulation or privatization, and even for the principles of "the market" and "the enterprise system." Let me illustrate with an anecdote.

About ten years ago, I was making a presentation to a group of corporate planners and professors on the general topic of "the state of corporate social responsibility." At the conclusion of my presentation we became involved in a discussion about among other things the merits of the Reserve Mining case (the company had been charged with dumping iron ore tailings into Lake Superior and had fought a long and acrimonious legal delaying action to keep operations going as long as possible). Toward the end of the session I called for a show of hands on two questions. One of the questions was as follows: "Was Reserve Mining's strategy a sound one, from the company's point of view, given that the delays enabled them to continue profitable operations for several years?" On this question the vote was, as I remember, about evenly divided. On the second question, "Was Reserve Mining's strategy a sound one from the point of view of the public's confidence in business and corporations' interest in sound regulation and enforcement?" not a single hand—not even from representatives of the business community—was raised in favor.

If corporations are to help ensure the future success and expansion of deregulation, privatization, and the market system, they will need to view their prospective policies and actions in this broader perspective. Taking the narrower and short term view will almost surely lead to a political backlash of greater regulatory control and diminished public trust and confidence.

6. *Recognize the critical role of measurement*: Setting goals and then measuring performance (both individual and component) against these goals is an integral part of the corporate management system. So goal setting and performance measurement should be enlisted in support of the new rules. Whatever emerges from the priorities exercise has to be translated into specific objectives with clear-cut targets, dates of accomplishment, and assigned responsibilities. Managers know now that they will be measured and rewarded

for their performance against profit and other financial objectives. It is critically important that we apply these same criteria to their performance against environmental, safety, diversity, and other similar nonfinancial objectives.

PROSPECTS FOR CHANGE

In the long history of the evolving relationship between the corporation and society, the new rules represent a new phase in the ever-rising standards that we expect the corporation to meet. It is the latest phase, but it will not be the last. New formative forces that we cannot now foresee will develop; society's needs will change; and new values will coalesce around new issues. But for now these rules define how we wish our corporations to respond to some of the key issues that arise from the vortex of forces that are currently reshaping our world.

It is timely now to sum up the prospects for change. Will the new rules develop exactly along the lines discussed in these pages? Are they realistic and attainable? And how likely is it that the corporation will change as dramatically as these new rules would seem to indicate?

On the first count, I have already noted that I deliberately chose to state each rule as precisely as possible, more as a focus for discussion than as an exact forecast. With that said, however, I believe that the statements do capture the *essence* of the issue and the corporate responses that society requires. It would be surprising, for instance, if reform and empowerment of the board of directors were not a part of the governance issue, or sustainable development (or progress toward it) not a needed response to the environmental issue. And, clearly, redefining the roles of the public and private sectors is inextricably intertwined with the "power shift" that is already underway. So, on balance, I would ask the reader to take my phrasing of the new rules literally, but only as *approximations* of the outcome of this latest rewriting of the corporate social charter.

As to the realism and attainability of the new rules, I am sure that there will be widely differing reactions to much that I have written here. There will certainly be those who argue that the proposals advanced here are idealistic, impractical, and probably unnecessary; that the business of business is to attend to its economic agenda, not to act as a social welfare agency; and that the primacy of profit and shareowner interests must remain intact if the corporation is to continue as an effective engine of economic progress. The disagreements here may be over values rather than facts. It is unarguable that, as a matter of fact, corporations pay as much heed to the needs of customers, employees, dealers, and suppliers as they do to shareowners' desire for dividends and stock appreciation. Most corporate executives may not subscribe to the stakeholder concept as a matter of theory; but in practice they recognize the stake that they and these other constituencies have in common in successful and mutually beneficial operations.

Further, the new rules do not seek to challenge the preeminence of the corporation's economic role nor to impose a social agenda that the corporation would be ill equipped to carry out. And to say as I do that profit is a means, a motive, and a measure of corporate performance, but not its primary purpose, is not to downplay the importance of profit; it is only to place it in its true perspective—as many executives before me have done. For a final word on this point, let me cite George Merck, the founder of the global pharmaceutical firm, Merck: "We try never to forget that medicine is for the people. It is not for the profits. The profits follow, and if we have remembered that, they have never failed to appear. The better we have remembered that, the larger they have been."

On the other hand, there will be those—fewer, I am sure—who will say that I have *under*estimated the degree of change that will be needed to adapt the corporation to the new demands placed upon it by more sophisticated consumers, more stringent environmental requirements, more self-conscious employees, and more demanding citizens, not to mention more aggressive competitors. The disagreement here, if any, is one of degree rather than direction. I have described the evolution of the new rules within the context of four possible scenarios that might govern the future economic and political climate. But focusing on the consequences of any *one* of these scenarios would almost certainly heighten or accelerate the impact of these new rules in some particular way. A scenario of economic upheaval followed by populist countermeasures, for instance, would surely result in tougher restraints on executive compensation and corporate governance systems than any I have suggested here. Or a heightening of problems stemming from global climatic change would toughen energy conservation measures or accelerate progress toward "sustainable development"—or both. So, yes, I could agree that, in certain circumstances, my assessment of the new rules might understate their future impact on the corporation.

And then there will also be those who look at the wide range of corporate initiatives that have already been taken and conclude that I am not predicting anything new—that the future I describe is already here. However, the fact that I am able to cite current examples of the measures that the new rules entail should not be taken as evidence that the task of transformation has been completed. In truth, it has only just begun. The great majority of corporations have still a long way to go; and even the leaders have for the most part made only selective progress. No one company has yet "put it all together."

Finally, there will be those who agree, in principle, with the thrust of the new rules, but who are intensely skeptical of corporations' willingness and ability to change, and believe that my description of the future is largely an exercise in wishful thinking. They are convinced that corporations are too preoccupied with meeting the new intensified competition, that their culture too rooted in a "profits—first, last, and always" credo, and that their executives are too self-centered for them to be capable of the sort of transformation I have outlined in these pages. However, their observations, although pertinent, overlook the overriding fact that the corporation may have no option but to change. Or, more exactly, it may have just one option: Change voluntarily and proactively, or be compelled to change by regulatory fiat or public pressure.

The changes that I refer to will occur, not just because they are desirable (although I believe they are), nor because the corporation has become a philanthropic institution (it hasn't—and shouldn't). They will occur because they are needed responses to changes in the social climate. *The new rules are driven by societal change, not by corporate initiatives.* The corporation is, as I have noted, a social institution, charged with an economic purpose; as such, it is not, and should not be, an *initiator* of social change. Its task is to perform its economic function within the parameters of socially acceptable standards of behavior. As these standards change, so too must corporate conduct.

We should never underestimate the capacity of the corporation to change, to adapt to changing market conditions, to adopt new technologies, and to accommodate shifts in the social and political environment. Sometimes it has changed quickly and exuberantly, as with a plunge into new markets; sometimes slowly and reluctantly, as with its response to new social demands; but almost always with ultimate success. It has demonstrated a flexibility that has eluded virtually every other institution; and, in doing so, it has served society well. Over the past century, it has, as we have seen, assimilated a remarkable succession of social initiatives thrust upon it by an ever more demanding public. And still it has prospered.

Paradoxically perhaps, the greatest impediment to further change may spring from the fact that globalization and the power shift are, as we have seen, presenting the private sector with a historically unparalleled opportunity to grow and prosper, and to do so with greater freedom from government surveillance. But with greater freedom comes greater responsibility; and many corporations seem more willing to embrace the former than the latter. And trend is not destiny. For every trend, there is evidence of a countertrend. The triumph of global capitalism is shadowed by growing doubts and questioning over the way it has operated in recent years. So we should not presume that the future is necessarily foreshadowed by the present. Uncertainty is the most prevalent feature of our times. That is why we need to look at alternative scenarios, and at different possibilities.

On balance, I am convinced that the new rules are both realistic and attainable. The fact that many leading corporations have already begun to experiment with initiatives along these lines is a persuasive indicator that the rules are not unreasonable, nor the task impossible. But the changes envisaged by these new rules will come only with time and effort, for in total, they represent a transformation of the corporation over the next twenty years or so that is as great as that of the past thirty years has been.

For my part, I consider myself to be neither an optimist nor a pessimist on these matters. I remain a confirmed "possibilist." Given the extent and complexity of the uncertainties we inevitably face in contemplating the future, no other philosophy is realistic. Although the future is not preordained, it is most surely full of possibilities. Taking a fixed point of view on it, whether as Pollyanna or as Cassandra, is misleading. Recognizing that there *are* possibilities, and that we *can* make choices, is perhaps as much optimism as we should allow ourselves.

For the corporation moving into the new millennium, there exists the shining possibility of their timely and positive response to "a tide in the affairs of men / Which, taken at the flood, leads on to fortune," but which, omitted, can mire them "in shallows and in miseries." The possibility exists. The choice is theirs.

NOTES

1. The following list provides only brief references as to the nature of possible actions that the corporation might take. For more complete descriptions—together with the rationale for these actions—see the appropriate chapter.

2. The time horizon for this vision will, of course, vary with the nature of the business, but typically lies in the range of five to ten years.

3. Ram Charan, "Managing Through the Chaos," *Fortune*, November 23, 1998, pp. 283–290.

Part IV

APPENDIXES

— A —

The Debate on "Bigness": Arguments for and against the Large Corporation

No institution is more characteristic of the modern industrial—or postindustrial—economy than the large private corporation. This has been and remains the principal economic mechanism for marshalling the people, materials, know-how, machinery, and money to produce in adequate volume the wide range of products and services needed to satisfy the requirements of a large and growing population.

However, as with any significant institution in society, the large corporation has given rise to endless debate and frequent criticism of its objectives, methods, and morality. In the United States in particular, there has long been a traditional distrust of any concentration of power, wherever located, and a preference for multiplicity and diversity among our institutions. Most people still have a deep-seated, often unconscious, empathy with the "little guy"—the underdog.

This appendix summarizes the key arguments in this debate, comparing the arguments pro and con, side by side, under sixteen headings. Many—perhaps most—have remained relatively constant over the years, with changes mainly in the details of topical references. Some, like the debate over environmental impacts, get added to the list as new issues and concerns arise. Others, like arms sales and the "merchants of death" charge, get dropped for lack of relevance or downplayed in light of more pressing concerns.

The arrangement presented does provide the convenience of a broad overview of the debate, even though it cannot engage in a detailed, point-by-point examination of the charges and rebuttals.To simplify matters even further, the various arguments are stated categorically, without evaluation, and without the tedious repetition of phrases like "Critics charge . . ." and "Proponents rebut. . . ."

There are limitations to this analysis. Quite obviously, only the gist of the arguments used by both sides can be sketched in here, but these are the basic points around which topical details and shadings of emphasis tend to focus. In attempting to group material under these headings, some difficulties are encountered due to the fact that two or more themes are frequently interwoven into a single line of argument. However, for convenience of analysis, the individual threads have been separated out.

This summary is intended to provide a historical background to the themes examined in this book. By looking backwards, we can see more clearly both the origins of the new rules and the extent of their differences from the debates of the past.

INDEX OF ISSUES

1a. Concentration of Economic Power

In many (some would say most) industries, economic power is being concentrated in fewer and fewer corporations. Mergers, acquisitions, and alliances are still proliferating, and concentration ratios (the percentage of industry sales or assets controlled by the top four companies) are increasing. We are thus moving further away from the ideal economic system in which individual competitive units are small and subject to the workings of a free market.

Any concentration of power, whether political or economic—and in this case it is both—is subject to abuse. "Power corrupts"; even the potential for abuse is corrupting. Antitrust violations, unilateral pricing decisions, suppression of innovation, undermining of smaller competitors—these are only a few of the abuses that concentrated economic power makes possible. To leave so much economic decision-making power in the hands of a limited number of corporations is inconsistent with the economic basis of democracy and a regrettable departure from the workings of a market in which no single unit exercises significant influence.

1b. The Benefits of Scale, and the Reality of Competition

Any modern economy depends on large-scale organization for essential elements of its production and progress. This need for scale and for continuing growth stems from the increasing complexity of business and technology, which can only be resolved by the integration of large scientific, technical, management, and capital resources. Thus, no one really envisages the possibility of organizing automobile manufacturing, airlines, global communications, or finance on a small-scale basis. The two ideas are quite simply incompatible. Economies and corporations have grown and progressed together. Indeed, corporations have become large because they have been successful, rather than being successful because they are large.

Large corporations can be and are highly competitive. Traditional "concentration ratios" are totally inadequate measures of the level of competition in an industry. For one thing, they focus on domestic companies and neglect the increasingly important role of offshore suppliers. For another, they place excessive emphasis on numbers of competitors and on price alone as the criteria for the existence of competition. They overlook the fact that competition is not limited to price, but extends to many other factors such as durability, safety, service, and styling. They disregard the diversity of markets in which customers can choose not only among different brands of products, but also between alternative products (e.g., aluminum versus copper, oil versus natural gas, cable versus wireless). The dimensions and intensity of competition have little to do with size per se.

2a. Concentrated Control of Corporations

Not only is economic control of markets being concentrated in fewer corporations, but control of these companies is itself also highly concentrated, in at least three ways. To begin with, despite corporations' claims of widespread shareownership, the real power is wielded by large institutional investors, including other companies' pension funds, who account for large and growing percentages of corporate stock and are more interested in high returns on their investment than in the overall social performance of corporations. Second, directors sit on multiple boards, often in interlocking relationships with banks and other corporations, further removing control from the average shareowners.

Finally, even directors are, for the most part, "management's pet rocks" (in Ross Perot's famous phrase), rubber stamping management's decisions, because the complexity of business is such that only the corporate executives can grasp the details and nuances of important decisions. Thus, in the final analysis, real power and the control that goes with it resides in the hands of a relative handful of corporate executives.

Economic power, unlike political power in a democracy, is not answerable to the public, and it is both unhealthy and unwise to leave this power in so few hands.

2b. Diffused Control and the Balance of Power

Any complete consideration of the extent and control of corporate power must include a recognition of the reality and extent of "countervailing power" in a market economy. No company, especially no large company, can act without regard to the economic role of government, the demands of customers, the strategies of competitors, the bargaining power of unions, the rights of shareowners, and the sometimes ill-defined "mood of the times" and public opinion. All these factors, to a greater or lesser degree, are exercised as checks and balances to management's powers.

The history of the past ten years shows clearly that both boards of directors and institutional investors are playing more active roles in examining and passing judgment on management's strategies and behavior. Recent moves in corporate governance have resulted in greater balance, power, and independence for boards, even to the point of ousting existing management in a number of high-profile cases. Similarly, large institutional investors have not hesitated to seek to influence—even to vote against—management decisions, when they believed shareowner interests were being neglected.

Even internally the current picture has changed from the strict hierarchy of former days. The structure of most modern corporations provides a greater diffusion of control and greater opportunity for individual initiative than is generally recognized. Decentralization is now generally recognized, not merely as an unavoidable necessity, but as a positive contribution to corporate efficiency and as a form of a "checks-and-balances" system.

3a. Excessive Profits

Money is the root of all evil, and profits are the root of all that is wrong with the corporation. It is the single-minded emphasis on the bottom line, using profit and loss as the ultimate measure of what is right and what is wrong, that distorts and corrupts the whole system.

Money is the centerpiece of managerial calculus. Whatever contributes to the bottom line is maximized; whatever detracts from it is minimized. That is why the use of cheaper materials, labor-saving processes, and offshore sourcing are promoted aggressively, while environmental protection, and employee and consumer health and safety are regarded as expenses to be avoided if possible and minimized if not. Even when some feature such as automobile safety is promoted, it is done because it is seen as a way to promote sales and increase profits, not because it is the right thing to do.

It is not merely the fact, but the scale of corporate profits that is so corrupting. The sheer size of corporate reserves makes them virtually invulnerable to all but major executive miscalculations, while making it easier to drive smaller competitors out of business by lowering prices—and then raising them again when the competition has been eliminated. Then again, it has been the increases in corporate profits in recent years that has led to the outrageous inequities between executive compensation and that of the average employee.

However, perhaps the greatest casualty in all of this is the level of ethical performance among corporate executives. Scarcely a day goes by without the business press reporting on ethical lapses, nearly all of which can be traced back to the unrelenting drive to maximize profits.

3b. The Productivity of Profits

Profit is both a motivator and a key resource. The potential for profit (there are no guarantees) is what attracts both individuals and companies to serve markets and meet consumer and corporate needs. Earned profits are the lifeblood of corporate well-being and expansion, providing the funds for research and innovation, for new plants and more efficient machinery, and for the creation of new jobs, as well as for a reasonable return on shareowners' investment. Without profits, a company will fail, and its failure will hurt customers, employees, owners, and business partners, as well as communities.

Profit, particularly short-term profit, is not the be-all and end-all of corporate motivation. A reading of any annual report will demonstrate that intermediate factors, such as sales growth, product leadership, the opening of new markets, and even support for community activities influence executive decisions, even when the consequence might be a reduction in profit margins.

Profit has a special role to play in the corporation's legal obligation to its shareowners, because dividends and stock appreciation are the mechanism for paying owners for the use of their capital. However, two points need to be stressed. First, a growing share of ownership is now in the hands of institutional investors who have a sophisticated and balanced assessment of corporate performance. Second, with the growth of employee shareownership, the benefits of profitable operations are more widely shared with those who make them possible.

Finally, it should be pointed out that most corporations do not make unreasonably large profits—as a percentage of sales or return on investment. Historically, opinion surveys have shown that the public typically thinks that 10-percent profit on sales is reasonable. And the great majority of corporations make far less than that.

4a. The Abusive Power of Money

There has been in the public mind a historic distrust of "moneyed interests," whether it is Wall Street, holding companies, or the financial resources of large corporations. Nothing has changed in this regard since President Teddy Roosevelt, with his finger on the public pulse, lashed out at the "malefactors of great wealth."

These financial resources play a greater role than superior technology or management skill in ensuring and enlarging the success of corporations. Because capital formation presents fewer problems for corporations than for small business, notwithstanding the growth of venture capital, they can buy their way into any line of business they choose or expand existing facilities. Because of their financial reserves, they can undersell small competitors—and then raise prices when competition has been driven out. Because of their financing affiliates, some of them can gain unfair competitive advantage through their ability to offer easy credit terms. Because of reciprocity arrangements with other large industrial and financial institutions, they can pre-empt important segments of markets and money sources.

4b. Gains from Large-Scale Investment and Credit

First, it should be noted that corporate tie-ins with financial institutions have been greatly reduced by the fact that nowadays capital investment programs are funded predominantly by reinvested earnings, rather than by new stock issues. (Certainly this is the case in the United States; the *keiretsu* linkages in Japan between manufacturing and banking remain largely intact.) Trends in corporate governance have also weakened these linkages as boards of directors excluded from membership representatives of banks with whom the corporation does business.

The important fact, however, is that society benefits from the productive application of corporate assets. Most important is the ability of large companies to adopt a long-term view in investing the huge sums of money needed to support progressive research programs and to translate the findings of the laboratory into commercial products. Prime examples are the development of pharmaceuticals, jet aircraft, and the computer. Such investments require continuity and stability for their success: They are a stabilizing factor in production and employment and when realized become the means of meeting the higher living standards of a growing population. Overall, corporate capital spending has become what *Fortune* called the "mighty multiplier" in the economy.

Large accumulations of funds have also sparked dynamic consumer spending through the widespread use of credit. Though temporary excesses have occurred, the large scale use of credit has been intelligent, creative, and responsive to the needs of business, individuals, and communities.

5a. Domination of Small Business

With the concentration of economic power in fewer and fewer hands, large corporations are crushing small business. They effectively control many so-called "independent" businesses, such as dealers and distributors; they are entering fields, such as product servicing, that might be better served by small companies; they force small suppliers to conform their designs and delivery to corporate needs; and they are driving small competitors to the wall. And, by doing all this, they are destroying a socially and economically desirable way of life.

Small businesses are agile, efficient, friendly, and responsive to customers and the market. But they are engaged in a David and Goliath struggle in which Goliath holds all the power and advantage.

5b. Interdependence of Large and Small Business

Basically, the size of organization is and should be determined by the requirements of the work to be performed. To take extreme examples, the local hardware store and the automobile manufacturing plant, or the TV service store and the television network, are each appropriately organized for the demands of their economic function. Both perform indispensable roles in their respective areas. Despite the general increase in scale of operations over the past fifty years, opportunities for small business have continued to expand. Nowhere is this more apparent than in the newly growing areas of software production and computer servicing.

Many small companies act as dealers, suppliers, subcontractors, and manufacturers of component parts for large companies, benefitting not merely from these sales, but also from the technical and management know-how that corporations share with them in the interests of more efficient relationships.

6a. Unwarranted Diversification

One advantage that corporate assets provide is the ability to enter new businesses, even those unrelated to a company's main line of business. There has been a recurrent pattern of such developments, from the growth of conglomerate manufacturing entities like General Motors and General Electric, to their diversification into financing affiliates, to the recent mergers of television, cable, and publishing operations.

Frequently these diversification efforts have failed, mainly for lack of management and organizational skills to manage such diversity, with resulting social costs in disrupted production, employment, and consumer service. But even when they have succeeded, it has been through the backing of deep-pocket corporate reserves rather than through any inherent competitive strength. Indeed, in virtually every case the diversification effort has resulted in a lessening of competition and a reduction in consumer choice.

6b. Social and Economic Benefits of Diversification

Bringing together diverse operations under a single roof increases the efficiency and stability of operations and improves consumer choice. Thus, for instance, producing a wide range of consumer or industrial products enables a corporation to stabilize production and, importantly, employment by switching from one product line to another as the market dictates. And bringing together product, financing, and product service in a single package is a convenience to the purchaser and makes for closer and better relations between buyer and seller.

Diversification can also increase competition by enlarging the "freedom of entry" into established markets. Frequently these markets pose barriers to entry that smaller companies could not surmount: Only larger corporations have the resources and know-how to enter such closed markets, thereby increasing competition. A recent example has been the entry of cable, Internet, and wireless companies into the field of telephonic communications, shaking up the established phone companies.

7a. The Distorting Power of Advertising

The ability of "big business" to expend large sums on advertising, far beyond the means of small business, produces a twofold advantage. It expands and strengthens market position by its massive impact on consumers' buying habits, and it so influences the editorial policy of the press and other mass communications media that they in effect become company spokesmen.

The glossy half-truths of corporate advertising mislead rather than inform the consumer. They create wants for nonessential goods and services. They distort consumer spending and thinking. They contribute to a materialistic view of life. They drown out the efforts of smaller competitors.

The influence of advertising on editorial policy is there for all to see. While straight business reporting deals with the unfavorable along with the favorable news, editorials overwhelmingly tend to lend support to large companies, especially those whose presence is the mainstay of local economies. (Only when the fault is too glaring to be whitewashed will criticism be offered.) In this way one of democracy's most cherished features—the freedom of the press—is tainted.

7b. The Constructive Role of Advertising

Advertising expenditures are unarguably large, but they do not—and cannot—have the overwhelming impact on consumer behavior that is often assumed. For one thing, competitive advertisements often tend to cancel each other out. For another, consumers also have access to other sources of information, including consumer groups' reports. Finally, a great deal of advertising serves mostly to stimulate general awareness and demand in a given product or service area.

To the extent that advertising does build up recognition and acceptance of national brands, the evidence of consumer surveys indicates that customers recognize the value and convenience of having such standard, recognized goods widely available—and, in a free market, companies will always seek to respond to consumer demands.

It is completely unjustified to infer a causal relationship between advertising expenditures and editorial policy. The press is vigilant in guarding its independence and builds strict policy guidelines to separate the editorial from the business side of the business. It is insulting to the media to suggest that they are incapable of taking care of any would-be intrusion on their freedom and independence.

8a. Social Domination

Corporations exercise a pervasive form of "thought control" in many ways: through the power of advertising in consumer markets, through control of the press, and through their influence in community organizations. By the subtle use of its power, by donations, by membership in community boards, and by community action, they seek to exert their influence over education, churches, hospitals, and other local organizations, seeking to promote a probusiness–procorporate point of view.

Take corporations at their word: They claim that profits are the sole motivating force in business. If that is so, all community action by large companies must have an ulterior motive—in this instance, to preserve their profits while conducting a whitewash campaign through opinion leaders, stifling criticism, and helping create a favorable business climate. Corporate giving to colleges and aid to schools must also be suspect since "he who pays the piper calls the tune," inducing these institutions to conduct research and education programs that will produce the ideas and the employees that corporations need.

In a more subtle way, corporations seek to permeate society with business values. In a pluralistic society, it is wrong and inconsistent with the system, for any one institution to gain such a degree of ascendancy over others. And it is abhorrent to our ideals to measure the feasibility or worthwhileness of all social action simply in terms of economic efficiency and financial profit.

8b. Social Responsibility

A great deal has changed since the "public-be-damned" days of William H. Vanderbilt, although many critics do not seem to acknowledge this. More appropriate terms to describe the current corporate philosophy are "corporate conscience," "social responsibility," the professionalization of management," or "enlightened self-interest." The fact is that, with the separation of ownership and management, the cartoon-style capitalist has been replaced by a new generation of managers with a strong and practical sense of responsibility to the public who recognize the need for a corporation to factor into its decisions the interests of the many groups it depends on in an ever more complex society.

Yes, corporations do aid schools and colleges, organize open houses, encourage their employees to participate in political and community activities. Why? It is because companies are corporate citizens with an awareness of their obligation to contribute to society and their communities more than economic benefits, important though these are.

Yes, corporations do speak out on economic issues, not because they desire to indoctrinate society, but because they have a right and an obligation to express their point of view on the impacts of social and political action on the working of the economy. In a real sense, freedom is indivisible: If we want to preserve political freedom, we must also maintain economic freedom—and an understanding of the economics of private enterprise.

9a. The Power of Political Influence

Although corporations seek to influence public and consumer opinion (as already indicated), their really corrupting influence is to be found in the political arena. The evidence of this influence is to be found everywhere: at every level and in every branch of government; in lobbying and drafting legislation; in the negotiation of government contracts; in the presence of executives as full-time government officials or consultants; and above all, in their financial contributions to party coffers.

Regardless of which party happens to be in power, big business is always politically active, seeking to promote its own ends: negotiating probusiness legislation or "giveaway" contracts with right-wing parties; or, lobbying against socialists' social programs. Political scandals, from the Teapot Dome affair in the United States seventy years ago to the corruption of Italian politicians more recently, are only the tip of the iceberg. Corporate influence on the processes of government are normally more subtle and less well publicized—and so more successful.

9b. Public Service

Corporations have the same right that any organization does to make known its views on the pending legislation that affects its operations. Indeed, on the whole, they do not exercise political influence proportionate to their economic standing—far less in fact than that exercised in many countries by farmers, unions, and government workers. Corporate executives in general and those in larger companies in particular have traditionally been reluctant to get involved in the political arena, partly from a distaste for politics, and partly due to a well-justified fear of public misrepresentation of their motives.

Economic issues have always played a major role in determining the political course of nations; and today, with the impacts of trade, technology, and restructuring, is no exception. Business viewpoints on these issues make an important contribution to political debate before policy decisions are taken, and the validity of these viewpoints on issues as diverse as free trade, taxation, and regulatory reform has been clearly demonstrated on the social and economic balance sheets of nations.

10a. Inefficiency

Large organizations, like large masses, have an inherent inertia which it is virtually impossible to overcome, or which, if overcome, gives way to uncontrollable momentum. They are unwieldy, inflexible, bureaucratic, and virtually unmanageable. From a social point of view, they are out of control and inefficient.

Big business is inefficient because it is too big. If it should be successful, it is because of its monopoly power and financial reserves. If it does succeed without actually monopolizing a market, "social efficiency" is still impaired by the loss of small companies that it puts out of business.

Bureaucracy is as rampant in large corporations as it is in big government. Standardized responses couched as "company policy," a plethora of forms, and a mind-boggling hierarchy are the norm, as any consumer with a complaint quickly discovers.

Size contributes to unmanageability. The sheer number of people involved makes it virtually impossible to harmonize their actions, so that even well-intentioned policies are left unimplemented. Still less is it possible to control the "rogue" manager or employee. Put together the drive for profits with the ability to hide actions in a huge organization, and you have a breeding ground for corruption.

10b. Contributions to Productivity and Management

Whatever the exact relationship between size and efficiency, the public overwhelmingly believes that large companies have managed to lower prices to consumers through their mass production and distribution techniques and thus have contributed substantially to the rise in standards of living. To achieve economic production on this scale clearly requires relatively large resources and facilities, and in most industries the lowest limit at which efficiency is achieved is high on the size scale. A general pattern can be discerned in industrial history of a company first achieving efficiency through size and then further increasing in size due to its efficiency.

To maintain this efficiency and manage the growing enterprises, large corporations have drawn on the best available technical, professional, and managerial talent, on whose training and development considerable expense is incurred.

In a large organization, executives are better able to think in broader terms and on a longer term basis, while technical and professional specialists focus on developing new products and improving production and other methods.

One key point: Too much is made of the sheer size of large companies—and, with globalization, aggregate size is tending to become even larger—without recognizing the extent of their cellular structure. Decentralization, delegation, and networking—these are not mere management buzz words: They are now essential conditions for efficiency in the modern organization, pushing decision-making power and responsibility closer to the "front line" of contact with the market.

11a. "Inhuman Relations"

The human resources policies of large corporations are better described as "inhuman (or inhumane) relations." Large organizations are not only inefficient, they are also impersonal, authoritarian, and lacking in the warm, close relationships that are the hallmark of smaller companies.

Employees become mere ciphers, unable to achieve even a limited self-realization, for their personal goals must be subjected to those of the corporation. It is not necessarily that managers deliberately set out to suppress individuality—they are victims themselves. But there is an inherent contradiction between the self-reliant independence of the individual and the degree of authority that must be exercised to ensure a corporation's profitability. At best, such a conflict leads to a numbed and thwarted "half-life"; at worst, it throws an employee on the scrap heap of layoffs whenever profits dictate a cutback or reorganization of production. "Downsizing," "rightsizing," and "restructuring" have become the managerial euphemisms for the ruthless cutbacks that characterize our age.

Big business has steadfastly resisted every advance in employee relations in the past century. Minimum wage, a shorter work week, pensions, health care, occupational safety, equal opportunity, and day care—the list goes on—each advance was bitterly opposed by large corporations and came to pass only through union negotiations, legislation, or the pressure of public opinion.

11b. Leadership in Human Resource Development and Compensation

It is in large companies that there is the most acute awareness that employees are many-dimensioned individuals, and that their work in a corporation forms the major outlet for imaginative and creative activity and should be treated as such. An authoritarian organization is not only abusive of individual dignity and expression, but is also (and for that reason) inefficient. That is why there is so much current emphasis in large corporations on the values of decentralization and delegation, individual and team development, and training and retraining. The complex problems of modern industrial technology, production, and distribution demand the fullest development of individual talents and a pooling of efforts and knowledge that can only be fully achieved in an atmosphere of trust and responsibility.

On the material side, the benefits enjoyed by employees in large corporations—such as wages and salaries, pensions, health-care coverage, and vacations—are almost always greater than those in smaller businesses. Frequently corporations have taken the leadership in these areas, moving ahead of public-policy requirements, and this tradition continues in areas such as day care, and flextime and flexwork arrangements that seek to create a better balance between work and family life.

12a. The Myths of Corporate Research

Corporate apologists would have the public believe that only large companies are equipped financially and technically to engage in the large-scale research and development necessary for our continuing economic and technological progress. But quantity (dollars spent) does not necessarily mean quality (breakthrough ideas). In fact, the bulk of corporate R&D expenditures goes to product development rather than to basic research. The really important discoveries of our age have been made in universities or by lone researchers, not by giant laboratories. (A recent favorite example is the development of the Apple computer by Jobs and Wozniak in a garage.)

Corporations typically acquire most of their patents (on which they so pride themselves) from individuals or by buying up small firms, finding that it is cheaper to acquire technical know-how this way rather than develop it in-house. They are then in a position either to withhold the benefit of these patents from the public until their existing product lines have been fully exploited or to use the patents to tighten their hold on market position.

Given these facts, it makes no sense for governments to continue allocating research contracts, either for defense or other purposes, to such inefficient institutions.

12b. The Real Benefits of Corporate Research and Development

Corporate research plays a key role at each of the three stages of research and development that the economist Joseph Schumpeter identified: invention, innovation, and "imitation."

Inventions—breakthroughs in basic research—are developed in large laboratories. Both General Electric and Bell Laboratories have produced Nobel Prize winners, and many patents are granted to corporate research workers. However, the peculiarly characteristic contribution of large-scale research lies in the area Schumpeter called *innovation*, the initial application of inventions to practical use. The essential function of large-scale R&D organizations—

the work that they alone make possible—is the pooling of knowledge, the expenditure of time and money, and the ability to absorb failures in the perfecting of new products and new technologies for the market. Examples abound—from DuPont's development of nylon, through RCA's work on color TV and GE's development of aerospace and nuclear power systems, to Merck's and Pfizer's investments in the development of pharmaceuticals. In each case, years of work and many millions of dollars were invested in these innovations.

Imitation, or the widespread application of perfected innovations, is ultimately the creator of new markets, new business, and employment opportunities involved in the production and distribution of new products. This is the stage of widespread diffusion of the benefits of corporate research.

Far from putting a damper on technological progress and competition, corporate research breeds competition, and competition breeds more research, creating a benign cycle of development.

13a. Environmental Destruction

Ever since the Industrial Revolution, large manufacturing companies have been engaged in a persistent rape of the environment, pillaging natural resources, polluting the air and water, and spreading wastes indiscriminately. More recently, since the first Earth Day marked the beginning of a new era of social awareness of and commitment to the need for a new approach to our relations with the environment, these companies have resisted change, opposing every new regulatory initiative and employing every delaying tactic available to them to put off compliance for as long as possible.

The root of this problem is to be found in corporations' singleminded commitment to maximizing profit and in their adherence to a belief that natural resources—air and water, for example—are inherently "free goods." By this calculation, every new measure to protect or restore our environment is an added cost and so should be subject to a cost–benefit analysis prior to its adoption—although they are reluctant to put dollar figures on the benefits side of this calculation.

This same financial calculus has led them to engage in "green marketing" and spurious public-relations campaigns. Turning some usually superficial product improvement to their marketing advantage, they seek to persuade consumers that their new product or service is "good for the environment" but are reluctant to have their claims tested or verified. Or they launch great advertising campaigns focusing on activities peripheral to their main operations in an effort to distract public attention and create the illusion that they are truly "green" companies.

With the onset of globalization, corporations in the developed nations have found new opportunities to circumvent the environmental regulations of their home countries and take advantage of the looser policies of developing economies. On the one hand, they are able to gain new markets for existing products that would be banned or unattractive in their domestic markets. On the other hand, they can move their more polluting operations offshore where new manufacturing plants are being welcomed.

13b. Matching Growth with Ecology

Consumers around the world have made clear that they want *both* growth (higher material living standards) and a clean environment. And corporations are giving both to them.

The environment is manifestly cleaner in most countries—certainly in the developed nations—than it was in 1970. For example, air and water are manifestly purer; energy efficiency has greatly increased; acid rain is decreasing; and the materials intensity of many products has been greatly reduced. Meanwhile, in the past thirty years, the material standard of living has improved dramatically, doubling in some cases. These improvements are the result of efforts by corporations, not by governments.

Once environmental improvement became a social priority, corporations recognized that some form of regulation would be necessary to ensure that all companies "played by the same rules." They have consistently advocated particular forms of regulation—flexibility; an emphasis on results rather than methods; the use of pollution trading rights; and cost–benefit analysis—to help ensure that economies can in fact continue to deliver both growth and a cleaner environment. These and similar reforms are now widely accepted by many government agencies and environmental interest groups, with whom corporations work to create new, jointly developed standards.

14a. "Big Business" and "Big Government"

"Big business" has been responsible, as much as any other factor, for the growth first of "big government" and then of "big labor." Any concentration of power is undesirable and incompatible with true democratic values, but the growth of large corporations left society with no alternative but to develop institutions with "countervailing power."

If corporations had not accumulated such power and had behaved more responsibly, then competition and the marketplace could have been relied on to provide the necessary checks and balances. But history has shown the need for government to intervene, curbing corporate power and regulating its potential for abuse. As the economy has grown and become more complex, so government regulatory agencies have had to multiply and increase their powers in order to keep pace with the increasing reach of corporate operations.

If corporations had not opposed unions so strenuously, and had voluntarily improved wages and working conditions, then unions might have remained localized and still able to negotiate on a more or less equal footing. But again, history has shown that business opposition led to the growth of international labor as unions sought an equal voice at the bargaining table.

Both big government and big labor grew out of control themselves and have to be checked. But the origins of these threats to true democracy are clearly to be found in the rise and abuses of large corporations.

14b. Corporate Support for Decentralized Power

The increase in the size and powers of government can more accurately be traced to the growth of populations and economies and to changing social conditions, rather than to the rise of the large corporation. The enlargement of all three types of organization reflects the expansion of population and its demands, rather than to any conscious attempt to develop institutions of countervailing power.

Corporate executives have strongly and consistently advocated the decentralization of power, not only in industrial organizations, but in governments and unions. They have argued that, only by devolving maximum responsibility and authority at the grassroots level, can we protect individual rights, promote flexibility, and increase accountability. These are essential characteristics and requirements for a democratic society.

Freedom, it has been said, is indivisible. Freedom of economic choice—in employment, consumption, and location—is an integral part of the structure of liberty. And this most surely has been a consistent theme in corporate philosophy and action.

15a. Excessive Materialism

On the moral plane, modern industrialism subverts our whole system of values by elevating material values over values of the mind and spirit. Desire for more, bigger, and better "things," encouraged by corporations for their own profit, has become an end in itself, instead of being regarded as of secondary value or as a means to the good life.

Advertising and planned obsolescence are two prime tools in the hands of corporations to keep the materialist cycle going. The massive advertising expenditures of large corporations are the not-so-hidden persuaders that are used to induce consumers to spend rather than save. Planned obsolescence—the use of less than optimum materials and the annual introduction of new models (e.g., automobiles)—is designed to accelerate the cycle by appealing to consumers' status-conscious need to have the latest model.

15b. Progress on Nonmaterial Values

Whether in marketing or in other corporate decisions, maximization of profits is not the sole consideration. Many other considerations, many of them nonmaterial, are factors in the way corporations behave.

In dealing with consumers, for instance, product design considers the aesthetic appearance as well as the functionality of the product. Labor-saving devices eliminate a great deal of drudgery in the home and so contribute to greater leisure. Trust, consumer responsiveness, and the building of continuing relationships are central when marketing to increasingly sophisticated consumers.

In dealing with employees, corporations recognize that the material factors of employment—such as wages, benefits, hours, and safety—establish only a basic "floor" in the relationship. Nearly all of the true motivators lie in the nonmaterial arena: respect, trust, dignity, recognition, and educational and training opportunities.

In the largest sense, the high standard of living to which corporations contribute so much is "high" in large part because it now contains so many nonmaterial aspects. To that extent corporations do enable nations to support good schools and hospitals, and recreation and artistic facilities, a good measure of leisure and vacations. This is as true as its opposite: that in developing countries, smaller-scale, less efficient industrial organizations and lower living standards go hand in hand.

16a. The Erosion of Ethics

The most pervasive and damning fault in large corporations is the steady erosion of ethical standards in the pursuit of profits. The "jungle law" of competitive behavior, maltreatment of employees, fraudulent advertising, "cutting corners" (if not outright breaking of the law), and social irresponsibility—these are but some of the overt signs of an ethical malaise that besets business. And they are inevitable, given the current emphasis on profit as the be-all and end-all of corporate performance.

The system corrupts individuals. Even the ethical "organization man (or woman)" is forced to abandon principles at some stage, and sooner rather than later; they cannot be true both to themselves and to the corporate motives that govern their business lives for long.

16b. The Ethical Responsibility of Corporations

The business system is not driven solely by the profit motive. Its root purpose is to serve the economic needs of society, and its success in attaining that purpose can only have been achieved by adhering to ethical and socially responsible principles. If that were not so, the large corporation would not have endured, but would long since have been legislated out of existence.

Corporations, like any institution, are a reflection of the current values of the society of which they are a part, because they derive their members and their charters from that society and are governed by its laws and mores. Like any institution, too, they have their share of misguided or unprincipled individuals, but that is no reason to condemn the institution as a whole.

— B —

European Social Charter

The European Social Charter is a declaration, not a binding convention, which summarizes elements of European social policy, some of which are or may be incorporated in social and labor legislation. The current version of the charter, adopted at Strasbourg on May 3, 1996, builds on an earlier version, opened for signature in Turin on October 18, 1961, and is designed to "update and adapt the substantive contents of the Charter in order to take account in particular of fundamental social changes which have occurred since the text was adopted."

The governments, who are members of the Council of Europe, accept as the aim of their policies the following thirty-one rights, "to be pursued by all appropriate means both national and international."

1. Everyone shall have the opportunity to earn his living in an occupation freely entered upon.

2. All workers have the right to just conditions of work.

3. All workers have the right to safe and healthy working conditions.

4. All workers have the right to a fair remuneration sufficient for a decent standard of living for themselves and their families.

5. All workers and employers have the right to freedom of association in national or international organisations for the protection of their economic and social interests.

6. All workers and employers have the right to bargain collectively.

7. Children and young persons have the right to special protection against the physical and moral hazards to which they are exposed.

8. Employed women, in the case of maternity, have the right to a special protection.

9. Everyone has the right to appropriate facilities for vocational guidance with a view to helping him choose an occupation suited to his personal income and interests.

10. Everyone has the right to appropriate facilities for vocational training.

11. Everyone has the right to benefit from any measures enabling him to enjoy the highest possible standard of health available.

12. All workers and their dependents have the right to social security.

13. Anyone without adequate resources has the right to social and medical assistance.

14. Everyone has the right to benefit from social welfare services.

15. Disabled persons have the right to independence, social integration and participation in the life of the community.

16. The family as a fundamental unit of society has the right to appropriate social, legal and economic protection to ensure its full development.

17. Children and young persons have the right to appropriate social, legal and economic protection.

18. The nationals of any one of the Parties have the right to engage in any gainful occupation in the territory of any one of the others on a footing of equality with the nationals of the latter, subject to restrictions based on cogent economic or social reasons.

19. Migrant workers who are not nationals of a Party and their families have the right to protection and assistance in the territory of any other Party.

20. All workers have the right to equal opportunities and equal treatment in matters of employment and occupation without discriminations on the grounds of sex.

21. Workers have the right to be informed and to be consulted within the undertaking.

22. Workers have the right to take part in the determination and improvement of the working conditions and working environment in the undertaking.

23. Every elderly person has the right to social protection.

24. All workers have the right to protection in cases of termination of employment.

25. All workers have the right to protection of their claims in the event of the insolvency of their employer.

26. All workers have the right to dignity at work.

27. All persons with family responsibilities and who are engaged or wish to engage in employment have a right to do so without being subject to discrimination and as far as possible without conflict between their employment and family responsibilities.

28. Workers' representatives in undertakings have the right to protection against acts prejudicial to them and should be afforded appropriate facilities for their functions.

29. All workers have the right to be informed and consulted in collective redundancy procedures.

30. Everyone has the right to protection against poverty and social exclusion.

31. Everyone has the right to housing.

Although this charter is intended to be a framework and an expression of desired goals for public policy, its implications for private corporations are obvious. More than half the rights, for instance, pertain to employment, working conditions, and employees' rights.

The complete text of the European Social Charter, as revised at Strasbourg on May 3, 1996, is available on line at http://www.coe.fr/eng/legaltxt/163e.htm.

— C —

The "CERES Principles"

The Coalition for Environmentally Responsible Economies (CERES) is a coalition made up of hundreds of institutional investors, fifteen of the largest environmental groups, and almost sixty endorsing companies who support the following statement of principles as a guideline for environmental responsibility.

By adopting these principles, we publicly affirm our belief that corporations have a responsibility for the environment, and must conduct all aspects of their business as responsible stewards of the environment by operating in a manner that protects the Earth. We believe that corporations must not compromise the ability of future generations to sustain themselves.

We will update our practices constantly in light of advances in technology and new understandings in health and environmental science. In collaboration with CERES, we will promote a dynamic process to ensure that the Principles are interpreted in a way that accommodates changing technologies and environmental realities. We intend to make consistent, measurable progress in implementing these Principles and to apply them to all aspects of our operations throughout the world.

Protection of the Biosphere

We will reduce and make continual progress toward eliminating the release of any substance that may cause environmental damage to the air, water, or the earth or its inhabitants, We will safeguard all habitats affected by our operations and will protect open spaces and wilderness, while preserving biodiversity.

Sustainable Use of Natural Resources

We will make sustainable use of renewable natural resources, such as water, soils and forests. We will conserve nonrenewable natural resources through efficient use and careful planning.

Reduction and Disposal of Wastes

We will reduce and where possible eliminate waste through source reduction and recycling. All waste will be handled and disposed of through safe and responsible methods.

Energy Conservation

We will conserve energy and improve the energy efficiency of our internal operations and of the goods and services we sell. We will make every effort to use environmentally safe and sustainable energy sources.

Risk Reduction

We will strive to minimize the environmental, health, and safety risks to our employees and the communities in which we operate through safe technologies, facilities and operating procedures, and by being prepared for emergencies.

Safe Products and Services

We will reduce and where possible eliminate the use, manufacture or sale of products and services that cause environmental damage or health or safety hazards. We will inform our customers of the environmental impacts of our products or services and try to correct unsafe use.

Environmental Restoration

We will promptly and responsibly correct conditions we have caused that endanger health, safety or the environment. To the extent feasible, we will redress injuries we have caused to persons or damage we have caused to the environment and will restore the environment.

Informing the Public

We will inform in a timely manner everyone who may be affected by conditions caused by our company that might endanger health, safety or the environment. We will regularly seek advice and counsel through dialogue with persons or communities near our facilities. We will not take any action against employees for reporting dangerous incidents or conditions to management or to appropriate authorities.

Management Commitment

We will implement these Principles and sustain a process that ensures that the Board of Directors and Chief Executive Officer are fully informed about pertinent environmental issues and are fully responsible for environmental policy. In selecting our Board of Directors, we will consider demonstrated environmental commitment as a factor.

Audits and Reports

We will conduct an annual self-evaluation of our progress in implementing these Principles. We will support the timely creation of generally accepted environmental audit procedures. We will annually complete the CERES Report, which will be made available to the public.

• • •

These Principles establish an environmental ethic with criteria by which investors and others can assess the environmental performance of companies. Companies that endorse these Principles pledge to go voluntarily beyond the requirements of the law. The terms may and might in Principles one and eight are not meant to encompass every imaginable consequence, no matter how remote. Rather, these Principles obligate endorsers to behave as prudent persons who are not governed by conflicting interests and who possess a strong commitment to environmental excellence and to human health and safety. These Principles are not intended to create new legal liabilities, expand existing rights or obligations, waive legal defenses, or otherwise affect the legal position of any endorsing company, and are not intended to be used against an endorser in any legal proceeding for any purpose.

Bibliography

The new rules are a work in progress, so accounts of their evolution are most frequently carried in the day-to-day reporting of such publications as *Business Week, The Economist, Financial Times, Fortune*, and *The Wall Street Journal*, as well as corporate annual reports and proxy statements. These documents have been a prime source of information for me as the frequency of citations in the text will attest.

For insights into the conceptual foundations of the new rules, I have found the following sources to be of especial value.

Argyris, Chris. "Empowerment: The Emperor's New Clothes." *Harvard Business Review* 76, no. 3 (May–June 1998): 98–105.

Bolman, L. G., and T. E. Deal. *Leading with Soul: An Uncommon Journey of Spirit.* San Francisco: Jossey-Bass, 1995.

The Business Roundtable. "Statement on Corporate Governance." Washington, D.C.: The Business Roundtable, 1997.

———. "Statement on Corporate Responsibility." Washington, D.C.: The Business Roundtable, 1981.

Campbell, Andrew, Marion Devine, and David Young. *A Sense of Mission.* London: Century Business, an imprint of Random Century Limited, 1990.

de Geuss, Arie. *The Living Company: Survival in a Turbulent Business Environment.* Boston: Harvard Business School, 1997.

Easterbrook, Gregg. *A Moment on the Earth: The Coming Age of Environmental Optimism.* New York: Viking, 1994.

Fukuyama, Francis. *The End of History and the Last Man.* New York: Free Press, 1992.

Gates, Jeffrey. *The Ownership Solution: Toward a Shared Capitalism for the Twenty-First Century.* New York: Addison-Wesley, 1998.

Ghoshal, Sumantra, and Christopher A. Bartlett. *The Individualized Corporation: A Fundamentally New Approach to Management*. New York: Harper Business, 1997.

Halal, William E. *The New Management*. San Francisco: Berrett-Koehler, 1996.

————. *The New Capitalism*. New York: John Wiley & Sons, 1986.

Handy, Charles. *The Hungry Spirit: Beyond Capitalism—A Quest for Purpose*. New York: Broadway, 1997.

Harman, Willis, and Maya Porter, eds. *The New Business of Business*. San Francisco: Berrett-Koehler, 1997.

Korten, David C. *The Post-Corporate World*. San Francisco: Berrett-Koehler, 1998.

Kuttner, Robert. *Everything for Sale: The Virtues and Limits of Markets*. New York: Alfred A. Knopf, 1996.

Luttwak, Edward. *Turbo Capitalism: Winners and Losers in the Global Economy*. New York: HarperCollins, 1998.

Osborne, David, and Peter Plastrik. *Banishing Bureaucracy: The Five Strategies for Reinventing Government*. Reading, Mass.: Addison-Wesley, 1997.

Osborne, David, and Ted A. Gaebler. *Reinventing Government: How the Entrepreneurial Spirit Is Transforming the Public Sector*. Reading, Mass.: Addison-Wesley, 1992.

Porter, Michael E., and Claas van der Linde. "Green *and* Competitive." *Harvard Business Review* 73, no. 5 (September–October 1995): 120–134.

Rost, Joseph C. *Leadership in the 21st Century*. New York: Praeger, 1991.

Schmidheiny, Stephan (with the Business Council for Sustainable Development). *Changing Course: A Global Business Perspective on Development and the Environment*. Cambridge, Mass.: MIT Press, 1992.

Scientific American. *Managing Planet Earth* 261, no. 3 (September 1989), special edition.

Stewart, Thomas A. "Will the Real Capitalist Please Stand Up?" *Fortune*, May 11, 1998.

————. "A New Way to Think about Employees," *Fortune*, April 13, 1998.

Thurow, Lester C. *The Future of Capitalism: How Today's Economic Forces Shape Tomorrow's World*. New York: William Morrow, 1996.

————. *Head to Head: The Coming Battle among Japan, Europe and America*. New York: Warner Books, 1993.

Tibbs, Hardin B. C. "Industrial Ecology: An Environmental Agenda for Industry," *Whole Earth Review* (Winter 1992): 4–19.

Index

ABOUT THE AUTHOR

Ian Wilson is an international management consultant, author, and authority on scenario planning and strategic management. Principal of Wolf Enterprises, a consultancy in San Rafael, California, he started his career in England and later joined General Electric in the United States. There, he was a member of the strategic planning staff, established GE's pioneering Business Environment Analysis component, and then became a public policy adviser to GE's chief executive officer. Later, as a senior management consultant with SRI International, he worked with senior management teams in a variety of industries.